THE
HANDBOOK
ON PRIVATE
FOUNDATIONS

Revised Edition

David F. Freeman
and the
Council on Foundations

THE FOUNDATION CENTER

AMI 1977 - 5/2
NPS - 410

Library of Congress Cataloging-in-Publication Data
Freeman, David F.
  The handbook on private foundations / by David F. Freeman and the Council on Foundations.
    p.   cm.
  Includes bibliographical references and index.
  1. Endowments—United States—Management.   2. Charitable uses, trusts, and foundations—United States.   I. Council on Foundations.   II. Title.
HV97.A3F73   1991
361.7′632′068—dc20   91-27436
                                                       CIP

Contents

Appendix Section One—Legal Issues

Appendix Section Two—Grantmaking Issues

Appendix Section Three—Standards

Appendix Section Four—Intermediary Organizations

Preface

Ten years ago, when David Freeman first wrote the *Handbook on Private Foundations*, foundations were just beginning to emerge from the difficult decade following the passage of the 1969 Tax Reform Act. Throughout the 1980s, the *Handbook* served as a staple for new as well as experienced private foundation trustees and staff. It has helped them through complex laws and regulations while providing basic information on starting a foundation and grantmaking program. And it has helped them to be more open and accountable to the public.

Although we normally think of the private foundation as a unique U.S. institution, its origin can be traced over several centuries and through various cultures and legal systems. Yet in the twentieth-century United States, the private foundation has assumed unprecedented social significance. Private foundations must not become complacent with this role: The twenty-first century poses a whole new set of circumstances that we must anticipate.

Private philanthropy is already making a transition into a new century and a new world. The private foundation model is being adopted and adapted by countries with cultures, legal systems, and economies vastly different from ours. In addition, more and more people of moderate means and from minority communities are starting private and other types of foundations. With society more diverse now than ever before, boards, staffs, and grantees increasingly reflect this pluralism.

Fortunately, private foundations are strong and flexible enough both to adapt to new demands and to precipitate change.

No book of this significance can be revised without the cooperation and hard work of many people. David Freeman graciously agreed to help us revise his original work. Carol Strauch, formerly director of information services for the Council on Foundations, managed this project. She and David Freeman worked for many months to revise the book. Elizabeth Boris, vice president for research, painstakingly read and commented on the manuscript many times. John Edie, vice president and general counsel, applied to the project his extensive knowledge of the laws and regulations governing private foundations. Many others, including Alice Buhl, Deborah Brody, and Robin Hettleman, contributed significantly to the completion of this book.

The revised *Handbook* reflects the combination of David Freeman's 40 years of foundation experience and sage advice, as well as the collective experience of the Council staff and membership. We are indebted to the original funder of this project, the Charles Stewart Mott Foundation, and to the members of the original advisory committee, chaired by James P. Shannon.

The text of the *Handbook on Private Foundations* provides basic information on many important subjects in a short, descriptive form to allow for quick reading. It is designed primarily for new foundation staff and trustees, although veterans who seek a quick review or reference will also find it helpful.

Extensive footnotes, an annotated bibliography for each chapter, and the appendices provide detailed information on the various subjects plus sample forms and letters.

I am confident that this book will continue to be the standard in the field for advice and information on private foundations.

James A. Joseph
Council on Foundations
June 1991

Introduction

Foundations on Firm Ground

In 1950, when I joined the small staff in the New York office of the Ford Foundation, organized philanthropy had already become an important part of the U.S. scene. The Carnegie and Rockefeller philanthropies, among others, had compiled a distinguished list of accomplishments. When I became president of the Council on Foundations 18 years later, foundations had become more visible, and—in Washington, D.C., at least—controversial, thanks in no small measure to the investigations led by the late Wright Patman and subsequent hearings by the Senate Finance Committee. These resulted in the watershed Tax Reform Act of 1969 and its voluminous regulations affecting private foundations.

When the first edition of this handbook was published ten years ago, the act seemed less onerous than had been feared at the time of its enactment, and some success had already been achieved in obtaining modifications. Responding to the exhortations of Robert Goheen, Alan Pifer, and other leaders of the Council on Foundations and individual philanthropies, foundations were making sincere efforts to tell their story to the public. Thus, the atmosphere in Washington, D.C., and throughout the country had greatly improved. The *Handbook* provided both a framework that could be used by foundation staff and trustees to manage their responsibilities effectively and a challenge to them to continue on this path of greater accountability. Recent events have illustrated that the need for such a handbook still exists—both for newly formed foundations and for existing ones.

During the 1980s, the Reagan administration placed new emphasis on the importance of volunteerism but cut back the federal government's share of financing for many traditional areas of philanthropic activity—housing, education, child care, and health care, to mention just a few. Frequently government officials asked foundations to help fill in gaps or to "match" federal dollars sometimes two or three to one. This has been especially true for the National Endowments for the Arts and Humanities.

During the last decade, tax policies affecting nonprofits have varied widely. Incentives to charitable giving increased only for the short time (from 1981 to 1986) when charitable gifts were deductible for tax payers who did not itemize. But most of the changes in the law or regulations directly affecting private foundations have been beneficial: the change in the required payout, the option to reduce the excise tax to one percent, and most recently the elimination of the complex limitation on administrative costs and the final lobbying regulations for foundations and grantees. This revision reflects all these changes.

Although this edition of the *Handbook* does not include the full text of the regulations affecting private foundations, a summary of the laws appears in Appendix 1. Readers interested in obtaining a complete set of the regulations are encouraged to contact a law or accounting firm (most will have them), or the office of the general counsel at the Council on Foundations.

These positive developments have in part resulted from foundations' increasing openness and in part from government officials' increasing recognition of the value of the nonprofit sector. Believed to have been dangerously low in the 1970s, the rate of creation of new private foundations has markedly increased. Meanwhile, new community foundations have been created and existing ones expanded at a remarkable rate.

What has this improved climate meant for private foundation executives and trustees? First, although the field is still closely regulated, society now views the "business" of giving away money as important and necessary. Second, with the communications revolution bringing opportunities and problems from all over the world to the attention of foundation trustees, many have recognized the need for foundation staff. The growth in the number of staff positions, the popularity of the workshops being offered to staff *and* trustees, and the startling increase in the number of "affinity groups of grantmakers" all testify to this.

Observers in the past ten years have also seen an increased emphasis on the concept of partnership with grantees. The grantor–grantee partnership is at the heart of any successful grant, yet it is often a real challenge to the foundation staff or board member to remember that the grantee is the one who must run with the ball. The second edition of the *Handbook* places more emphasis on this subject.

My own experience has reinforced an earlier concern that foundation people not become too wedded to an approach that emphasizes "proactive" grantmaking for individual projects. More than 80 percent of the grants I have worked on during the past decade have been for general support. This reflects the Scherman Foundation trustees' belief that in general, grantees can best make the decision about how to use their grants. This philosophy is particularly popular with grantees that are dependent for most of their support on project money from government or private sources.

In this new edition, the Council staff and I also discuss asset management in a new light, with Chapter 8 reflecting council-sponsored research on investments and the change in the payout requirement. Foundation trustees should pay close attention to this area. This is especially true as the uncertainties of our economy and numerous options for investment pose tough challenges for foundation managers wanting to ensure that their grantmaking base or its purchasing power are maintained for years to come.

We continue to urge foundations to consider program-related investments. As explained in Chapters 4 and 8, the Internal Revenue Code encourages foundations to make loans to nonprofits. Often ignored by grantor and grantee alike, program-related investments remain an excellent addition to the large foundation's program alternatives. They can also be used to extend a smaller foundation's "reach," particularly where the recipient understands the concept and presents an appealing investment opportunity.

For many years, foundations have cooperated on projects, although in the nervous days before the Tax Reform Act of 1969, some grantors feared an antitrust action if the larger foundations worked too closely together. Recently, foundations have renewed interest in joint approaches to problem solving, service delivery, or research, perhaps in part because staff working in a particular field have come to know one another through affinity group and regional association meetings. Some examples of recent collaborative projects include the AIDS Coalition and Partnership, the Robert Wood Johnson Foundation's requests for proposals, collaboration around community economic development, and collaboration in various communities around improving schools.

The Council's management surveys indicate that foundations are drawing more staff and board members from nontraditional groups. The majority of foundation staff are women, including more and more women chief executive officers. Staff and boards are also more ethnically diverse. Foundations are being challenged to adapt their policies and performance to meet new leadership needs and to promote outreach and training to more culturally diverse grantees.

Foundations have long been a vital part of the nonprofit sector and serve as models for other societies throughout the world. New opportunities for leadership are emerging in the Soviet Union, where the International Foundation for the Survival and Development of Humanity established its headquarters. And in Eastern Europe, for example, George Soros has started a network of foundations. We are also witnessing increased philanthropy by German, Japanese, and Taiwanese corporations, both in the United States and in their own countries.

These brief event snapshots suggest that this is a good time for the establishment or enlargement of private foundations. It is also a good time for foundation leaders to examine their own assumptions about the governance and grantmaking processes they employ and the effectiveness of their efforts. In this light, the Council staff and I have designed the *Handbook* to assist philanthropists and their associates in maximizing the opportunities and challenges that lie ahead.

David F. Freeman
New York City
April 1991

1

Foundations in the United States

The roots of philanthropy go back many centuries, and philanthropic organizations exist in many cultures. In the United States, many individuals, families, and corporations have chosen a unique institution—the private foundation—to carry out their charitable purposes. Private foundations have played an important role in U.S. history during the last century, supporting cultural, social, and scientific efforts. Today private foundations continue to offer donors special opportunities to contribute to society.

Foundations in the United States date from the end of the nineteenth century, when Andrew Carnegie, John D. Rockefeller, and other industrial pioneers first chose to apply parts of their accumulating wealth to public purposes. Unlike European philanthropists, they faced no governmental restrictions or royal monopoly on good works. The corporate form of organization had served them well in the pursuit of profits, and with no public agency to direct them otherwise, they found it only natural to adapt this same device for the achievement of charitable objectives.

These early foundations were created years before income or estate taxes became a serious factor. Moreover, when federal progressive taxes on income, gifts, and estates were enacted in the second decade of the twentieth century, our government not only exempted charities, including foundations, from income tax but also encouraged gifts to them by permitting donors' deductions from income, gift, and estate taxes. Such deductions, intended as incentives, had their desired effect. By the late 1980s, nearly 30,000 foundations were in existence, many of them created by persons of relatively modest wealth.

A prime reason for this remarkable growth has been the foundation's flexibility. It can respond to a need as it becomes manifest, it can strike out quickly in new directions, and it can give in a single community or throughout the world.

WHAT'S IN A NAME?

In 1956, two foundation watchers offered very different answers to the question, "What is a foundation?" To author Dwight MacDonald, the Ford Foundation was "a large body of money completely surrounded by people who want some."[1]

F. Emerson Andrews developed the second definition in his pioneering work, *Philanthropic Foundations*. It was adopted by the Foundation Center in the first edition of *The Foundation Directory* and remains substantially unchanged today:

> A foundation [is] a nongovernmental, nonprofit organization with its
> own funds (usually from a single source, either an individual, family, or
> corporation) and program managed by its own trustees and directors,
> which was established to maintain or aid educational, social, charitable,
> religious, or other activities serving the common welfare primarily by
> making grants to other nonprofit organizations.[2]

This definition readily fits most of the organizations described in this handbook. But the grantmaking field has no copyright on the name *foundation*—it is a term freely used by noncharitable organizations, by other kinds of charities, and increasingly by governmental agencies. Ordinarily this confusion is a minor irritant, making problems for statisticians of the field, but not a matter of general concern. On occasion, however, the public image of grantmaking foundations is damaged by the publicized misdeeds or excesses of other types of "foundations" not subject to the same close regulation.

Just as the presence of the word foundation in an organization's name is no guarantee that it is a grantmaking foundation, the reverse is also true. The titles of many foundations contain synonyms such as *fund, endowment,* and *trust,* but others use no such identifier at all—for example, Carnegie Corporation of New York; DeRance, Inc.; and Research Corporation.

DIMENSIONS OF THE FOUNDATION FIELD

There are nearly 32,000 grantmaking foundations of all types in the United States.[3] The vast bulk of these organizations is composed of independent foundations. Community foundations number near 300, and there are about 1,600 corporate foundations.

In 1989 (the latest year for which data were available at time of publication), the assets held by all foundations were estimated to total $137 billion. The combined annual giving of all foundations was close to $8 billion, but that constituted only about 6 percent of all philanthropic giving, most of which came from individuals.

The distribution of foundation assets is sharply skewed. There are some 7,500 foundations, each with assets over $1 million. These foundations, approximately 24 percent of the field, hold 96 percent of the field's assets. Seventy-three foundations each have assets over $250 million.

If one states the matter in reverse, there are over 24,000 foundations with assets of less than $1 million each. These foundations, 76 percent of the field, hold only 4 percent of the total assets. About 11,000 of these foundations each have assets of under $100,000.

TYPES OF FOUNDATIONS

The *independent foundation* is a term coined by the Council on Foundations to distinguish private foundations established and funded by individuals or families from those funded by corporations. Also adopted for statistical use by the Foundation Center, the independent foundation category is by far the largest and most varied. It includes the large, long-established foundations as well as the smallest foundations.

Most independent foundations are established by contributions from an individual donor or family. In many instances, the donor and other family members participate actively in the foundation's direction. Large foundations usually have professional staff, but the smaller ones typically do not and are run entirely by their directors or trustees on a volunteer basis. Over time, a foundation launched with close ties to a donor and family often tends to develop a character and style of its own, becoming less personalized and more of an institution in its own right.

Most independent foundations are endowed, that is, they have a principal fund and make their grants essentially from investment income. Some, particularly smaller foundations, make grants from funds that are contributed periodically by living donors. Foundations that operate initially on this pass-through basis often receive an endowment at a later stage.

Corporate foundations are those established by business corporations as a means of carrying out systematic programs of charitable giving. They are classified as private foundations and are legally separate from the corporation. Corporations, whether giving through a foundation or direct giving program, frequently focus on the educational, cultural, and social welfare needs of communities where the company facilities and employees are located. They often sponsor programs to match employee gifts to charity. The corporate foundation board of directors is usually composed of senior executives and directors of the company, and staff is often recruited from within the company—although in recent years some corporations have hired staff from outside the corporation who are experienced in community work. Few corporate foundations have large endowments. Most receive and distribute funds each year from current profits of the parent company and have endowments equivalent to only one or two years of annual giving.

Although corporate grantmakers will find parts of this volume useful, more specific information on corporate giving is available from the Council on Foundations. Several references are listed in the bibliography.

Community foundations differ significantly in structure and in other respects from independent and corporate foundations. Community foundations have multiple sources of funding and a local or regional focus in their giving. Commonly they administer investments and charitable distributions separately; investments are managed professionally, often by trustee banks. The grantmaking and other charitable activities are directed by a governing body or distribution committee representative of community interests. The assets of a community foundation consist of a number of component funds with varying charitable purposes.

Community foundations are classified as public charities under the 1969 Tax Reform Act and accordingly are subject to fewer and different regulations than private foundations. Gifts to them qualify for maximum income tax deductibility. The number and size of community foundations have grown tremendously in the last 20 years. This is in part because of the requirement that they raise funds to meet a public support test. It may also have partly resulted from the help provided to newly forming or revitalizing community foundations by special programs sponsored by the Council on Foundations, the Ford Foundation, and the C. S. Mott Foundation. However, a major reason for their popularity among donors is the ease with which funds can be established and the variety of giving options available to donors.

Additional information on community foundations is available from the Council on Foundations. This present volume concentrates instead on private independent foundations whose funds are received from one or a limited number of contributors, for example, an individual, family, or other contributor.

An *operating foundation* is a private foundation that primarily conducts programs of its own, expending its funds directly for the conduct of its own charitable activities rather than making grants to others. Examples include the J. Paul Getty Trust, which operates museum activities, and the Russell Sage Foundation, which conducts and publishes research. The distinction between operating foundations and those that are primarily grantmaking has long been recognized in the foundation field. The 1969 Tax Reform Act recognized this distinction by establishing a separate category, with more favorable tax status, for operating foundations. Approximately 3,000 organizations are classified by the Internal Revenue Service (IRS) as private operating foundations.[4] The vast majority of private foundations are classified as private "nonoperating"; we are primarily concerned with these grantmaking organizations in this book.

GENERAL AND SPECIAL PURPOSE FOUNDATIONS

Most donors charter their foundations with general purposes to support a wide range of charitable activities that change from time to time, as the directors or trustees determine. Others, either by choice of the managers or by virtue of the charter, may have one or more special purposes. A special purpose may be extremely broad, such as the advancement of science or health, or quite limited and specific, such as research into the causes and cure of alcoholism. Frequently, foundation managers select trustees and staff for a special-purpose foundation because of their interest or expertise in the field of emphasis.

Whether or not they incorporate geographic limitations into their charters, most small general-purpose foundations and a few large ones restrict their giving to a region, state, or city. Many special-purpose foundations and the largest of the general-purpose foundations, however, give regionally, nationally, and internationally.

FOUNDATIONS IN SOCIETY

The Andrews/Foundation Center definition of a private foundation, cited earlier in this chapter, is helpful in describing the range of organi-

zations in which we are primarily interested. However, it fails to position foundations in the voluntary sector of our society. The voluntary,
independent nonprofit, or third sector, as it is variously called, is an important partner with government and business in the myriad activities
that collectively make up our way of life. Within the voluntary sector,
foundations play both a supportive and an innovative role, serving as
important channels through which profits earned by individuals and
businesses are distributed to the public in goods and services. Their influence within the voluntary sector is not dependent on the dollar volume of their grants, which is small in comparison to government
spending. Rather, it lies in their flexibility in responding to needs, their
willingness to take risks, and in the pluralistic nature of foundation decision making.

No other country has so many alternatives to government funding
for a good idea or a new approach to an old problem. The value of
foundations as alternate funding sources lies in the likelihood that at
least one grantmaker will be willing to take a chance on a particular organization or individual, making possible an experiment that may gain
public acceptance and broad support.

This is not to suggest that it is easy to get a grant from a foundation.
Some of the staffed foundations that keep track of the number of qualified requests they decline each year report the percentage of turndowns
is about 85 percent and rising. This trend is partly due to increased demand for private contributions in the wake of government cutbacks
during the 1980s. But the adage, "if at first you don't succeed, try, try
again," is still sound advice to the grantseeker.

The range of activities recognized by the IRS as within a charitable
organization's exempt purposes constantly widens. Even contributions
to businesses that operate for profit can qualify as charitable if made,
for example, to help racial minorities establish themselves in the free
enterprise system. Foundation grants have triggered other extensions of
the definition of what is charitable, such as special guidelines including
public interest work in law and voter education activities.

There is much discussion among scholars and practitioners about
foundation grantmaking philosophy. Some say foundations are more
concerned with research on the underlying causes of social or health
problems, while others contend that they are more involved in funding
the delivery of needed services. It is probably more accurate to say that
they are concerned with both. Thus, while some foundations working
on the problems of the inner city may fund studies of economic or demographic trends, others seek to help new community organizations

wrestling with immediate problems such as homelessness, drug abuse, or unemployed young people.

We can learn valuable lessons from the relatively short experience of organized grantmaking. For example, a few foundations have traditionally shown considerable willingness to stay with a particular problem or project over a period of years—a capability that distinguishes them from most government funding sources. The Rockefeller Foundation's long and successful battle against yellow fever is a favorite example. That same foundation and others have shown equal persistence in the funding of agricultural research leading to the miracle rice and grain strains that have increased crop yields so markedly as part of the "green revolution" in Asia, Africa, and Latin America. And, in future years we may find that long-term commitments from private foundations such as the Robert Wood Johnson Foundation and others will be instrumental in finding a cure and developing prevention strategies for AIDS.

Although grantmaking may be their primary function, many foundations offer more than money. Staffed foundations and actively involved trustees of unstaffed ones frequently develop expertise in a special area of interest and become informal clearinghouses of information about new approaches to problems and funding sources other than their own. Often foundations bring together people working in the same or related fields for mutually helpful discussion and planning.

Although most foundations are blessed with broad charters, in practice many narrow their areas of current interest. This sharpening of focus serves several useful purposes. If these interests are clearly defined and publicized, it helps grantseeking agencies to target their appeals for support. And the grantmaker, having become familiar with both the problems and the imaginative people who are working toward solutions in a special field, is able to make better-informed grant decisions.

Examples of both the "staying power" of foundations and the advantages of selecting areas of special interest (taken from a long list of past accomplishments) include reform of medical education, early work on population problems, and development of policy-oriented research institutes such as the Brookings Institution and the Institute of Medicine of the National Academy of Sciences.[5]

Nonprofit organizations look to grantmaking foundations to provide funding for experimental and high-risk projects. But with many research, educational, and service agencies heavily dependent on government project funding, general support grants from smaller foundations are also vitally important. In these and many other ways, foundations are demonstrating their continuing usefulness.

FOUNDATIONS AND GOVERNMENT

Much has been written about the degree to which government has "taken over" the funding of the voluntary sector. It is true that government support of nonprofit institutions equals that of private contributions, and government spending on charitable activities such as health care and job training dwarfs private spending.[6] But since foundations are able to change the direction and emphasis of their programs with little or no lead time, many new opportunities have opened up *because* of heavy government funding in fields traditionally thought of as the concern of the private sector. For example, government funding of health services through Medicare and Medicaid has created demand for new types of health practitioners; Robert Wood Johnson, Commonwealth, Kaiser, and other foundations have conducted studies, made grants to educational institutions, funded demonstration projects, and otherwise moved to help identify ways to meet the demand.

In the environmental field, foundations have long played an important role by preserving wilderness areas, barrier islands, and historic buildings. This function continues to be an important one, especially because of the speed with which foundations and grantees such as the Nature Conservancy and Trust for Public Land can move. In addition, foundations monitor government conservation programs and allow environmental disputes between government agencies to be ventilated. And on occasion, powerful coalitions of public interest law firms and voluntary membership organizations (many of whom were launched by or are funded by foundations) generate lawsuits to force corporations or government agencies to comply with environmental protection laws and regulations. Foundations have been willing to take risks in this area and in others through support of pilot projects, studies, and investigative reporting. These and similar activities have often influenced or changed public policies.[7]

Trends in the 1980s indicated that government funding in certain areas may have reached its limit, resulting in a larger demand for foundation dollars for basic services, especially for the disadvantaged. Foundation boards and staffs find themselves in new roles, sometimes working in tandem with government agencies to fund programs. Foundations are also contributing more dollars to issues such as public education—areas that have traditionally been considered to be the concern of the public sector.

LEGAL STATUS OF FOUNDATIONS

Foundations in the United States typically are created and organized under state law either as corporations or trusts and enjoy federal tax exemption under the Internal Revenue Code.[8] Neither these laws nor others give the term *foundation* a precise or fixed legal meaning. Indeed, many of the state statutes under which foundations are created and operate do not use the word at all.

The Internal Revenue Code refers to foundations in various contexts related to not-for-profit organizations, but it leaves the term undefined. However, the relatively new phrase *private foundation*, introduced by the 1969 Tax Reform Act, does have a technical meaning. Unfortunately, the code defines private foundations not by what they are, but by what they are not. Moreover, the phrase private foundation creates confusion because the word *private* tends to blur an essential fact: Foundations are committed to public purposes, even though their assets are derived from private sources.

The code's definition by exclusion of private foundation operates in this fashion. Starting with the universe of voluntary organizations described in Section 501(c)(3), the code excludes broad groups such as churches, schools, hospitals, government, and publicly supported charities and their affiliates. (Publicly supported charities derive much of their support from the general public and reach out in other ways to a public constituency.) The code refers to all of the above kinds of excluded organizations as *public charities*. Section 501(c)(3) organizations remaining after these exclusions are considered private foundations.

Thus, organizations are included in the remainder as private foundations that are not really grantmaking foundations at all. These may include museums, homes for the aged, and libraries, among others. The IRS considers these organizations private foundations if they have been endowed by an individual or a single family or if they were established as public charities and lose that status by failing to prove that they have received ongoing financial support from the general public.[9]

NOTES TO CHAPTER 1

1. Dwight MacDonald, *The Ford Foundation: the Men and the Millions* (New York: Reynal and Company, 1956), p. 3.

2. Stan Olson, ed., "Introduction," *The Foundation Directory*, 1991 Edition (New York: The Foundation Center, 1990), pp. vi. See also F. Emerson Andrews, *Philanthropic Foundations* (New York: Russell Sage Foundation, 1956), p.11, for a definition and discussion of the meaning of the term *foundation*. For a comprehensive definition of terms, see John A. Edie, *First Steps in Starting a Foundation* (Washington, DC: Council on Foundations, 1987, rev., 1989).

3. Loren Renz, ed. *Foundation Giving: Yearbook of Facts and Figures on Private, Corporate and Community Foundations*, 1991 Ed. (New York: The Foundation Center, 1991).

4. *Ibid.*

5. Council on Foundations, "Private Foundations and the 1969 Tax Reform Act," in *Research Papers*, Volume III, Commission on Private Philanthropy and Public Needs (Filer Commission) (Washington, DC: Department of the Treasury, 1977), p. 1576. See also Saul Richman, "Down the Highways and Byways with American Philanthropy," *Foundation News* 21, no. 1, January/February, 1980, p. 13. For a sampling of the types of support provided by foundations today, see also the Council on Foundations' publication, *How We Helped*.

6. Virginia A. Hodgkinson and Murray S. Weitzman, *Dimensions of the Independent Sector: A Statistical Profile*, 3rd Ed. (Washington, DC: Independent Sector, 1989). 220 pages.

7. For discussion and examples of such grants, see James Joseph, "Private Philanthropy and the Making of Public Policy" (Washington, DC: Council on Foundations, 1985); and Frank Karel and John Edie, *Foundations and Public Policy* (Washington, DC: Council on Foundations, 1985). In light of new lobbying regulations, see also John A. Edie, *Foundations and Lobbying: Safe Ways to Affect Public Policy* (Washington, DC: Council on Foundations, 1991).

8. Sections 509(a) and 501(c)(3).

9. In order to maintain their "public" status and avoid reclassification as private foundations, public charities must meet a variety of tests established by the Internal Revenue Code. The most common test used in this regard is the *public support* test under section 170(b)(1)(A)(vi). An organization may be considered publicly supported if it normally receives on a continual basis a substantial part of its support from the general public, government, or a combination.

The 1984 Tax Reform Act introduced a new hybrid classification of foundations labeled *exempt operating foundations*. This new legal category was designed to benefit those public charities that, after many years of successful public involvement, now find it difficult to meet the public support test. By meeting specific requirements, they can obtain reclassification as exempt operating foundations. They are then relieved from the burdens of the support test and are exempt from the private foundation excise tax and expenditure responsibility requirements if grants are made to them by nonoperating foundations. Very few organizations qualify for this special status.

ANNOTATED BIBLIOGRAPHY–CHAPTER 1

WHAT'S IN A NAME?

Andrews, F. Emerson. *Philanthropic Foundations* (New York: Russell Sage Foundation, 1956). 459 pages.

Andrews, a respected foundation scholar, provides a comprehensive overview of the management, formation, and operations of foundations.

Commission on Foundations and Private Philanthropy (Peterson Commission). *Foundations, Private Giving and Public Policy* (Chicago: University of Chicago Press, 1970). 287 pages.

This is a report written by 15 distinguished private citizens in response to an attack against philanthropic foundations by congressional leaders and others. The report focuses on five pressing concerns: the role of philanthropy in a changing society, the needs of U.S. charitable organizations, tax incentives for philanthropy, the need for public confidence, and the proper role of foundations vis-à-vis government as agents and initiators of progress.

Commission on Private Philanthropy and Public Needs (Filer Commission). *Giving in America* (Washington, DC: Department of the Treasury, 1975). 240 pages.

The Filer Commission, established in 1973, studied the role of both philanthropic giving in the United States and the voluntary "third sector" of U.S. society. The commission sets forth its recommendations to the voluntary sector, to Congress, and to the U.S. public concerning ways in which the sector and the practice of private giving can be strengthened and made more effective.

Commission on Private Philanthropy and Public Needs (Filer Commission). *Research Papers* (Washington, DC: Department of the Treasury, 1977). 3,087 pages.

Six Volumes: *History, Trends and Current Magnitudes,* Vol. I; *Philanthropic Fields of Interest* (part 1, Areas of Activity, part 2, Additional Perspectives), Vol. II; *Special Behavioral Studies, Foundations and Corporations,* Vol. III; *Taxes,* Vol. IV; *Regulation,* Vol. V. *Research Papers* consists of 91 studies sponsored by the Filer Commission. The studies were designed to establish a base of information on past and present giving trends, the relationship between public and private financial support for philanthropic activities, and the effect of the tax system on the capacity of the private voluntary sector to meet public needs in a time of change. The first part of Volume I provides a technical explanation of the commission's recommendations and discusses means of implementing the recommendations. It is followed by a report from the Donee Group that criticizes some of the commission's recommendations and offers alternatives.

Council on Foundations. *Recommended Principles and Practices for Effective Grantmaking.*

This brochure includes eleven recommendations for how foundations can operate openly and effectively in order to best accomplish their mission in society.

Cuninggim, Merrimon. *Private Money and Public Service: The Role of Foundations in American Society* (New York: McGraw-Hill Book Company, 1972). 267 pages.

Cuninggim, president of the Danforth Foundation from 1961 to 1972, has an intimate knowledge of how a large foundation functions. This book comments in a frank style on both the problems that confront foundations and the tasks that face them now and in the future. Topics discussed include political activism of foundations, secretiveness, achievements of foundations, and the Tax Reform Act of 1969.

Heimann, Fritz F., ed. *The Future of Foundations* (Englewood Cliffs, NJ: Prentice-Hall, for the American Assembly, 1973). 278 pages.

This book contains nine useful articles dealing with different aspects of foundations. There is a historical account of the accomplishments of foundations and the controversies surrounding their activities by Thomas Parrish. Jeffrey Hart, Fritz Heimann, and John G. Simon discuss the role and rationale behind foundation giving. John R. Labovitz discusses the general provisions of the 1969 Tax Reform Act and effects of the legislation. Boris I. Bittker refers to the distinction in treatment between foundations and other types of charitable organizations. Richard E. Friedman examines private foundation versus government spending. H. Thomas James provides an overview of foundation administration, discussing trustees, staffing, methods of program development, ways to monitor grants, and foundation reporting. Orville G. Brim looks at program evaluation.

Olson, Stan, ed. "Introduction." *The Foundation Directory*, 1991 Edition (New York: The Foundation Center, 1990). 35 pages.

The introduction provides most recent data on the scope and dimensions of the foundation field, including detailed statistics on those foundations having assets of more than $1 million or total contributions of $100,000 or more. The *Directory* covers grant program areas, assets, and gifts.

DIMENSIONS OF THE FOUNDATION FIELD

Duffy, Maureen. *Annual Survey of Corporate Contributions*, 1991 Ed. (New York: Conference Board). +50 pages.

This is a collection of survey data for the calendar year 1987. It attempts to measure the flow of corporate-contribution dollars during the year. It relates contributions to key indicators, including pretax income, assets, number of employees, and industry classification. It identifies trends in the distribution of dollars among the major areas of funding such as education, health, and the arts.

Foundation Giving, 1991 Ed. (New York: The Foundation Center, 1991) (updated periodically).

This book contains a summary of facts and figures on foundations and trends in foundation giving.

Giving USA: A Compilation of Facts and Trends on American Philanthropy. Annual Report. Nathan Weber, ed. (New York: American Association of Fund-Raising Counsel). 193 pages.

This is an extensive compilation of facts and trends in U.S. philanthropy. It puts foundation giving for each year into context with statistics on individual and corporate giving.

Hodgkinson, Virginia A., and Weitzman, Murray S. *Dimensions of the Independent Sector: A Statistical Profile*, 3rd Ed. (Washington, DC: Independent Sector, 1989). 162 pages.

This is a statistical profile that provides a framework for describing the way the sector fits into our society, the various functions it performs, and the people it services.

Murphy, C. Edward, ed. *National Databook of Foundations*, 1991 Edition (New York: The Foundation Center, 1990). 2 vols.

The introduction contains data on the number and type of grantmaking foundations. The bulk of the volumes contains a state-by-state listing of independent, company-sponsored, and community foundations.

Olson, Stan, ed. *The Foundation Directory*, 1991 Edition (New York: The Foundation Center, 1990). 1444 pages.

The *Directory* provides statistical data on the number of foundations, trends in giving, staffing, growth of the field, and other topics. A careful analysis accompanies the data, resulting in a good overview of characteristics of the foundation field. The bulk of the *Directory* contains information on foundations with assets of over $1 million or that make grants in excess of $100,000 per year. Entries include name, address, types of grants awarded, restrictions, and other basic information useful to grantseekers and grantmakers alike. The index contains listings for staff, trustees, types of programs, and grants.

TYPES OF FOUNDATIONS

Council on Foundations. *Corporate Philanthropy: The Business of Giving* (Washington, DC: Council on Foundations, 1982). 158 pages.

This book provides insight into the business of giving through the viewpoints, concerns, motivations, and policies of leading corporate executives, foundation directors, grant applicants, and others involved in grantmaking.

Foote, Joseph. "No, They're Not Foundations." *Foundation News* 27, no. 5, September/October 1986; pp. 40–44.

The author discusses grantmakers' concerns over the use of the title *foundation* by organizations that seek grants or solicit charitable contributions.

Foote, Joseph. "Service Unlimited." *Foundation News* 26, no. 4, July/August 1985, pp. 11–19. Also, "You Name It, They Do It." *Foundation News* 26, no. 5, September/October 1985, pp. 14–25.

These are feature articles describing private operating foundations and their varied contributions to philanthropy and society.

Freeman, David F. "Personality Traits of Small Foundations." *Foundation News* 21, no. 5, September/October 1980, pp. 11–12.

Freeman examines the characteristics of small foundations from a sampling of those with assets under $1 million.

Hopkins, Bruce. "Types of Private Foundations." In *The Law of Tax-Exempt Organizations*, 5th Ed. (New York: John Wiley and Sons, 1987). p. 478.

Hopkins discusses the types of foundations from a legal perspective.

Keele, Harold, and Kiger, Joseph, eds. *Greenwood Encyclopedia of American Institutions: Foundations* (Westport, CT: Greenwood Press, 1984). 516 pages.

These are concise histories of major U.S. foundations.

Treusch, Paul E. *Tax-Exempt Charitable Organizations*, 3rd Ed. (Philadelphia: American Law Institute, 1988). 705 pages.

See Chapter 8, "Private Foundations: General Rules," p. 453, which defines private foundations; and Chapter 10, "Special Organizations," p. 559, which discusses trusts, operating foundations, conduit foundations, etc.

Ylvisaker, Paul N. *Small Can Be Effective* (Washington, DC: Council on Foundations, 1989). 12 pages.

The author illustrates how small foundations can be and have been both creative and effective by inventive use of their money.

FOUNDATIONS IN SOCIETY

Bremner, Robert H. *American Philanthropy* (Chicago: University of Chicago Press, 1988). 291 pages.

Bremner provides a social history of U.S. philanthropy from colonial times to the present day. The book also includes a bibliographical essay to guide the reader on literature in the philanthropic field.

Council on Foundations. *What Lies Ahead for Philanthropy.* (Washington, DC: Council on Foundations, 1986). 16 pages.

An assessment of philanthropy's future in this country. The report suggests that increased demand for private charitable funds will lead to special challenges and opportunities for foundations in the future.

Magat, Richard, ed. *Philanthropic Giving: Studies in Varieties and Goals* (New York: Oxford University Press, 1989). 310 pages.

This work contains an interdisciplinary collection of papers that explores the historical and philosophical origins of giving, the methods by which donations reach their intended beneficiaries, and the consequences of the philanthropic tradition. Parts IV and V focus on foundations and corporations. Sponsored by Yale University's Program on Non-Profit Organizations.

Nielsen, Waldemar A. *The Golden Donors: A New Anatomy of the Great Foundations* (New York: E. P. Dutton, 1985). 468 pages.

Nielsen critiques the recent histories of the 36 largest foundations in the United States (whose assets exceed $250 million). He deals with public reporting, administration, grantmaking, leadership, and other issues. This is an update and expansion on ideas first presented in his earlier book, *The Big Foundations* (1972).

O'Connell, Brian. *Philanthropy in Action* (New York: The Foundation Center, 1987). 337 pages.

The main portion of this work is dedicated to anecdotes on philanthropy's impact on a broad range of fields. The book serves as an excellent immediate resource on grantmaking and includes a bibliography.

O'Neill, Michael. *The Third America* (San Francisco: Jossey-Bass, 1989). 215 pages.

O'Neill provides a thorough discussion of the nonprofit sector including information on religion, research, health care, and the arts.

Odendahl, Teresa, ed. *America's Wealthy and the Future of Foundations* (New York: The Foundation Center, 1987). 325 pages.

This book examines the complexity of attitudes, motivations, economic forces, and regulations that lead wealthy people to commit private resources to public endeavors. It includes historical trends that lead to the formation of foundations and their subsequent growth.

Odendahl, Teresa. *Charity Begins at Home* (New York: Basic Books, Inc., 1990). 299 pages.

Odendahl argues that philanthropy by wealthy individuals perpetuates economic inequality by supporting institutions largely benefiting the upper class.

Payton, Robert. *Philanthropy: Voluntary Action for the Public Good* (New York: American Council on Education/MacMillan Publishing Company, 1988). 279 pages.

Payton provides a thoughtful overview of the philanthropic tradition in the United States through a collection of essays on challenges facing philanthropy. The author explores ethical issues and poses questions for trustees and staff of foundations and other nonprofits. The book also includes an essay on nonprofit sector research by Virginia Hodgkinson.

"Philanthropy, Patronage, Politics." In *Daedalus: Journal of the American Academy of Arts and Sciences* 116, no. 1, Winter 1987. pp. 1–177.

This entire issue of Daedalus is devoted to the philanthropic field. Six articles are presented by outstanding members of the philanthropic field.

Pifer, Alan. *Philanthropy in an Age of Transition* (New York: The Foundation Center, 1984). 239 pages.

This book is a compilation of essays by the author, the president of the Carnegie Corporation from 1965 to 1982. They reflect his evolving ideas and concerns about the philanthropic field. The essays were first published as introductions to the corporation's annual reports.

Powell, Walter W., ed. *The Nonprofit Sector: A Research Handbook* (New Haven, CT: Yale University Press, 1987). 464 pages.

This publication brings together the Yale Program on Non-Profit Organizations accumulated research knowledge, from outside as well as inside the program. The 24 chapters are written by different scholars and practitioners in the nonprofit field and cover organizational theory, dimensions of the sector, functions, and sources of support. Included in the section on sources of support are a chapter on foundations by Paul Ylvisaker and a chapter on corporate philanthropy by Michael Useem.

Salzman, Jack. *Philanthropy and American Society: Selected Papers* (New York: Center for American Culture Studies, Columbia University, 1987). 185 pages.

This is a collection of papers commissioned by the center to study the philanthropic field in a systemic way. The book contains eight articles from members of the field as well as a brief bibliography.

Whitaker, Ben. *The Philanthropoids: Foundations and Society* (New York: William Morrow and Company, Inc., 1974). 256 pages.

An investigation of the world's foundations and their effects on society plus a critique of their aims, politics, economics, and achievements. The book investigates foundations, both large and small, and answers questions such as the following: What are the various motives of their founders? How much truth is there in the rumors of CIA infiltration of foundations? Why should organizations ostensibly so well-intentioned arouse so much criticism and suspicion? Have foundations become an elite subsidizing elites? Who controls foundations?

FOUNDATIONS AND GOVERNMENT

Council on Foundations. "Private Foundations and the 1969 Tax Reform Act." In *Research Papers Volume III* (Filer Commission), p. 1564.

See Part III, "The 1969 Tax Reform Act and Its Effects," for a discussion of the Tax Reform Act provisions and the effect on foundations as reported in a survey of foundation members of the council.

Edie, John. *Congress and Private Foundations: An Historical Analysis* (Washington, DC: Council on Foundations, 1987). 35 pages.

The pamphlet details the efforts made by Congress over the years to regulate public and private charities with special emphasis on the grantmaking sector. This booklet is an excerpt from *America's Wealthy and the Future of Foundations*, cited earlier in this bibliography.

Edie, John. *Foundations and Lobbying: Safe Ways to Affect Public Policy* (Washington, DC: Council on Foundations, 1991). 135 pages.

Edie discusses the 1990 lobbying regulations, published by the Treasury Department, which provide greater clarity about what is permitted and increased flexibility for foundations to be advocates in the public policy debate.

Eisenberg, Pablo. "Monitoring Government: Issues/Challenges/Approaches." *Foundation News* 20, no. 2, March/April 1979, pp. 43–47.

Eisenberg presents a case for citizen monitoring of government programs and how to approach it. He encourages foundations to become active in the financial support of such organizations.

Friedman, Richard E. "Private Foundation–Government Relationships." In *The Future of Foundations*, Fritz F. Heimann, ed. (Englewood Cliffs, NJ: Prentice-Hall, for the American Assembly, 1973). pp. 56, 163.

This book reviews the relationship of foundations to government with reference to human services projects. It looks at the constraints that impede a productive relationship between foundations and government. It discusses the role of the IRS.

Joseph, James A. *Private Philanthropy and the Making of Public Policy* (Washington, DC: Council on Foundations, 1985). 36 pages.

Joseph discusses foundations' roles in shaping public policy. He explores how foundations transcend government, transform government, work in partnership with government, and are regulated by government.

Karel, Frank, and Edie, John. *Foundations and Public Policy* (Washington, DC: Council on Foundations, 1985). 55 pages.

This background information kit outlines the key questions in how foundations can help shape public policy. Case studies are included.

LEGAL STATUS OF FOUNDATIONS

Fremont-Smith, Marion R. *Foundations and Government: State and Federal Law and Supervision* (New York: Russell Sage Foundation, 1965). 564 pages.

This is an older but still useful comprehensive treatment of the foundation as a legal entity. It covers the history of foundations, the law of charitable dispositions, the trust and corporate form of organization, and federal and state regulation of foundations.

Hopkins, Bruce R. *The Law of Tax-Exempt Organizations,* 5th Ed. (New York: John Wiley and Sons, 1987). 949 pages.

Part IV deals with private foundations and includes an introduction to regulatory topics such as disqualified persons, self-dealing, and excess business holdings.

Treusch, Paul E. *Tax-Exempt Charitable Organizations,* 3rd Ed. (Philadelphia: American Law Institute, 1988). 705 pages.

This is a helpful source on many topics related to tax-exempt charitable organizations. It gives the requirements for qualifying as a tax-exempt organization as well as the limitations and liabilities of this IRS status. It discusses the effect of terminating an exempt status, the tax consequences of unrelated business operations of exempt organizations, and the differences between various categories under which tax exemption may be sought. It includes relevant sections of the IRS code and the Tax Reform Act of 1969.

2

Why Create A Foundation?

THE DONOR'S OPTIONS

To carry out charitable purposes, a donor has many options. Direct tax-deductible gifts can be made to schools, colleges, churches, museums, or other institutions. A charitable trust can be established and managed by a bank. Here, the donor can establish precise instructions or broad general guidelines as to how the trustee will handle both the capital and the income and for what purposes. A community foundation can establish and administer a fund providing similar flexibility. An operating foundation can be created to carry out directly certain designated charitable or educational objectives. Or the donor can create a grant-making foundation designed to receive and hold, in perpetuity or for a designated time span, funds the donor wishes to use primarily to support charitable activities.[1]

The idea of establishing foundations first became popular in the United States during the late nineteenth century. Andrew Carnegie, John D. Rockefeller, and Margaret Olivia Sage were among the field's pioneers. Over the years, many wealthy donors chose the foundation as a way to systematize their charitable giving. The rate of establishing new foundations reached a peak in the 1950s and slowed in the following three decades. Researchers cite changing attitudes and changing tax laws, particularly the Tax Reform Act of 1969, as reasons for the decline.[2]

However, data from the Foundation Center now show that the private foundation is gaining again in popularity, for both individuals and corporations.[3] Among the factors that have contributed to this reversal are the positive attitudes of government policymakers, as evidenced by a series of helpful amendments to the 1969 legislation by Congress and the educational efforts of the Council on Foundations, the Foundation Center, and regional associations of grantmakers.

INDEPENDENT FOUNDATIONS

When and why does it make sense to create an independent grantmaking foundation? As noted in the preceding chapter, the flexibility of the grantmaking foundation has been a major factor in the growth of the field. But research shows that other important considerations have also influenced thousands of donors to make it their chosen charitable instrument.[4]

"You know what I wish? I wish there was a foundation that gave grants just to lie fallow for a year or so."

Drawing by B. Tobey; © 1960
The New Yorker Magazine, Inc.

Most donors cite their strong personal philosophy as a primary reason for establishing a foundation. A sense of altruism or social responsibility is at the heart of their decision to give to charity. However, the

choice of a foundation over other available vehicles is often made because the donor desires to maintain more control over distributing the
charitable assets. Donors may wish to choose the foundation's initial
board, serve on that board, and establish the foundation's purposes.
They may do so under the rules governing private foundations. Tax advantages are also a part of the rationale for starting a private foundation, although the tax laws treat gifts to a private foundation less
favorably than direct gifts to public charities.[5]

The donor's charitable objective is a particularly important factor to
weigh in selecting the appropriate instrument. Typically, donors have a
number of different interests, are undecided about priorities, and want
to maintain flexibility in their giving program as they develop their
philanthropic objectives. The private grantmaking foundation is the
most flexible option available and can be established with broad or
narrow purposes spelled out in its charter or trust instrument. It can be
created in perpetuity or with a limited life. The governing board can be
large or small. If it is staffed, generalists can be recruited to manage a
diversified giving program, and specialists can be brought in as consultants when needed. If the charter purposes are broad, the board can revise the direction of the foundation's giving program to meet changing
needs.

Foundations provide living donors with flexibility as to the timing of
gifts. For instance, a donor may in one year have particularly high income and wish to take full advantage of the 30 percent of income deductible for a cash gift to a foundation, without deciding in that same
year on the final charitable recipients. In a subsequent lean year, the
foundation will have available for giving additional funds that, in the
meantime, have been earning virtually tax-free income.

Still another form of giving to a private foundation is through the
creation of a charitable remainder trust. Through such an arrangement,
a donor could realize a deduction in the year of the trust's establishment but continue to receive income from the trust for life, with the
foundation receiving the assets after the donor's death.[6]

Also, for a donor wishing to make substantial charitable gifts, the
careful planning of a giving program could require staff or consultants.
The IRS recognizes their compensation as a necessary administrative
expense for a grantmaking foundation. For example, the Wieboldt
Foundation, established in 1921, concentrates its giving of about
$550,000 a year in the Greater Chicago area, emphasizing help to dis-
advantaged groups, mostly minorities. With an experienced executive
director and one additional staff member, it gives time and attention to
requests from less established and sophisticated applicants. And it
monitors and evaluates their performance. Periodically, the foundation

reviews its overall program, occasionally with the assistance of a team of outsiders knowledgeable about grantmaking.

A staffed foundation can also provide a buffer between the donor and other board members and the many requests for funding they regularly receive. By channeling the requests through the foundation, the donor and the grantseekers can be assured of a thoughtful, systematic consideration of each request.

One question potential donors often ask is "What minimum amount of assets do I need to start a foundation?" There is no simple answer to this question. Foundations vary in their purpose, the number and types of grants they award, the way they carry out programs, and the degree to which their boards are involved in the operations. Each foundation must also meet reporting and other requirements, which usually involve services from legal or accounting professionals. The costs of doing business vary a great deal.

As John Edie states in *First Steps in Starting a Foundation,* "One must determine the amount of funds likely to be available annually, and then ask what amount will be left for grants after paying for necessary administrative costs. . . . Can the new foundation accomplish its purpose given the resources available while using responsible procedures?"[7]

This analysis might cause one to argue for a large endowment or assurance of substantial annual donations at the outset. However, an extremely active board of directors or pro bono services from a lawyer or accountant are among the factors that enable small foundations to succeed. There are also situations where trustees anticipate a substantial endowment from the donor's estate. Then the small foundation created during the donor's lifetime serves as a useful device for exploring different areas of philanthropy, interesting and training younger members of a family in the business of giving money away, and developing a responsible board in which the donor has confidence. It is worth noting that two of the largest foundations, Ford and Robert Wood Johnson, were relatively small until they received bequests from the estates of major donors. The John D. and Catherine T. MacArthur Foundation and the Knight Foundation are other recent examples of this "phasing-in" process.

Another important factor to consider is the type of assets to be conveyed to the foundation. Many of today's large foundations were funded with stock of a single company founded or controlled by the donor family. The ability to place large blocks of stock in "friendly hands" and reduce the impact of estate and inheritance taxes by charitable bequests helped preserve family control of many companies. Private foundations no longer offer an attractive option for this type of estate planning. Section 4943 of the Tax Reform Act of 1969 requires divestiture of substantial portions of such holdings (termed *excess business holdings*) by private foundations within five years of the distribution of such bequests by the estate to the foundation. In addition, the payout requirements of Section 4942, though modified in 1976 and 1981, may force gradual liquidation of blocks of stock when the dividend yield is less than 5 percent of market value.[8]

Small foundations continue to provide a convenient means for donors to give blocks of stock or other assets to charity. Typically, these "flow-through" foundations will sell the assets promptly and distribute the proceeds in cash to charitable grantees, some of whom might have difficulty in handling direct gifts of stock or real property.[9]

OTHER OPTIONS

In some situations, the private operating foundation, the community foundation, or some other public charity may be the donor's instrument of choice. For instance, the operating foundation model might be most appropriate if the donor family has a clearly defined charitable activity in mind, and members of the family wish to be directly involved in the foundation's program work. The donor may wish to attract funds from friends or the general public to support a particular charitable activity. In such cases, establishing a publicly supported organization may be the logical choice. The donor may also wish to explore the possibility that an existing community foundation or other public charity with a proven track record could pursue better the donor's objectives, perhaps through setting up a named fund.[10]

If the assets to be dedicated to charity consist principally of real estate or other property best suited for some particular purpose (e.g., acreage suitable for camping, experimental farming, a nature preserve, or an art collection that might become the nucleus of a small museum), an operating foundation or a new or existing public charity may be the logical choice. If the donor's interest is primarily in one community with an established community foundation, then an unrestricted gift to or the creation of a named fund for that foundation will provide flexibility. It will also assure responsible investment management, allow savings in administrative costs, and provide continuity of leadership in carrying out the donor's specific or general charitable purposes.

Still another option, less well known, is the "supporting organization." As outlined in Section 509(a)(3), a supporting organization is created primarily to fund the activities of one or more existing public charities.[11] As the name implies, there must be a close relationship to one or more such public charities. If that is acceptable to the donor, then the supporting organization will preserve some of the independence and identification with a donor's family typical of a private foundation while avoiding some of the limitations. For example, the Sherwick Fund is a supporting organization of the Cleveland Foundation. The Sherwick Fund enjoys the same favorable tax status as the community foundation while preserving its own identity and publishing a separate annual report.[12]

Finally, prospective donors may decide that they do not need these various alternatives. If the assets to be given to charity are readily marketable, why not give them away directly and use the more favorable deduction available to individuals for charitable gifts?

More than 83 percent of the $104 billion in private giving during a recent year went directly from individuals to churches, schools, hospitals, and similar local charities. While the bulk of this huge amount comes from lower- and middle-income givers, some wealthy individuals and families prefer to give to such institutions directly, either because they feel it is more personal or perhaps because their attorney, accountant, or other advisor has discouraged them from exploring the foundation route.[13]

There are also some situations where direct giving has real advantages, even though no charitable deduction is available. For example, a donor interested in a particular cause may wish to lobby for specific legislation. The individual donor may directly support lobbying activities and even (within prescribed limits) political candidates.[14] Or there may be times when charity begins at home—for example, the donor may wish to provide friends or relatives with financial assistance, even though gift taxes may be incurred. In these and other similar circumstances, direct giving by the individual is the only safe course. Nevertheless, giving through a foundation still offers a number of advantages over individual giving.

CORPORATE FOUNDATIONS

Corporations today use a variety of tools to demonstrate their commitment to community involvement. They can make donations or social investments directly from corporate programs, or they can establish a legally separate foundation. Today many corporations use both vehicles.[15]

While some of the arguments that have persuaded individual philanthropists to create foundations are also valid for corporations, there are several special considerations that corporations have found convincing. Most frequently cited is the leveling, from year to year, of the flow of contributions. By building a reserve or "cushion" of assets in the foundation during years when the parent company has high earnings, a relatively level flow of contributions from the foundation can be maintained even when the parent company's earnings fall off. This cushioning effect permits the corporation to reduce its taxes in good years through larger deductions, and to reduce its contributions to the foundation in lean years when it may have other pressing needs. The foundation can dip into its reserves at times when operating charities are likely to be suffering cutbacks in individual giving and are particularly in need of sources of support.

The legal restrictions applicable to private foundations pose few problems for this pattern of corporate foundation giving. Since most function with relatively small endowments, receiving annual contributions from the parent corporation and paying out similar amounts in grants, they are little affected by either the mandatory payout requirement or the excise tax on investment income.

The opportunity to use a charitable deduction and to build endowment makes the foundation attractive to a corporation for another reason. The immediate deductibility of gifts to the foundation means that in good years, a corporation can "endow" its foundation, and, as the earnings of that endowment build up, use those earnings to supplement the grants made possible by the corporation's annual contribution to the foundation. Thus, the corporation creates what might be termed an inflation hedge. The earnings on the foundation's endowment make possible increased annual giving, even when the corporation's annual contribution to its foundation remains unchanged.

Senior corporate officers are visible targets for fundraisers and are frequently importuned by those seeking corporate contributions. The corporate foundation serves as a buffer and makes possible better organized and more selective giving than is usual where a senior officer's only intermediary is a contributions committee of the board. Fundseekers assume, often incorrectly, that the chief executive officers control such committees, whereas they see corporate foundations, particularly if they have adopted and published guidelines for their giving, as more independent. This more independent status does not necessarily mean that the corporate foundation will require more staff time than is needed for direct giving by the corporation.

Corporate donors have cited several other factors as reasons for creating a separate foundation. Establishing a foundation, whether general or specific in purpose, can be seen as a formal statement by the corporation that it is committed to a program of social responsibility. And, reflecting the current times, a corporate foundation may also be more likely to survive a company merger or acquisition. While new management may see a direct corporate giving program as only one more budget area to undergo scrutiny and cutbacks, a separate foundation, especially one with an endowment, is more likely to continue its programs. Finally, reflecting the new consciousness of the global business markets, corporations are becoming more interested in making grants overseas. By following specific requirements, a foundation may make grants to foreign donees, but if a company were to make the same donation directly, it would not be allowed to deduct the gift as a charitable contribution.[16]

Finally, the process of establishing the foundation provides an opportunity for a useful reappraisal of philanthropic objectives and the upgrading of the giving function within the corporation. Such steps should bring about a more effective use of charitable dollars and justify any added administrative expenses.

Certain 1969 Tax Reform Act rules, such as the tight restrictions on self-dealing between donor and foundation and the threat of various penalty taxes that may be incurred by the foundation and its managers, even for inadvertent missteps, fall on the minus side of the ledger in a consideration of whether to form a corporate foundation. Also, since the 1969 Tax Reform Act, the foundation has lost some of its attraction as a recipient of appreciated property. These rules initially had a chilling effect on corporate foundations (and on private foundations generally), but the field has learned to live with them.[17]

Some grey areas remain where the corporate foundation may not be the most appropriate donor, and the corporation may prefer to make contributions directly. For example, research closely related to the corporation's business, even though conducted at a university, might best be funded as a direct corporate contribution. Scholarships and tuition loans for employees or their children, though permitted for a corporate foundation, must be handled under complex guidelines approved in advance by the IRS and may be somewhat easier to administer as a direct corporate activity.

Corporate giving frequently involves more than contributions of money. Gifts of inventory are deductible under 1976 rules governing such gifts, but the corporation must make them directly.[18] It is also best if the corporation itself handles loans of personnel and technical assistance to operating charities, another increasingly popular expression of corporate social responsibility. However, opportunities for such help and for volunteer work by company personnel may be identified by corporate foundation staff.

These and other considerations have led a number of corporations to channel a significant part of their annual giving through a corporate foundation. Still, they continue to use direct corporate gifts where that seems more appropriate. Except in the largest corporations, the same staff usually handles both types of giving.

To give away money wisely is never easy, but an institutionalized approach provides more opportunity for careful decision making and insulation from friendly arm twisting and emotional appeals. Grant-making foundations are a vital part of the voluntary philanthropic sector with a distinguished record in the social history of this country. Although now the most heavily regulated part of that sector, they have maintained most of their flexibility and merit careful consideration by today's donors and their advisors.

NOTES TO CHAPTER 2

1. John A. Edie, *First Steps in Starting a Foundation* (Washington, DC: Council on Foundations, 1987, rev. 1989.) This resource contains a comprehensive description of the options available in organized philanthropy.

2. Teresa Odendahl, ed., *America's Wealthy and the Future of Foundations* (New York: The Foundation Center, 1987), pp. 4–5, and subsequent chapters. Also, see Chapter 7 of this handbook for a full discussion of the legal requirements and restrictions for private foundations, resulting from the 1969 Tax Reform Act and amendments to its provisions in subsequent years.

3. Stan Olson, ed., "Introduction," *The Foundation Directory,*1991 Edition (New York: The Foundation Center, 1990), pp. v–xii.

4. Teresa Odendahl, ed., *America's Wealthy and the Future of Foundations,* pp. 78–82 and pp. 236–246. See also David R. Frazer, "Of Lasting Duration," *Foundation News,* January/February 1988, pp. 25–29.

5. As explained in Chapter 6, the general rule is that individuals may deduct up to 30 percent of gross income and corporations up to 10 percent of taxable income for cash gifts to private nonoperating foundations. Special rules apply to gifts of appreciated property, both by individuals and corporations. *Bequests* to private foundations, however, have no such limitations, and when coupled with the use of the marital deduction, remain an attractive method of estate planning.

6. *Tax Economics of Charitable Giving* (Chicago: Arthur Andersen & Co., 1987), and David Westfall, *Estate Planning Law and Taxation* (Boston: Warren, Gorham, and Lamont, Inc., 1984, and subsequent updates) are among the resources available on the topic of trusts.

7. John Edie, *First Steps in Starting a Foundation,* p. 41.

8. Because estate administration commonly requires a period of several years, particularly where a substantial asset of the estate is closely held stock, the period for planning divestiture is in reality longer than the five years provided by the statute, but the foundation cannot hold the stock permanently. For a discussion of the impact of payout requirements on investment policy, see Chapter 8.

9. When the foundation completely distributes or "flows through" all gifts and income within two-and-one half months of the end of the tax year in which it receives the gifts, the gifts qualify for maximum (50%) deductibility. Section 170(b)(1)(E)(ii).

10. Section 509(a) lists the categories of organizations that are public charities. These include organizations that are publicly supported under either the test set forth in Section 509(a)(2) or Section 170(b)(1)(A)(vi).

11. A supporting organization can also be established in conjunction with a civic league or labor or business organization exempt under Sections 501(c)(4), (5), or (6) if the organization is publicly supported under the test set forth in Section 509(a)(2). See Regulations 1.509(a)–4(k).

12. The pooled fund described in Section 170(b)(1)(E)(iii) is also recognized by the 1969 Tax Reform Act; a few have been set up by community foundations and colleges. Where available, this type of fund offers donors control over charitable expenditures during their lifetimes and maximum deductibility.

13. In the late 1980s, the Council on Foundations and several regional associations of grantmakers established programs to educate advisors about the benefits to their

clients of establishing private foundations. The Council and the associations make available upon request packets of material that describe the benefits of and the steps to be taken in establishing private foundations.

14. Private foundations are generally prohibited from lobbying by Section 4945(d)(1). However, under Section 501(c)(3) and liberalized, optional rules enacted in 1976, Section 501(h), public charities may engage in limited lobbying activities. Both they and private foundations are prohibited from intervening in political campaigns. See Chapter 4 for additional information on lobbying restrictions.

15. *Why Corporate Foundations Make Sense* (Washington, DC: Council on Foundations, 1988) contains a comprehensive discussion of the advantages and disadvantages of corporate foundations and corporate direct giving programs. This resource also contains information on how to establish a corporate foundation. For general statistics on corporate giving trends, see Linda Cardillo Platzer and Maureen Neven Duffy, *Survey of Corporate Contributions* (New York: The Conference Board, 1989).

16. Foreign subsidiaries of U.S.-based corporations may make charitable contributions locally, but the tax deductibility of such gifts will depend on the laws of the country in which the subsidiary operates.

17. Bruce Hopkins, Edward Beckwith, and Jana DeSirgh, *Company Foundations and the Self-Dealing Rules* (Washington, DC: Council on Foundations, 1987). A summary appears in "Tax Traps for the Company Foundation," *Foundation News*, November/December 1987, pp. 64–66. For a discussion of deductibility of appreciated property, see Chapter 6.

18. Baker & Hostetler, *Corporate Giving: A Compendium of Applicable Federal Tax Laws* (Washington, DC: Council on Foundations, 1987), pp. 17–26. See also Alex Plinio and Joanne Scanlan, *Resource Raising: The Role of Non-Cash Assistance in Corporate Philanthropy* (Washington, DC: Independent Sector, 1986.)

ANNOTATED BIBLIOGRAPHY–CHAPTER 2

THE DONOR'S OPTIONS

Edie, John. *First Steps in Starting a Foundation* (Washington, DC: Council on Foundations, Inc., 1987). 126 pages.

The author defines types of foundations and discusses issues to consider in setting up a foundation. Included are legal requirements, sample materials, and a reference list. This book is helpful for both potential donors and their advisors.

Odendahl, Teresa, ed. *America's Wealthy and the Future of Foundations* (New York: The Foundation Center, 1987). 325 pages.

This book examines the complexity of attitudes, motivations, economic forces, and regulations that cause wealthy people to commit private resources to public endeavors. It includes historical trends that lead to the formation of foundations and their subsequent growth.

INDEPENDENT FOUNDATIONS

Arthur Anderson & Co. *Tax Economics of Charitable Giving* (Chicago: Arthur Anderson & Co., 1985). 215 pages.

This provides comprehensive coverage of the economics of giving with examples. It covers deductions, outright gifts, deferred giving methods, annuities, bequests, and foundations. And it gives the legal and tax implications of many alternative methods of giving to charity.

Frazer, David R. "Of Lasting Duration." *Foundation News* 29, no. 1, January/February 1988, p. 24.

This is an excellent overview of the function and potential of private foundations.

Goulden, Joseph C. *The Money Givers* (New York: Random House, 1971). 341 pages.

In Chapter 2, "Founders and Their Motives," Goulden gives a series of reasons why individuals create foundations. He also provides historical examples.

Odendahl, Teresa, ed. *America's Wealthy and the Future of Foundations* (New York: The Foundation Center, 1987). pp. 78–82, 236–246.

Chapter 8 is entitled "Wealthy Donors and Their Charitable Attitudes." It includes information from interviews on the many reasons why donors choose the foundation vehicle versus other forms of giving.

Pekkanen, John. "The Great Givers, Part I and Part II." *Town & Country*, December 1979, p. 141, and January 1980, p. 37.

A general survey of foundation history and accomplishments up to 1980.

Russell, John M. *Giving and Taking: Across the Foundation Desk* (New York: Teachers College Press, 1977). 90 pages.

Chapter 2, "Are Foundations Really Necessary?" discusses what a foundation is and what it does. Russell stresses foundation work that government cannot do and gives examples.

Treusch, Paul E. *Tax-Exempt Charitable Organizations*, 3rd Ed. (Philadelphia: American Law Institute, 1988). 705 pages.

See Chapter 1, "Introduction to Tax Aspect of Philanthropy," p. 1, and Chapter 2, "Threshold Decisions," p. 33, for help in sorting out alternative methods of giving and applicable regulations.

Troyer, Thomas A. *Private Foundations Today: The Rebirth of an Estate Planning Option* (Washington, DC: Council on Foundations, 1982). 18 pages.

Reprinted from the proceedings of the 16th Annual Institute on Estate Planning, it discusses the various restrictions on private foundations established in 1969 together with the developments since that date. Troyer also gives advantages of private foundations and tips for estate planners.

Vanguard Public Foundation. *Robin Hood Was Right: A Guide to Giving Your Money for Social Change* (San Francisco: Vanguard Public Foundation, 1977). 148 pages.

This is a "how-to" manual for wealthy donors who might like to set up an activist or social change foundation. It contains chapters on three activist foundations, how to make a will, and how to set up a foundation.

Weaver, Warren. *U.S. Philanthropic Foundations: Their History, Structure, Management, and Record.*

Chapter 8, "Reasons for Establishing Foundations," includes an extensive list of reasons for forming a foundation.

CORPORATE FOUNDATIONS

Council on Foundations, Inc. *Why Corporate Foundations Make Sense* (Washington, DC: Council on Foundations, 1988). 46 pages.

This resource for grantmakers examined the advantages of establishing or expanding a corporate foundation. Although this publication explores several management structures, it devotes most of its attention to the corporate foundation. Also included is information on legal considerations in establishing a corporate foundation.

Clearinghouse on Corporate Social Responsibility. Washington, DC. "Corporate Foundations—A Charitable Alternative." *Response*, March 1980, p. 3.

Includes a brief history of company foundations and reasons for establishing one.

Council on Foundations. *Corporate Giving: A Compendium of Applicable Federal Tax Laws* (Washington, DC: Council on Foundations, 1987). 55 pages.

This resource for grantmakers includes all significant changes made by the 1986 Tax Reform Act.

Hopkins, Bruce; Beckwith, Edward; and DeSirgh, Jana. *Company Foundations and the Self-Dealing Rules* (Washington, DC: Council on Foundations, 1987). 28 pages.

This pamphlet explores the problems caused by the self-dealing rules in the context of company foundations. It includes guidelines for what is safe and what is not, an executive summary, and a 14-page technical analysis of the self-dealing rule as an appendix.

3

First Steps

Once one makes the decision to establish a foundation, how does one go about it? The legal and accounting professions play important roles in creating the appropriate corporate entity or trust, obtaining tax-exempt status, determining the timing of gifts to the foundation, and setting up accounts and records. Several other issues must be dealt with also. What will be the size and composition of the governing board? What is an acceptable amount or percentage of expenditures to budget for administrative costs? What qualifications should the executive staff have?

No book can provide answers to all the questions that will arise, but this chapter and Chapter 6 deal with some of these administrative matters. In Chapter 9 we suggest sources of up-to-date information and advice that the organizers of a new foundation may turn to for additional help. Although the material in this chapter will be familiar to attorneys who have created exempt organizations, it may be useful as a checklist for them and as a guide for those who have not been through the process.[1]

Since foundations are organized under state law, the first question is: Which state? The second question is: Shall we create the foundation as a charitable trust, or in corporate form? State regulation of foundations is uneven. Generally, those states with large numbers of foundations have active regulatory bodies but do not require much more information than that included in the federal returns. Some states also have filing or reporting fees, but the amounts involved are usually minor. Thus, there is not much incentive to "shop" for a lenient jurisdiction, and foundations are usually set up in the state where the business of the foundation will be conducted. To incorporate in one state and have the principal office in another will require the filing of annual information returns—and whatever else the states may require—with two states.[2]

What legal form will the donor choose for the foundation? A majority of foundations have been established as nonprofit corporations, although many continue to be formed as charitable trusts. Each form has its advantages, though; the charitable trust is very simple to create and usually requires no approval by a governmental agency. The law of trusts, based on common law, is not as precise and certain as incorporation laws. Trustees of a trust may be held to a higher standard of fiduciary responsibility than directors of a nonprofit corporation. Delegation of responsibility, particularly with regard to investment decisions, may be more difficult for trusts. Program activities managed "in-house," such as the operation of a clinic or conference center, are usually handled more simply under the corporate form.[3] Finally, enlarging the governing board or replacing its members is handled much more effectively under the corporate form. However, a valid argument in favor of the trust is its flexibility in receiving and disposing of real property. Under some state laws this is a cumbersome process for a nonprofit corporation.[4]

CERTIFICATE OF INCORPORATION

Let us assume that the foundation is to be incorporated under state law. The proposed name should be cleared with the appropriate state authority, and the "certificate of incorporation" must be prepared in accordance with state law. In order to meet federal requirements for exempt status as a private foundation, the certificate should include the following:

a. in its purpose clause, language establishing its charitable, educational, or similar purpose;

b. a statement that the earnings of the corporation shall not result in any private benefit to its members, trustees, or officers (except for reasonable compensation for services rendered);

c. a statement that no part of the corporation's activities shall consist of attempts to influence legislation and that it shall not participate in political campaigns;

d. a clause providing that on dissolution the assets shall be disposed of for charitable purposes; and

e. a statement that the corporation will comply with the requirements of Sections 4941, 4942, 4943, 4944, and 4945 of the Internal Revenue Code.

This last provision is designed to make the pertinent provisions of the Internal Revenue Code enforceable by state authorities. Foundations in existence at the time of the passage of the 1969 Tax Reform Act were required to amend their charters to include such language unless state laws were enacted that treated the required provisions as contained in the foundations' charters. Most states have passed such statutes, but it is good practice to include the language in the certificates of new foundations.

Having dealt with these formalities, and others that may be required by particular states, what substantive matters should the certificate of incorporation address? Many purpose clauses are drafted in very general language, "kissing the statute," as the saying goes, to simplify the process of obtaining tax exemption and to provide the foundation's governing body with maximum flexibility to make and modify policy as future needs, opportunities, and changing interests dictate. However, a donor anxious to assure that a foundation will adhere closely to the particular philanthropic objectives that motivated its creation may wish to have those objectives stated in the certificate. But too great a degree of specificity should be avoided, lest the foundation's managers in future years find themselves locked into a program for which there is no longer pressing need.

Limited Life or Perpetuity?

Most states give perpetual life to corporations created by statute while providing for ways that their members and others can terminate them. Unlike trusts created for the benefit of individuals, trusts for the benefit of charity can in most states be created in perpetuity. Lawyers who advise donors generally suggest these flexible options rather than proposing the creation of an organization that will have a limited term. However, some donors have established foundations for a limited period of time, requiring in the charter that the assets be distributed after a certain number of years.[5]

Factors to consider in reaching a decision on the length of life of a foundation might include:

a. Charitable purpose—The donor may wish to provide for a stream of gifts to charity far into the future to meet society's changing needs. Or the donor may wish the foundation to have a maximum impact in a particular field for a limited time and may require that the principal and income be expended over a specified number of years.

b. Family participation—If younger family members show interest in carrying foundation activities into the future, the donor may wish to establish the foundation in perpetuity to enable the family tradition to continue after his or her death. If future family involvement is unlikely, the donor may still feel confident that other board members can be found to carry on. If not, the donor may provide for the foundation's termination at a specified future time.

c. Size of the foundation—If the donor can provide a significant endowment to carry the foundation into the future, or if future gifts from family or other donors can be expected to provide substantial funds, the foundation may operate for many years. However, foundations established with limited assets and no expectation of additional gifts may become too small to achieve significant results. Costs of administration and inflation could reduce the value of their giving.

Governing Body

The incorporation process provides the donor with the opportunity to make important decisions about the foundation's governing body. Donors should immediately resolve issues such as the size, method of election, and tenure of the governing body because they can relate directly to the degree and duration of family control. Unless state law requires otherwise, it is probably best to keep the certificate of incorporation short and general, spelling out specifics in the more easily amended bylaws. For instance, if the donor wishes to limit the tenure of board members in order to ensure gradual infusion of new blood and new ideas, the limitations should be spelled out in the original bylaws, and the original board members invited to serve on that basis. Limits may be based on length of service, age, or both. This will avoid possible later embarrassment, misunderstanding, or the need to design complex "grandfather" clauses exempting the original trustees from tenure limitations.[6]

Sooner or later, many independent foundations face the question of family control. Many have debated this question over the years. Legislators proposed statutory "solutions" limiting family dominance in 1965, but they received little congressional support.[7] Within the field there are divergent views on the subject.[8] Some donors feel that unless their family can continue to exercise major influence in the policies and administration of their foundations, they would rather do something else with their money. Others feel that the gradual dilution of family control is a healthy thing. John Nason, himself a trustee many times over, examines the issue in a balanced way in *Foundation Trusteeship: Service in the Public Interest.* He concludes that for the many small foundations that make up the majority of the field, "family decisions might be enlarged and improved by nonfamily advice, but it would be counterproductive to eliminate family control."[9] However, he and others in the field argue strongly that foundation boards should try to achieve a balance and diversity of points of view and to reach out for additional experience. This helps ensure that foundations continue to be responsive and creative in their programs.

Membership corporations, provided for in many state not-for-profit corporation laws, offer flexibility since the members of the corporation need not be synonymous with the directors or trustees. For example, the members, whose primary function is to elect the directors, may be invited to serve for life. But the directors may be limited by the bylaws to two consecutive terms of four years and then rotated off for at least a year. Directors who have served eight years would remain members and be asked to attend the annual members' meetings and to participate in the selection of successor directors. Thus, "retired" directors keep in touch with the foundation, and family influence in the important selection process can remain strong even when the majority of the directors are not family.

The bylaws should not be excessively detailed. But they should contain authorization for appointing committees of the board, electing officers, notice and waiver of notice of meetings, and similar provisions dealing with the foundation's administration. Without trying to provide detailed guidelines for every eventuality, they should make clear that the board has authority to run the foundation. For example, indemnification of directors and officers is permissible in most circumstances despite the self-dealing rules of the Internal Revenue Code. Spelling out these circumstances in bylaws serves a useful purpose.[10]

Organizational Meeting

Under state law, corporations are required to hold an initial meeting to accomplish several specific tasks. The meeting can be held as soon as the state has approved the foundation's application for exemption, making the foundation a legal entity. Although state laws differ, typically the incorporators, named or potential board members, and the foundation's legal counsel will meet together to:

a. elect directors.
b. elect officers.

c. adopt the bylaws of the corporation.

d. pass a resolution to open bank accounts and sign signature cards.

e. establish the fiscal year.

f. adopt a corporate seal.

g. provide for recruitment of initial or interim staff.

h. record the minutes of this meeting and place them in a book along with subsequent meeting minutes to be kept for the life of the foundation.

The board may also want to begin work in other areas such as setting up investment accounts, discussing grantmaking goals, establishing a set of principles and practices for grantmaking, naming committee members, and other matters. All this depends on how much time the board wants to take at this first meeting and how frequently the board expects to meet.

FILING FOR EXEMPT STATUS WITH IRS

Once the certificate of incorporation has been approved by the appropriate state authorities, the foundation is ready to seek exemption from federal income tax, a status that will assure deductibility for contributions to it. This is done by filing Form 1023 with the appropriate district director. Whenever possible, the form should be filed within fifteen months of the foundation's organization under state law.[11] Such timely filing will make subsequent IRS recognition of exempt status retroactive to the date of organization. And it will ensure the deductibility of contributions that may have been made to cover organizing costs.

At first glance, Form 1023 is a bit overwhelming. With its various schedules, it currently runs fourteen pages. Fortunately, private foundations need worry about only six of those pages, and one of the six concerns only those foundations seeking "operating" status. (The form is also used by the wide variety of organizations seeking 501(c)(3) status as publicly supported organizations. Much of the form is applicable primarily to them.) Along with its Form 1023 application, the private foundation must file for an employer identification number on Form SS-4, even though it may not expect to have any employees. It should also indicate which activities code numbers best describe its purposes or activities.[12]

Form 1023 may be used to request IRS approval of grant procedures for any grants to individuals for travel, study, or similar purposes by completing Schedule H. However, failure to request such approval as a part of the request for recognition of exemption will not foreclose the foundation from submitting its criteria for such grants to individuals later, although IRS approval must be obtained before such grants are made.[13]

New or existing private foundations seeking recognition of their status as private operating foundations should complete Schedule E of Form 1023. The instructions in the Form 1023 package are not much help. But the somewhat complex tests are fully described with examples in IRS Publication 557, *Tax Exempt Status for Your Organization.*

Having completed and filed Form 1023, the foundation should mark time until it receives a determination letter from the IRS. If the application is a routine one that is handled at the appropriate IRS district office, the determination letter should be received within a few months. The transfer of substantial assets to the foundation before the determination letter is received is risky, even though a favorable determination letter in response to a timely application will be retroactive to the date of organization.

While waiting for the determination letter, the foundation must file its Form 990-PF with the IRS and the appropriate state authorities on or before the due date, as if its status had been determined. For a checklist of filing and other requirements a new foundation must meet, see Appendix 3.

Despite the numerous technical details, starting a private foundation is not burdensome. A donor who becomes familiar with the relevant issues and retains experienced legal counsel should have little difficulty taking the first steps outlined here.

NOTES TO CHAPTER 3

1. For a more in-depth discussion of the options available to donors and specific legal steps in starting a foundation, see John A. Edie, *First Steps in Starting a Foundation* (Washington, DC: Council on Foundations, 1987, rev. 1989).

2. The managers of a private foundation must furnish copies of the foundation's federal returns to the attorney general of the state in which the principal office of the foundation is located, the state in which the foundation was incorporated, and any other state to which the foundation reports. Section 6056; Regulation 1.6056–1(b)(3).

3. Marion Fremont-Smith, *Foundations and Government* (New York: Russell Sage Foundation, 1965), Chapters III and IV.

4. Edith L. Fisch, "Choosing the Charitable Entity," *Trusts and Estates* (December 1975), p. 875.

5. A recent example of a limited-life foundation is the Lucille P. Markey Charitable Trust, established through Mrs. Markey's will to fund medical research. The trust must spend both principal and interest by July 1997 (fifteen years after her death). Another well-known foundation of this type was the Rosenwald Foundation. In 1928, donor Julius Rosenwald enumerated the following reasons for requiring the trustees of his foundation to expend all its funds within 25 years after his death:

   > I am not in sympathy with this policy of perpetuating endowments and believe that more good can be accomplished by expending funds as Trustees find opportunities for constructive work than by storing up large sums of money for long periods of time. By adopting a policy of using the Fund within this generation, we may avoid those tendencies toward bureaucracy and a formal or perfunctory attitude toward the work which almost inevitably develop in organizations which prolong their existence indefinitely. Coming generations can be relied upon to provide for their own needs as they arise. (From F. Emerson Andrews, *Philanthropic Foundations* [New York: Russell Sage Foundation, 1956, pp. 55–56.])

6. Statistics on the number of foundations that provide for terms of office for board members, the length of terms, and other subjects are included in the *Foundation Management Report* (Washington, DC: Council on Foundations). The report is published every two years and is based on a survey of Council members and other grantmakers.

7. U.S. Congress, *Treasury Department Report on Private Foundations* (Washington, DC: 89th Congress, 1st Session, February 2, 1965). See also Donee Group, "Private Philanthropy: Vital and Innovative or Passive and Irrelevant?" *Research Papers*, Volume I (Filer Commission) (Washington, DC: Department of the Treasury, 1977), p. 65.

8. Compare Carl A. Gerstacker, "Let 'Outsiders' Control Family Foundation Boards," *Foundation News* 16, no. 5, September/October 1975, pp. 16–18; and Robert M. Johnson, "The Family Board," *Foundation News* 15, no. 1, January/February 1974, p. 4.

9. John W. Nason, *Foundation Trusteeship: Service in the Public Interest* (New York: The Foundation Center, 1989,) p. 46.

10. See John A. Edie, *Directors and Officers Liability Insurance and Indemnification* (Washington, DC: Council on Foundations, 1989.)

11. With Form 1023 a fee of several hundred dollars and Form 8718, "User Fee for Exempt Organization Determination Letter Request" are to be filed.

12. The Activity Code, found in the instructions for Form 1023, is designed to cover the activities of all Section 501 (c)(3) organizations. Many of the activities listed would be inappropriate or illegal for private foundations, and a few, such as "support, oppose or rate political candidates," would probably be illegal for any Section 501(c)(3) group. A grantmaking foundation, whether general purpose or with limited program interests, is best described by checking number 602: "gifts, grants, or loans to other organizations." Other code numbers will be more appropriate for operating foundations, e.g., number 120, "Publishing Activities," or number 199, "Other Scientific Research Activities." Activity Code Numbers 560 or 561 should be checked if the donor plans to have the foundation make grants directly to individuals. If the individual grants are to be used for scholarships, number 040 should be used.

13. See Chapter 4 for a brief discussion of these requirements. For a more comprehensive discussion, see Bruce R. Hopkins, et. al., *A Guide to the Making of Grants to Individuals by Private Foundations* (Washington, DC: Council on Foundations, 1987.)

ANNOTATED BIBLIOGRAPHY–CHAPTER 3

Edie, John. *First Steps in Starting a Foundation* (Washington, DC: Council on Foundations, 1987). 126 pages.

The author defines types of foundations and discusses issues to consider in setting up a foundation. Included are legal requirements, sample materials, and a reference list. This book is helpful for both potential donors and their advisors.

Marshall, Maxine. "Building a Foundation." *Foundation News* 30, no. 6, November/December 1989, pp. 56–58.

Marshall relates her and her husband's experiences in starting a family foundation. It is an enlightening article that takes the reader step by step through the process of starting a foundation.

CERTIFICATES OF INCORPORATION

Fisch, Edith L. "Choosing the Charitable Entity." *Trusts and Estates,* January 1974. p. 875.

Fisch discusses legally significant differences that apply to charities depending upon the form of organization—a trust, a corporation, or an unincorporated association. These differences affect creation, administration, and termination of the charity.

Fremont-Smith, Marion R. *Foundations and Government: State and Federal Law and Supervision* (New York: Russell Sage Foundation, 1965). 564 pages.

This is a comprehensive study of foundations as legal instruments, including requirements for foundations organized as trusts or corporations, registration and supervision at the federal and state levels, field surveys of regulation in operation, and discussion of the several congressional investigations of foundations.

Hopkins, Bruce. *The Law of Tax-Exempt Organizations,* 5th Ed. (New York: John Wiley and Sons, 1987). p. 611.

See Chapter 32, "Form of Organization and Governing Instruments," for a discussion of the organizational tests for achieving exempt status for foundations.

LIMITED LIFE OR PERPETUITY?

Embree, Edwin R., and Waxman, Julia. *Investment in People: The Story of the Julius Rosenwald Fund* (New York: Harper & Brothers, 1949). 291 pages.

A historical account dealing with the creation, operation, and accomplishments of the Julius Rosenwald Fund. In 1948, the foundation closed its doors according to Rosenwald's wish that the money be spent within 25 years of his death.

GOVERNING BODY

Boris, Elizabeth, Brody, Deborah, et al. Council on Foundations, Inc. *1990 Foundation Management Report* (Washington, DC: Council on Foundations, 1990). 181 pages.

This biennial report, based on a survey, conducted by the Council, provides in-depth information on foundation staffing, compensation, benefits, governing boards and other management policies. The information is provided for all types and sizes of foundations (both with and without paid staff) and contains additional information for corporate grantmakers and community foundations.

Council on Foundations. *Trustee Orientation Packet* (Washington, DC: Council on Foundations, 1991). 70+ pages.

This resource is designed to provide new foundation trustees with a basic understanding of their role and responsibilities. It includes several publications of the Council related to trusteeships. It also includes a suggested reading list.

Donee Group. "Private Philanthropy: Vital and Innovative or Passive and Irrelevant?" In *Research Papers*, Volume I (the Filer Commission), Part I, p. 49.

This recommends that foundation boards be required by law to have no less than one-third public members originally and after five years, no less than two-thirds public members. It calls for more ethnic and racial diversity on foundation boards.

Edie, John. *Directors and Officers Liability Insurance and Indemnification* (Washington, DC: Council on Foundations, 1989). 35 pages.

This guidance memorandum is prepared in a question and answer format, and is designed as a basic introduction to directors and officers insurance and the indemnification option.

Gerstacker, Carl A. "Let 'Outsiders' Control Family Foundation Boards." *Foundation News* 16, no. 5, September/October 1975, pp. 16–18.

Gerstacker recommends that nonfamily members should be allowed onto family foundation boards and into positions of leadership within those foundations.

Johnson, Robert M. "The Family Board." *Foundation News* 15, no. 1, January/February 1974, pp. 4–5.

The author addresses the issues of being too much of a family foundation. He discusses the pros and cons of both all-family boards and boards with nonfamily members.

Nason, John W. *Foundation Trusteeship: Service in the Public Interest* (New York: The Foundation Center, 1989).

Nason identifies the roles of foundations and trustees today, including a discussion of foundations' public and private development within a changing society. He also discusses board composition and the dynamics of effective boards, including board size, roles of members, and length and frequency of meetings and agendas. Nason addresses questions on board staffing, management, and compensation. The study includes a discussion of the new tax laws and their effects on foundations. This book updates his original findings in the 1977 book *Trustees and the Future of Foundations*.

Treasury Report on Private Foundations. Submitted to the Senate Committee on Finance and the House Committee on Ways and Means, February 2, 1965.

This is an examination of the major criticisms of foundations with generally sympathetic conclusions. Part II identifies several problems relating to foundation management, including the potential for the donor to wield substantial influence over the foundation.

U.S. Human Resources Corporation. "U.S. Foundations and Minority Group Interests." In *Research Papers*, Volume II (The Filer Commission), Part II, pp. 1, 165.

This study of the response of foundations to the needs of ethnic minorities concludes that foundations have not sufficiently provided for their needs. It discusses how to keep foundations aware of these needs and accessible to minorities and concludes that to fulfill the role of creative responsive philanthropists, foundations must have representation of broader interests in decision-making positions.

FILING FOR EXEMPT STATUS WITH THE IRS

Internal Revenue Service, Department of the Treasury. *Application for Recognition of Exemption*. Federal Package 1023.

This contains forms and instructions necessary to file for exempt status.

Internal Revenue Service, Department of the Treasury. *How to Apply for and Retain Exempt Status for Your Organization*. Publication 557.

The IRS describes the procedure for obtaining exempt status and the filing requirements for tax-exempt organizations.

Internal Revenue Service, Department of the Treasury. *Tax Information for Private Foundations and Foundation Managers*. Publication 578.

This is a detailed explanation of the tax rules that apply to private foundations. It includes explanations of items such as determining status, filing, notices, and other requirements. It provides information on terminating private foundation status, tax on net investment income, tax on taxable expenditures, tax on failure to distribute income, tax on self-dealing, tax on jeopardizing investments, and tax on excess business holdings.

4

Grantmaking and Other Charitable Activities

THE CHALLENGES AND REWARDS OF GRANTMAKING

When the donors make the decision to create a new foundation, they *giving it is not easy!* may at first feel that giving the foundation's money away will be easy. The common experience of many philanthropists and their associates is that it is not, although few would echo Andrew Carnegie's lament, "Pity the poor millionaire, for the way of the philanthropist is hard."[1] Grantmaking can and should be both challenging and rewarding to the grantmaker. Natural instincts of altruism and generosity, when channeled in an organized way toward, for example, solving important social problems or increasing cultural opportunities for the public, provide great personal satisfaction to those involved in the giving process.[2] The range of opportunities open to even the smallest foundation is so great that the process of selection among worthwhile undertakings can become an exciting challenge.

Grantmaking can also be a process of continuing education for the foundation manager who has the patience to be a good listener. Those who seek foundation support, for their own or their organization's efforts to make some improvement in the human condition or add to the sum of knowledge, tend to be well informed and refreshingly enthusiastic about their work. Foundation giving often comes down to a bet on *purpose* an individual. Not all such bets pay off, of course, but very few turn out so badly that the foundation manager feels funds were wasted.

SETTING GRANTMAKING POLICY

Where should a new foundation concentrate its grants? Are the programs of an existing foundation still responsive to the needs of its community? What are the new and emerging problems to which it should be attentive? Should the grants be made on a local, national, or international basis? These and similar questions are probably the most important a foundation board can ask. They are based on an assumption that has been at the heart of successful grantmaking for many years: Foundation giving differs from most individual giving because it is planned. This planning process may be, and for small foundations usually is, a very informal one, but it should be a conscious effort to determine how best to accomplish the foundation's purposes.

Many foundations, large and small, are created with very broad purpose clauses, but at an early stage in their development, they may begin to concentrate on certain areas of giving and to rule out others. The favored areas often reflect the particular charitable interests of the donors, the most pressing needs of a geographical area as perceived by the board, or the opportunities presented to the board by staff or consultants with experience in one or more segments of the voluntary foundation sector. Whatever the initiative that produces this concentration, the manager should recognize it as an important and distinguishing characteristic of the foundation, and it should be stated as a guideline for the foundation's constituency.

Because we all do best what we most want to do, trustees of a newly formed foundation should feel no compunction in choosing to emphasize those programs most interesting to them. In making choices, however, it is of utmost importance that the range of possibilities be well examined. Such a review can be an eye-opening and exhilarating opportunity to learn about different ways of meeting human needs and finding solutions to problems.

The choice among fields is a principal duty of a foundation board, and its members should be willing to expend money and time on the process. What the foundation decides at this stage is basic to all else it will do. At the same time, the difficulty of choosing among program fields can produce dissent among board members of new foundations. The process of winnowing down the infinite possibilities requires great good will, tolerance, and willingness to yield and compromise. After all, a foundation can achieve much good in many charitable fields. Therefore, it may be wiser for a majority on the board to accommodate the interest of one member or a minority of the board, at least for a trial period, by adding a program rather than voting it down.[3]

In seeking answers to the question, "Where shall we concentrate our giving?'' many foundation boards have turned to outside consultants.[4] This is a particularly appropriate route for a new foundation that intends to employ staff but has not completed its selection. The choice of fields of concentration should help determine the job description of the executive and give prospective applicants for the position some conception of the challenges and opportunities that the job will offer.

Another, perhaps more customary, opportunity for conscious choice among program areas arises when the foundation employs the first, or a new, executive director. If the executive is charged with helping a new foundation's board make these choices, that person's task will be quite similar to that of an outside consultant. Others in the field will readily provide suggestions and advice, and the staff of the Council on Foundations can help make referrals. There should also be ample opportunity in the early stages for conferences with individual board members to help the new executive develop rapport with the board and to determine areas of special interest to particular directors.[5]

Where the new executive is inheriting an established program, the change in staff, or the move from an unstaffed to staffed operation, offers an ideal opportunity to reappraise past programs and plan for the future. In many large staffed foundations, program reviews are

"*Oh, nonsense—hundreds of people have exhausted their grants and gone on to live happy, productive lives.*"

Drawing by Donald Reilly; © 1978
The New Yorker Magazine, Inc.

made every few years as a matter of course, often with the help of outside consultants and under the direction of special board committees.
In smaller foundations, usually staffed by a single executive or managed only by the trustees, such stocktaking may be hard to fit into a
typically crowded schedule. It may also be difficult to justify to a board
comfortable with existing programs. Hence, it is important that the new
executive make the most of the transition period.

PHILOSOPHIES AND TECHNIQUES OF GRANTMAKING

One of the challenges all foundation managers face is the choice between active and passive roles. A number of foundations have been established as, or converted into, operating foundations. Their funds are
devoted primarily to the active conduct of charitable programs. But
grantmaking foundations need not sit back and wait for grantseekers to
find them. Some foundations or groups of foundations take the initiative to study a particular problem and then seek out existing agencies or
else create new ones to work toward the problem's solution.[6] Others
conduct formal needs assessments in areas of interest. Some call meetings or ask assistance of agencies active in a field and invite presentations from them about its importance and the opportunities for
foundation activity.[7]

Another much-discussed issue within the foundation field is (in
oversimplified terms) the choice between preserving excellence and encouraging constructive change. Foundations fund a variety of organizations representing each characteristic, although some prefer to combine
these approaches by funding well-known institutions that wish to test
innovative ideas or move into new program areas.

Whichever approach they may favor, foundation managers should
be responsive to changing circumstances, emerging needs, and fresh
approaches to old problems. This is sometimes done through participation of board members and staff in meetings to which the grantseeking
public is invited.[8] Another way of keeping in touch with new developments is by attending periodic meetings or workshops on particular
program activities and interests.[9] The periodic evaluations of programs
and policies suggested in Chapter 5 are also important.

Although foundations have been faulted by some critics for excessive
caution and lack of sensitivity to social problems in their grantmaking,
others find many foundations overly liberal and too involved with
social change. Such charges have also been made by members of Congress. As in other fields, generalizations are not very useful in describing the social or political orientation of grantmakers. They are a

remarkably heterogeneous group, and there is opportunity for many different points of view to be supported.[10]

Whatever the philosophy of a particular governing board, few would disagree with Alan Pifer's conclusion, after a discussion of foundations and public policy that:

Foundations do have a legitimate role to play in public policy formation, although no one should doubt that there are some risks involved. But if that role is played openly, conscientiously, and with integrity, the chances are good the public will not only be tolerant of foundations, but will even come to see them as essential to the well-being of the nation.[11]

Grantmaking foundations also frequently play the role of broker. Having made a grant to a particular organization and being convinced that the money was well invested, a foundation may invite other foundations with similar interests to learn more about that organization's work. Or, convinced of an agency's worth but unable to fund it directly, the interested foundation may provide useful leads to other funding sources. A foundation can also take the lead in bringing together community leaders or separate factions to work on joint solutions to problems. These activities are often more easily undertaken by a staffed foundation than one where the directors handle the giving program as volunteers.[12]

Project versus General Support Grants

Many operating charities seek foundation support for experiments in service delivery or specific research proposals. Less frequently, a foundation persuades an operating agency to take on a new program and makes a commitment to that program for a long enough period to enable the agency to hire qualified staff, develop the program, and demonstrate its effectiveness. This type of giving, whether at the foundation's initiative or in response to a proposal originated by the agency, is referred to as a *project grant*. It is a way for the foundation manager to direct funding to a specific target and, perhaps, to attract additional support from other foundations or from government if the project is effective. Project grants also give the grantmaker maximum flexibility to move to other problems or program areas when a project is completed. The project grant has the advantage of an agreed cutoff date beyond which the foundation has no commitment. Not surprisingly, though, successful projects are soon built into an agency's ongoing program. Unless government picks up the new activity or the agency terminates other activities, it will need more private funding, and the agency may well knock on the initiating foundation's door again. To reduce this likelihood, some foundations encourage their grantees to develop additional sources of support during the life of the project. Others virtually require this by reducing annual payments during the last years of multi-year grants or by requiring that its contributions be matched from other sources.[13]

The _general support grant_ is typical of unstaffed foundations, although many staffed foundations provide general support as well. This type of funding is often the most valuable kind of support from the point of view of an operating agency, especially if the agency is already the recipient of project grants. Within the foundation's chosen program areas, the board picks one or more operating charities in a particular field for general support, on the premise that the leaders of the agencies are in a better position to determine priorities and pick targets than the foundation itself.[14]

The two approaches are, in a sense, complementary: An agency entirely dependent on project funding may have trouble meeting its core budget, while one that receives only general support may become set in its ways and be reluctant to try new ideas. Similarly, the same foundation may use both approaches, fitting a particular grant to the general needs of the agency or the problems being addressed.

Duration of Grants

Foundations seldom make commitments to a particular program or agency for longer than three years. They are reluctant to tie up funds far in advance, so they are able to shift their support to fields as circumstances change. Some foundations feel grantees will be more accountable if they allow only a short period requesting renewal. Even on three-year commitments, it is common practice to require at least annual reporting and to make payments for the second and third years contingent on satisfactory progress reports. Where one foundation is the principal source of an agency's funding and that foundation has limited staff, it may review its commitment every second year, and, if appropriate, renew it for another three-year term.

Some argue that foundations _should_ be willing to make long-term commitments because government agencies usually are not able to do so. But foundations that provide building and endowment funds, such as the Kresge Foundation, _are_ making long-term bets on the recipient institutions, even though the funds are paid out over a relatively short period. Other foundations may make long-term commitments to program areas where few service agencies exist or to organizations doing work in areas that, although important, do not have much popular appeal.

The Grantmaking Process

Having made policy decisions on areas of concentration and types of grants, it is important that a foundation communicate these decisions and suggest to its potential constituency how the foundation plans to carry out its program. Will the foundation require applications on a prescribed form? Will there be deadlines for consideration of requests at a particular meeting? Will interviews be encouraged or discouraged? Before exploring these questions, let us look at a "flow chart" (pp. 52–53) and see what is involved in processing a grant request. Although the chart was prepared by a staffed foundation, the tasks assigned to staff may be handled by one or more board members in a foundation managed solely by trustees.

Handling Initial Requests

As the chart shows, there is a preliminary screening process to eliminate requests that clearly fall outside the foundation's stated guidelines. Requests that fail to survive this screening should be promptly declined. Since the volume of such requests may be considerable and can be burdensome for small foundations, a few rules of thumb may be helpful. First, form letter grant requests with facsimile signatures could be turned down with a form postcard or letter. Second, requests for annual reports or guidelines should be honored, but sometimes it may be useful to include a partial form letter indicating that on the basis of the information furnished, the inquiring agency probably would not qualify for support. Third, requests that demonstrate some knowledge of the foundation's interests deserve a prompt reply, particularly if the request indicates the writer plans to follow up with a phone call. Computerized form letters that can be tailored to different situations make this process quite simple.

Working up the Application

When the request is one the foundation wishes to consider for a possible grant, the flow chart suggests a number of steps to be taken in the work-up and review.[15] Some of the questions that usually need to be answered can be handled by the use of an application form or the listing of such items in the foundation's printed guidelines. Other questions involving the agency's competency or future funding of the project may require a meeting with the applicant, checks with other foundations, or consulting an expert in a particular field (sometimes a phone call will provide the answer).

Many of the steps suggested in the chart can and probably should be eliminated where, for example, the request is for renewal of support to an established agency. Rigid insistence on an application form in such

Application Flow Chart

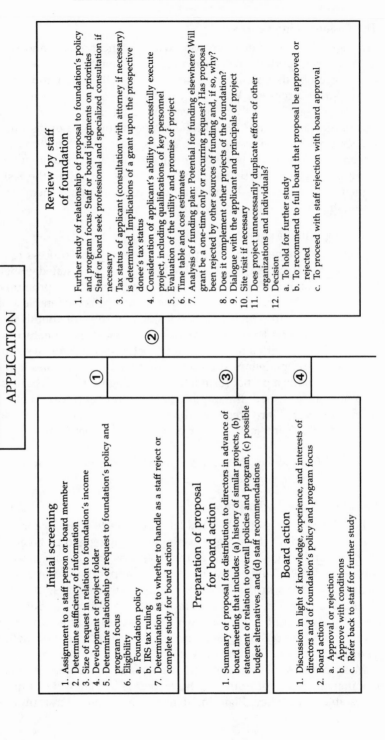

APPLICATION

①

Initial screening

1. Assignment to a staff person or board member
2. Determine sufficiency of information
3. Size of request in relation to foundation's income
4. Development of project folder
5. Determine relationship of request to foundation's policy and program focus
6. Eligibility
   a. Foundation policy
   b. IRS tax ruling
7. Determination as to whether to handle as a staff reject or complete study for board action

②

Review by staff of foundation

1. Further study of relationship of proposal to foundation's policy and program focus. Staff or board judgments on priorities
2. Staff or board seek professional and specialized consultation if necessary
3. Tax status of applicant (consultation with attorney if necessary) is determined. Implications of a grant upon the prospective donee's tax status
4. Consideration of applicant's ability to successfully execute project, including qualifications of key personnel
5. Evaluation of the utility and promise of project
6. Time table and cost estimates
7. Analysis of funding plan: Potential for funding elsewhere? Will grant be a one-time only or recurring request? Has proposal been rejected by other sources of funding and, if so, why?
8. Does it complement other projects of the foundation?
9. Dialogue with the applicant and principals of project
10. Site visit if necessary
11. Does project unnecessarily duplicate efforts of other organizations and individuals?
12. Decision
    a. To hold for further study
    b. To recommend to full board that proposal be approved or rejected
    c. To proceed with staff rejection with board approval

③

Preparation of proposal for board action

1. Summary of proposal for distribution to directors in advance of board meeting that includes: (a) history of similar projects, (b) statement of relation to overall policies and program, (c) possible budget alternatives, and (d) staff recommendations

④

Board action

1. Discussion in light of knowledge, experience, and interests of directors and of foundation's policy and program focus
2. Board action
   a. Approval or rejection
   b. Approve with conditions
   c. Refer back to staff for further study

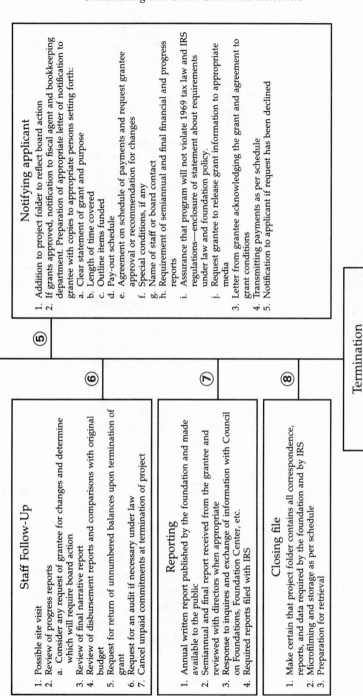

Notifying applicant

1. Addition to project folder to reflect board action
2. If grants approved, notification to fiscal agent and bookkeeping department. Preparation of appropriate letter of notification to grantee with copies to appropriate persons setting forth:
   a. Clear statement of grant and purpose
   b. Length of time covered
   c. Outline items funded
   d. Pay-out schedule
   e. Agreement on schedule of payments and request grantee approval or recommendation for changes
   f. Special conditions, if any
   g. Name of staff or board contact
   h. Requirement of semiannual and final financial and progress reports
   i. Assurance that program will not violate 1969 tax law and IRS regulations—enclosure of statement about requirements under law and foundation policy.
   j. Request grantee to release grant information to appropriate media
3. Letter from grantee acknowledging the grant and agreement to grant conditions
4. Transmitting payments as per schedule
5. Notification to applicant if request has been declined

Staff Follow-Up

1. Possible site visit
2. Review of progress reports
   a. Consider any request of grantee for changes and determine which will require board action
3. Review of final narrative report
4. Review of disbursement reports and comparisons with original budget
5. Request for return of unnumbered balances upon termination of grant
6. Request for an audit if necessary under law
7. Cancel unpaid commitments at termination of project

Reporting

1. Annual written report published by the foundation and made available to the public
2. Semiannual and final report received from the grantee and reviewed with directors when appropriate
3. Response to inquires and exchange of information with Council on Foundations, Foundation Center, etc.
4. Required reports filed with IRS

Closing file

1. Make certain that project folder contains all correspondence, reports, and data required by the foundation and by IRS
2. Microfilming and storage as per schedule
3. Preparation for retrieval

Termination

From *Foundation News*, November–December 1971. Included in article by Robert W. Bonine, "One Part Science, One Part Art," pp. 244–249.

instances may only produce unneeded paperwork. At a minimum, however, the foundation manager should be satisfied as to the current tax status and finances of the applicant and the competence of its management.

Many grant requests now routinely include a copy of the applicant's ruling letter from the IRS establishing its tax status. The importance of determining tax status stems primarily from the requirements of Section 4945 of the Tax Reform Act. Private foundations may make grants only to public charities, unless the grantor exercises "expenditure responsibility" as explained later in this chapter. Most charitable agencies qualify as public charities, either through the nature of their work (church, school, or hospital) or because they receive substantial support from the general public (the "support" tests of Section 509(a)(2) or 170(b)(1)(A)(vi)). Most have obtained the IRS letter stating that they are "not a private foundation."[16] Even new agencies can obtain tentative rulings to that effect, and grantors may generally rely upon these to cover legal requirements.

Where this is not volunteered, it should be requested, at least if the agency is new to the foundation. If the agency is well known, a check with the Treasury's *Cumulative List*[17] often will be sufficient to confirm its status. Some foundations go a step further by including a statement in the grant agreement to be signed by an official of the grantee organization saying, in effect, that the IRS letter provided is the latest communication from the IRS relevant to the tax status of the grantee.

The applicant's financial condition, usually available in its latest annual report or audited statement, is a good indication of the strength of the agency, its need for additional funding, and the percentage of its budget consumed by fundraising costs and administration.[18] The annual report may also define the organization's purposes, list its accomplishments, and identify its board and staff leadership. Occasionally the financial statement may disclose endowment or reserves so large in relation to the annual budget that the grantmaker may decide a grant is not really needed. Most charities count themselves fortunate if they have reserves equal to one year's operating budget.

When these routine items in the review process are out of the way, the toughest part of the foundation manager's job begins. Selecting the most promising proposal, or determining the most pressing need, is an art, not a science. Despite carefully articulated criteria and guidelines, subjective judgments become necessary when, as is usually the case, a foundation receives many more worthwhile proposals within its stated fields of interest than it can fund.

Perhaps the most important of these subjective judgments relates to the leadership of the agency or the project. This factor can be evaluated to some extent by looking at an established agency's track record, for example, the board's leadership and involvement in the agency and whether membership of the board and composition of the staff represent diversity. It is also sometimes helpful to look at the résumés of a new agency's executives. But if geography and time permit, there is no good substitute for an interview, or better yet, a site visit.[19]

If the request is for project support or to help launch a new agency, the foundation should ask another type of question. Are there other similar efforts already under way? What are the prospects for future funding from other private sources or from government? If the proposal is for a short-term study or demonstration, how will the results be shared with the field, and who will pay attention? How will the agency evaluate its success? Answers to these questions should reveal much about the planning that has gone into the proposal and help the foundation manager rank it on an informal priority list. These answers may also suggest other sources of information that managers can use to check their judgment.

TYPES OF GRANTS

Having decided that a proposal merits support, the foundation manager can recommend to the board one of several alternative types of grants. If the applicant has requested a specific amount within the range of the foundation's usual grants, intended for use over a short period of time, the recommendation can be simple. Frequently, however, the amount asked is larger than the foundation can afford, but the manager believes there are other likely funding sources. Or, sometimes a project is strengthened by a shared funding. In either case, a _matching grant_ may be in order. A typical response is, "We'll give you $5,000 toward the $15,000 budget for the project, provided you raise the balance from funders within six months." This type of grant serves several purposes. It enables the recipient to go to other grantmakers with tangible proof of the foundation's interest. It also assures the foundation that other appropriate funding sources are sharing the costs and that its money will not be spent until enough has been raised to fund the project.[20]

Matching grants can be used in a variety of ways. For example, one is to encourage a grantee to seek a broader base of support by matching only grants from new sources. Overuse of the device has its disadvantages. The National Endowments for the Arts and Humanities have been accused of using high matching requirements to "dictate" the programs of foundations interested in these fields. And local and regional foundations have occasionally made similar complaints about foundations with national giving programs.

The funder may on occasion be persuaded of the project's worth but feel that it needs some substantive change. Such doubts can usually be resolved by discussing them with the grantee. If not, the funder may recommend a conditional grant specifying the desired change. Such grants should be used sparingly, since they amount to telling the grantee agency "we know best."

When a foundation is convinced of the merits of a proposal but is not able to provide complete funding out of current income, it may wish to make a multiyear commitment. Appropriations providing for payments to be made in future years do not usually count in meeting the payout requirements under Section 4942 until payment is actually made to the grantee, but there is an exception in the law for *set-asides*. If the foundation demonstrates successfully to the IRS in advance that the funds set aside for future payments will in fact be paid within 60 months and that the project can better be accomplished by such a set-aside than by an immediate grant, the full appropriation may count in the first year.[21]

Expenditure Responsibility

So far we have discussed grants to public charities. Occasionally, a new agency or one receiving its principal support from one or two sources cannot qualify for this status even though it has 501(c)(3) status. Or a non-501(c)(3) organization such as a for-profit business may seek funding for a project that is clearly charitable in nature. The statute provides a specific set of rules under which a private foundation may still make a grant to such agencies. These rules have proved to be workable, and many foundations routinely make such *expenditure responsibility* grants.

Briefly, this process formalizes what is basically good practice. There must be a pregrant inquiry to determine the reliability of the grantee. The written terms of the grant must include commitments by the grantee to return unused funds, to submit full reports, to make financial accounts available, and not to use the grant for other than charitable purposes. If the grantee does not have a 501(c)(3) status, it must segregate and account separately for the grant funds. The purposes of the grant must be spelled out clearly in a grant agreement letter signed by the grantee. Additionally, under expenditure responsibility rules, the grantor must make a brief report to the IRS as an attachment to its annual Form 990-PF.[22]

One other requirement in the expenditure responsibility agreement is that the grantee not use any of the funds to influence legislation. In an excess of caution, some foundations have incorporated such a prohibition in their grant letters to public charities. This is neither necessary nor appropriate.[23]

Certain Earmarked Grants

Foundation managers inquiring into the tax status of a prospective grantee (let's call it the Y charity) are sometimes told, "We haven't received our exemption yet, but the X agency, recognized by the IRS as a publicly supported 501(c)(3) organization, will accept grants for us." On other occasions, the X agency will actively solicit funds for the programs of Y charity and other groups for which X agency acts as sponsor. Is the foundation that makes grants to X under these circumstances running any risk?

The regulations under Section 4945 dealing with grants to organizations cover these situations under the heading "Certain Earmarked Grants." They seem to say that in either of the two circumstances described, the foundation will be considered to have made its grant to the X agency if the grant is not earmarked for Y, and if there is no agreement between the foundation and X giving the foundation the power to select Y as the final recipient. The difficulty with the regulation is that in both situations, the foundation wants the grant to reach Y. The more assurance the foundation has that this will happen, the more likely it is that on audit the foundation will be challenged for having made its grant to Y, with possible penalty taxes for failure to exercise expenditure responsibility. However, as long as X agency takes full responsibility for the Y project, the grant *should* be considered as made to X for one of its charitable purposes. A safe and reasonable alternative is for the foundation to make the grant directly to Y and exercise expenditure responsibility.[24]

International Grantmaking

While most private foundations make grants on a local or national basis, an increasing number of foundations include grants for international purposes as part of their programs. The realization that we live in an interdependent world has caused foundations and corporations to look beyond our borders for worthy causes to support or to support U.S. organizations that operate programs outside this country. Making grants on an international basis can be incorporated into the foundation's existing interests, policies, and procedures. If the foundation has established application and grant monitoring procedures, both domestic and international grants can undergo similar scrutiny. As in the case with domestic grants, international grants must be made for exempt charitable purposes as defined by the Internal Revenue Code.

A private foundation may legally make grants for international purposes in a number of ways.[25] The simplest way is to make a grant to a U.S.-based organization with 501(c)(3) status that operates programs here or abroad or to a non-U.S. organization that has been granted 501(c)(3) status. In both these cases, the foundation can rely on the 501(c)(3) status of the organization to prove that its operations are charitable as defined by the IRS. Large and small foundations support a wide range of activities through such organizations. These include educational and cultural exchanges; international conferences on disarmament, environmental, and economic issues as well as family planning programs and technical assistance to agriculture in Third World countries. It includes support for similar programs conducted by organizations such as the Moscow-based International Foundation for the Survival and Development of Humanity.

Foundations may also make grants to foreign governments, provided they prove that the grant is made for charitable purposes and will not be diverted for other purposes. A foundation may also make a grant to a non-U.S. organization that is the "equivalent of a 501(c)(3) organization" in a foreign country. This status can be shown by obtaining a written opinion from an attorney who has applied criteria similar to those used by the IRS in determining tax-exempt status in the United States to conclude that the organization in question is the equivalent of a 501(c)(3) public charity. Based on an affidavit from the grantee, the same result can be obtained if the foundation makes a "good-faith" determination that the grantee is the equivalent of a 501(c)(3) public charity.[26]

For grants to an organization that does not fit any of the categories described earlier, a foundation must exercise expenditure responsibility and document that the grant will be used for charitable purposes.[27]

Grants to Individuals

Grants to individuals for educational or charitable purposes have a long and distinguished history in philanthropy. While gifts made directly to individuals are not deductible as charitable contributions when made by the individual taxpayer, they are clearly an approved activity for foundations. However, the 1969 Tax Reform Act requires that a foundation planning to make grants for "travel, study, or other similar purposes" obtain advance approval of its selection procedures from the IRS. And the procedures must be designed to assure objectivity in the selection process.[28]

There are three types of awards to individuals that foundations may make without going through the process of submitting procedures. First, grants may be made to educational institutions for scholarship purposes if the selection process is handled by the institution.[29] Second, the foundation may function as almsgiver, awarding grants directly to indigents to help them meet their living expenses, for example. Third, the foundation may contract with an individual directly to perform a research assignment or render other services connected with the foundation's program or administration.[30]

Special rules revised in 1977 and 1980 govern the awarding of grants by company foundations to employees or their children. In general, the rules described above apply, but the number of grants permitted is limited to 10 percent of the employees' children eligible to receive them, or to 25 percent of the number of eligible employees' children who apply, whichever is greater. Grants to employees are limited in any year to 10 percent of the number of eligible applicants.[31]

Loans and Program-Related Investments

Scholarship loans are included within the definition of "grant" and must meet the requirements for grants to individuals just described. When the loans are repaid, the funds are added to the foundation's 5-percent payout requirement for the year in which the loan is repaid. This is because they are counted as qualifying distributions when made.

Loans to operating charities are also a part of the grantmaking foundation's repertoire. These are typically handled in one of two ways. First, a group of funders may make grants or loans to a pool, perhaps established by the local or regional association of grantmakers, community foundation, or another publicly supported agency, which in turn loans funds at low or no interest to operating charities. Second, an individual foundation may make a *program-related investment* in an operating charity, or, under certain circumstances, to a for-profit entity.

This term program-related investment, added to the foundation manager's vocabulary by the 1969 Tax Reform Act, has opened up new opportunities for imaginative use of a foundation's resources.[32] Foundations have traditionally made a clear distinction between their investments and their grant program. Foundations plan investments to produce income and capital appreciation, while their grants carry out their charitable mission. Program-related investments lie somewhere between these two functions. Although made as loans or equity investments, they are motivated primarily by the hope of achieving the foundation's program objectives, not economic return. For example, if a foundation is concerned about the deterioration of an inner-city neighborhood, it may invest capital in a housing corporation engaged in rehabilitation work, even though the corporation hopes eventually to make a profit on its projects. By following the guidelines for such investments spelled out in the regulations, a foundation may count such an investment as a qualifying distribution. It will not be considered to have made a jeopardy investment under Section 4944, even though the investment is a risky one. Both large and small foundations have successfully invested in organizations in a variety of areas, including the arts, health, housing, social services, education, and the environment.

Operating Programs

So far this chapter has dealt primarily with grants to other organizations and individuals. Most foundations carry out their purposes through grants, but often it makes more sense for a foundation to "do it itself." This may be true with respect to a conference, research project, publication of research funded by the foundation, or construction of a building to serve as offices for local voluntary agencies. Such activities are entirely appropriate, and their costs count as qualifying distributions under Section 4942.[33]

If the foundation's programs develop to the point where most of its income is being expended directly on such activities, it may wish to qualify as a "private operating foundation." Successful reclassification brings with it different payout requirements and additional tax incentives for potential donors.[34] If a foundation obtains support for its programs from a number of donors, it may be possible to convert from the private category to that of publicly supported organization. For example, the Southern Education Foundation applied for and received reclassification from a private foundation to a public charity from the IRS. The foundation made the change to reflect its operations better, which include using grants from other donors as well as its own funds to accomplish the foundation's goals, and to make it unnecessary for such donors to exercise expenditure responsibility.

The Board Meeting

Once the staff (or perhaps a delegated board member) has decided on the requests and projects to recommend for board consideration, they prepare a docket for the board members well in advance of the meeting. Whenever possible, the docket should be discussed with the board chair before the meeting. Questions that the chair may have will be good preparation for staff members who will attend the meeting. Since the docket usually becomes the major part of the agenda, it is important that the presiding officer be familiar with it. The length and form of the board docket varies widely. One approach is to present the essence of a proposal in one or two pages, with attachments or excerpts from the grant request only where necessary. If the staff (or board) members who prepared the item are present at the board meeting, they can always be called upon to answer questions on matters not covered in the written summary. Another approach is to give board members more of the flavor of the proposal by including the request as an attachment to the analysis and recommendation.

Board meetings need not be limited to considering grant requests. They can also provide opportunities for board members to gain more information and understanding about the foundation's work and recent developments in its fields of interest. One way of doing this is to set aside a block of time at each meeting for discussion, perhaps with a grantee (whose grant is not up for renewal) or else with another knowledgeable "outsider" who can present an overview of activities related to one of the foundation's interests. Occasional board and staff retreats provide opportunities for more extended review of program and policies, as discussed in the next chapter.

Rocks and Shoals

The independent grantmaking foundation offers great flexibility and scope for creative philanthropy. There are, however, trouble spots, which can be avoided if the dangers are recognized in advance.

First, it is important the self-dealing rules of Section 4941 be observed in the grantmaking process. A grant by a foundation that satisfies a binding personal pledge by a foundation manager or other disqualified person is subject to penalty tax. Thus, if Tom Jones, founder of the Jones Foundation, signs a personal pledge to contribute $1,000 to the Jonesport Hospital, the Jones Foundation must not make a grant to the hospital to discharge Mr. Jones's obligation. But if authorized by his board, Mr. Jones can make a pledge on behalf of the foundation, which it can appropriately honor.

Second, grants to other private nonoperating foundations or to public charities "controlled" by the grantor foundation or its disqualified persons will count as qualifying distributions for the grantor only if the foundation expends the funds within the next tax year and meets reporting requirements. If Tom Jones and other directors of the Jones Foundation are also a majority of the board of the Jonesport Hospital, the foundation's attorney should look closely at Regulations 53.4942(a)-(3)(a) and (c) before the foundation makes a grant to the hospital.

Third, *any* expenditure by a private foundation to influence an election is subject to penalty tax under Section 4945. Additionally, a grant to a public charity, if it is earmarked for a prohibited purpose, will incur penalty taxes and jeopardize the foundation's exemption. The only "exception" is the carefully defined nonpartisan voter education activity, which may be funded by foundations through agencies meeting the requirements of Section 4945(f).[35]

Fourth, grants to influence legislation are also taxable expenditures under Section 4945, but here the definitions and the exceptions are quite liberal. Actions by executive, judicial, or administrative bodies are excluded from the definition of legislation. Foundations are permitted to lobby in their own defense on matters that might affect their existence, powers and duties, tax status, or the deductibility of contributions to them. They are also permitted to engage in or fund nonpartisan research and make the results available to the public and legislators. Foundation managers or their grantees may respond to written requests for technical advice or assistance from legislative committees. And most important to the activities of many operating agencies, foundations may make grants to public charities that are attempting to influence legislation. In these cases, the foundation should not earmark general purpose grants for lobbying. When a grant is being made to support a special project, no part of the grant may be earmarked for lobbying purposes, and the amount of the grant may not exceed the total expenditures in the budget of the special project for activities other than lobbying.[36]

Finally, when a foundation considers funding a new organization it should be careful about "tipping." Tipping occurs if the grantee must meet a public support test and the foundation's grant is so large in relation to other support as to cause the charity to fail the test and be "tipped" out of public charity status into private foundation status. For many years, the granting foundation was subject to penalty for tipping the charity unless it exercised expenditure responsibility. Now, with the advent of Revenue Procedure 89–23, no penalty applies to the grantor when tipping occurs so long as the grantee has a valid tax determination letter, the IRS has not published a change in the grantee's status, and the grantor does not control the grantee. For the grantee, being "tipped" out of public charity status can have serious consequences. So, if a foundation plans to make a large grant to a small organization, for example, the grantor should alert the grantee in advance to potential tipping problems. Rulings by the IRS also make provision for excluding "unusual grants" to help meet such problems.[37]

NOTES TO CHAPTER 4

1 J. F. Wall, *Andrew Carnegie* (New York: Oxford University Press, 1970), p. 796.

2. At the close of the first meeting of the Russell Sage Foundation, Mrs. Sage said, "I am nearly eighty years old and I feel as if I were just beginning to live." Quoted in F. Emerson Andrews, *Philanthropic Foundations* (New York: Russell Sage Foundation, 1956), p. 42.

3. One criterion frequently used in selecting program areas is stated by Robert F. Higgins (*Foundation News* 17, no. 3, May/June 1976, pp. 40–45) as "areas relatively underfunded by most other foundations." This can be a useful guideline but probably should not be an absolute requirement. For example, if several national foundations had become enthusiastic sponsors of public interest law programs, a regionally oriented small foundation might feel that the field was preempted and miss opportunities to support local initiatives that could lead to improvements in service delivery, better enforcement of local or state laws, or other steps that legal advocacy might accomplish.

4. See Chapter 9 for further discussion about consultants.

5. For the story of how one young foundation determined program goals, see Charles Rooks, "Developing a Grantmaking Program," *Foundation News* 28, no. 6, November/December 1987, pp. 60–63.

6. One example of the result of this technique is the advent in the 1980s of local education funds, many beginning as the result of small local foundations' study of opportunities for education reform, others encouraged by large national foundations. These funds are created with private money, support a variety of programs, and encourage more community participation in public schools. Another example is the Historic Wilson Block in Dallas, restored by the Meadows Foundation to meet its goal of creating a community of nonprofits that could share space and other resources. The National Arts Stabilization Fund was established by the Ford, Rockefeller, and Andrew W. Mellon Foundations, and supported by local donors, to develop a strategy for improving the long-term financial climate of the arts in communities across the United States.

7. The Bush Foundation, as part of a recent biennial retreat, called in several experts in the areas of homelessness and math/science education. The practitioners provided information that helped the board determine whether to make these areas a priority for the foundation. The Wieboldt Foundation, which funds community organizations, has held board meetings in neighborhood settings and has invited organization leaders to make presentations about trends and opportunities, all as a part of the board's effort to learn more about the types of organizations they fund.

8. See further discussion of this technique in Chapter 5 and footnotes.

9. The Council on Foundations includes program topic sessions as a regular part of its annual conference. Regional associations also include sessions in either annual conferences or other meetings and workshops throughout the year. Foundation staff and board members interested in specific funding topics have joined together as "affinity groups," which hold meetings and publish materials on various funding areas. See Chapter 9 and Appendices 16–19 for further information on these groups.

10. Various opinions are expressed by authors such as Waldemar Neilsen (*The Golden Donors* [New York: E.P. Dutton, 1985]); Paul Ylvisaker, "Is Philanthropy Losing Its Soul?" (*Foundation News* 28, no. 9, May/June 1987, pp. 63–65); or Michael Joyce,

"Philosophical Differences About Philanthropy" (*Philanthropy Monthly*, November 1989, pp. 13–15.) Within the field, opinions range from those of members of the Philanthropic Roundtable, who have criticized philanthropy for departing from traditional values, to those of members of the National Network of Grantmakers, who propose that philanthropy should advocate more for "progressive" change.

11. Alan Pifer, "The Foundation Role in Public Policy Formation," *Foundation News* 16, no. 4, July/August 1975, pp. 25–27.

12. For a thoughtful discussion of the many roles small foundations can play (including and going beyond grantmaking), see Paul Ylvisaker, *Small Can Be Effective* (Washington, DC: Council on Foundations, 1989.) The text of this publication appears in Appendix 13.

13. A knotty issue often encountered in project funding, especially for grants to complex organizations such as universities, is the appropriateness of taking into account some portion of the grantee's overhead or indirect costs as expenses of the project. For a discussion of various expense allocation and grantmaking practices, see Lance Buhl, "Shedding Light on Indirect Costs," *Foundation News* 27, no. 1, January/February 1986, pp. 56–59.

14. For a discussion of the pros and cons of project versus operating support, see Jennifer Leonard, "Best Supporting Role," *Foundation News* 30, no. 5, September/October 1989, pp. 42–46.

15. For a detailed analysis of the grant review process, see Teresa Odendahl and Elizabeth Boris, "The Grantmaking Process," *Foundation News* 24, no. 5, September/October 1983, pp. 22–31.

16. See Treasury Publication 557, *How to Apply for and Retain Tax Exempt Status for Your Organization*, and Summary of Tax Reform Act of 1969 as amended in Appendix 1.

17. *Cumulative List of Organizations described in Section 170(c) of the Internal Revenue Code of 1986*. Department of the Treasury Internal Revenue Service Publication 78. An annual with three quarterly supplements, it lists organizations to which contributions are deductible for income tax purposes, with key numbers indicating category (e.g., private foundation, public charity).

18. The National Charities Information Bureau (NCIB) has developed standards for good nonprofit management and governance, which it applies when evaluating nonprofits for its regular public reports. See Chapter 9 and Appendix 15 for more about NCIB's activities, and those of the Philanthropic Advisory Service of the Council of Better Business Bureaus, which also evaluates reports on nonprofits.

19. See Jim Gorman, "Adding the Human Dimension," *Foundation News* 28, no. 3, May/June 1987, pp. 32–37. See Appendix 5 for a checklist of items to observe when visiting a potential grantee.

20. Another type of matching grant is much sought after by fundraisers for capital campaigns. The grantor makes a grant to help launch the campaign and agrees to give additional funds after the grantee has raised a specified amount elsewhere.

21. Section 4942(g)(2). Set-asides are described, and the procedure for obtaining advance approval is outlined in Regulations 53.4942(a)–3(b). The exception was broadened in 1976. See Appendix 1—TRA as amended. Also, Treasury Publication 578, *Tax Information for Private Foundations and Foundation Managers*.

22. Regulations 53.4945–5(b)–(e) and 53.4945–6(c). See also Appendices 7 and 9 for further information and a sample grant agreement.

23. Section 501(c)(3) has long permitted lobbying that constitutes "no substantial part" of a public charity's activities, and the general prohibition in the 1969 Tax Reform

Act on lobbying by private foundations did not in any way deprive public charities of this right. However, the vagueness of the "substantiality" test in Section 501(c)(3) has been a continuing source of uncertainty and difficulty. In 1976, Congress sought to meet this problem by giving most public charities an option to subject their lobbying to a more specific and liberalized test based upon the amount of their lobbying expenditures rather than the substantiality of their lobbying activities [Sections 501(h) and 4911]. Final regulations implementing the 1976 legislation were issued in August 1990. For discussion of the impact of this amendment on grantors, see footnote 36, this chapter, and accompanying text.

24. See John Edie, *Use of Fiscal Agents: A Trap for the Unwary* (Washington, DC: Council on Foundations, 1989). Although written primarily for community foundations, this material is also useful to private foundations making contributions to organizations where the issue of earmarking may arise.

25. For a full discussion of legal and other technical issues, see *Making Grants Overseas* (Washington, DC: Council on Foundations, 1983).

26. Efforts are underway with the IRS and Treasury to publish procedures whereby a second grantor foundation can rely on such an equivalency affidavit obtained by the first grantor foundation.

27. Regulation 53.4945–5(b)(5).

28. This requirement for advance approval of procedures has proven workable. Section 4945(d)(3) and (g); Regulations 53.49454(a)(3); 53.4945–4(c) and 4(d). *A Guide to the Making of Grants to Individuals by Private Foundations* by Bruce R. Hopkins, Jerome P. Walsh Skelly, and Edward J. Beckwith (Washington, DC: Council on Foundations, 1987) provides a full discussion of the requirements and sample procedures. Also see "To Each His Own," by Roger Williams, *Foundation News* 30, no. 3, May/June 1989, pp. 26–31.

29. There is an earmarking problem here, analogous to that discussed in the preceding section. Generally, a grant to an institution will not be considered a grant to an individual if the grantee institution exercises supervision over the project and controls the selection of the individual. See Regulation 4945–4(a)(4) for useful examples. Stricter rules apply where the individuals selected are government officials [Regulation 53.4941(d)–1(b)(2)].

30. Regulation 53.4945–4(a)(4)(iv).

31. See Rev. Proc. 76–47, 1976–2 CB 670 (scholarship grants) and Rev. Proc. 80–39, IRB 1980–39, p. 22 (educational loans). The restrictions on scholarship grants have been criticized as unduly severe (Michael I. Sanders, "New Guidelines Tell When IRS Will Approve Company Foundation Scholarship Grants," *Journal of Taxation*, April 1977, pp. 212–216; Charles P. Sacher, "Rev. Proc. 76–47: Guidelines for Advanced Approval of Company Foundation Grants," *Trusts and Estates*, August 1977, pp. 541–543).

32. For more information, see Appendix 8. See also a resource developed by the staff of the Piton Foundation, *Program Related Investments: A Primer* (Washington, DC: Council on Foundations, 1986) and Melinda Marble, *Social Investing and Private Foundations* (Washington, DC: Council on Foundations, 1989.) Note also the discussion of jeopardy investments in Chapter 8.

33. Regulation 53.4942(a)–3(a)(2).

34. Gifts to private operating foundations qualify for the 50-percent and 30-percent limitations on individual contributions of cash and appreciated property, respectively. See Summary of Tax Reform Act of 1969 as amended, Appendix 1.

35. For a discussion of foundation involvement in nonpartisan voter registration activities, see the Funders' Committee for Voter Registration and Education publications,
"Handbook on Tax Rules for Voter Participation Work by 501(c)(3) Organizations"
(Washington, DC: 1988), by Thomas Troyer et al.; and *Funders Guide to Voter Education and Registration* (New York: 1984.)

36. Regulations 53.4945–2(a)(5). See also the favorable IRS private letter ruling issued to
the McIntosh Foundation in December 1977 (IRS No. 7810041) finding, in five common situations, no obstacle to grants by the foundation to public charities carrying
on legislative activities. For more information, contact the office of the general counsel, Council on Foundations. New regulations on this subject incorporating and expanding the McIntosh letter were made final on August 31, 1990 (*Federal Register*,
pp. 35579–35620).

37. See Revenue Procedures 81–6 and 81–7.

ANNOTATED BIBLIOGRAPHY–CHAPTER 4

Council on Foundations. *The Grantmaking Process: The Basics*
(Washington, DC: Council on Foundations, 1988). 110 pages.

This resource for grantmakers contains background articles, guidelines, checklists, and other supplemental information. It includes pregrant assessment, eligibility requirements, application procedures, proposal evaluation, financial analysis, and other topics. The book is a compilation of materials from various sources, including portions of this book and some articles listed in the bibliography.

THE CHALLENGES AND REWARDS OF GRANTMAKING

Council on Foundations. *Corporate Giving in the 1990s—The Next Generation* (Washington, DC: Council on Foundations, 1987). 26 pages.

This paper reconsiders the rationales and values behind corporate philanthropy and constructs a framework for corporate giving that fits today and can endure.

Evans, Eli N. "Creativity as the Cornerstone of Philanthropy." *Foundation News* 24, no. 3, May/June 1983, pp. 64–65.

This short essay stresses the need for foundations to maintain their long-range perspective while being willing to support untested programs and ideas.

Richman, Saul. "Down the Highways and Byways with American Philanthropy." *Foundation News* 21, no. 1, January/February 1980, pp. 13–17.

This discusses the achievements of philanthropic foundations in the United States.

Ylvisaker, Paul N. "Is Philanthropy Losing Its Soul?" *Foundation News* 28, no. 3, May/June 1987, pp. 63–65.

The author charts the transformation of grantmaking from charitable giving to the present day institutionalized philanthropy. According to Ylvisaker, this transformation requires constant self-assessment by every grantmaker. The article includes three lists to help grantmakers in their self-assessment.

SETTING GRANTMAKING POLICY

Coolbrith, Alison. "Setting Priorities: Why and How." *Foundation News* 25, no. 1, January/February 1984, pp. 48–49, 72.

Coolbrith explains that corporate giving programs must set priorities and increase the relevance, efficiency, and importance of grantmaking. Also, she gives the criteria for setting and maintaining priorities.

Council of Michigan Foundations. *Grant Focusing Workbook* (Grand Haven, MI: Council of Michigan Foundations, 1988). 59 pages.

This "cookbook" describes in detail the Muskegon Community Foundation's process to develop grantmaking priorities. It provides models for structuring the process, meeting agendas, and sample letters.

Council on Foundations. *The Grantmaking Process: The Basics.*

See Section Two, "Defining A Grantmaking Program," for articles and guidelines for planning and implementing a grantmaking process.

Nason, John W. "Programs By Default or By Design." *Foundation News* 30, no. 1, January/February 1989, pp. 74–77.

Nason suggests constant critical review of programs and a continuing willingness to reexamine established assumptions is good foundation practice. This article was excerpted from *Foundation Trusteeship.*

Rooks, Charles S. "Developing a Grantmaking Program." *Foundation News* 28, no. 6, November/December 1987, pp. 60–63.

The author describes in detail the process used by the Meyer Memorial Trust to determine its program goals. He also poses questions for foundation trustees and staff to consider as they embark on this important mission.

PHILOSOPHIES AND TECHNIQUES OF GRANTMAKING

The history and philosophy of individual foundations can be found in their annual reports, special reports, and books that chronicle a foundation's history. While too numerous to cite, these resources are available from individual foundations, historical societies, and university or public libraries.

Hart, Jeffrey. "Foundations and Social Activism: A Critical View." In *The Future of Foundations*, Fritz F. Heimann, ed. (Englewood Cliffs, NJ: Prentice-Hall, for the American Assembly, 1973). pp. 43–57.

The author regards foundations as vulnerable to the criticism that they wield irresponsible power when they become involved in social change activities. These types of activities fuel demands for the regulation of foundations. He advises funding that benefits all segments of society. He urges foundations to do more funding of the arts.

Johnson, Robert Matthews. *The First Charity: How Philanthropy Can Contribute to Democracy in America* (Cabin John, MD: Seven Locks Press, 1988). 234 pages.

The author builds a case for grantmaking that encourages democracy through citizen participation. Johnson provides both a theoretical discussion and a practical guide for grantmaking to community-based organizations.

Joyce, Michael. "Philosophical Differences About Philanthropy." In *The Philanthropy Monthly*, November 1989, pp. 13–15.

The author discusses the basic differences between a liberal and a conservative outlook and the effects of each outlook on philanthropic philosophy.

Krieg, Iris. "Interactive Philanthropy." *Foundation News* 30, no. 6, November/ December 1989, pp. 59–60.

Krieg describes the interactive approach to grantmaking that enables foundations to target resources while preserving flexibility within their grantmaking policies and procedures.

Miller, J. Irwin. "Time to *Listen.*" *Foundation News* 25, no. 3, May/June 1984, pp. 16–23.

Miller urges foundation trustees and staff to reconsider their role, to take more risks, and to recognize the world's interdependence.

Murningham, Marcy M. *Moral Values, Philanthropy, and Public Life: Recasting the Connections* (Boston: The Lighthouse Investment Group, 1989). 75+ pages.

This report identifies ethical concerns of the philanthropic field. Murningham addresses the moral environment of grantmaking, the ethical dilemmas of staff, and the need to examine the ideals and imperatives that drive foundation decisions.

Northern California Grantmakers. *Perspectives on Collaborative Funding* (San Francisco: Northern California Grantmakers, 1985). 72 pages.

Collection of reports and essays by foundation leaders in the Bay Area, providing the philosophy behind partnerships and successful techniques for collaboration.

Payton, Robert L. *The Ethics of Corporate Grantmaking* (Washington, DC: Council on Foundations, 1987). 30 pages.

The pamphlet examines the issues of ethics and behavior in the grantmaking field.

Pifer, Alan. "Speaking Out: Reflections on 30 Years of Foundation Work" (Washington, DC: Council on Foundations, 1984). 40 pages.

Speech presented by Mr. Pifer near the time of his retirement as president of the Carnegie Corporation of New York. He describes the challenges and rewards, dreams, and realities of private philanthropy.

Portnoy, Fern. "Collaboration: Go For It." *Foundation News* 27, no. 5, September/October 1986, pp. 59–61.

Portnoy offers strategies for developing successful funding partnerships.

Reisler, Raymond. "Going Out on a Limb." *Foundation News* 25, no. 1, January/February 1988, pp. 42–45.

Raymond urges grantmakers to take more risks and search for new ways to solve community problems.

Rogers, David. "On Building a Foundation." *Foundation News* 25, no. 4, July/ August 1987, pp. 48–51.

The author, at the time president of the Robert Wood Johnson Foundation, offers his reflections on successful foundation goal setting, management, and grantmaking.

Shellow, Jill. *The Grantseekers Guide* (Mount Kisco, NY: Moyer Bell Ltd., 1989). 858 pages.

This is a reference guide that describes funding interests of foundations that are members of the National Network of Grantmakers and described as committed to social justice. It includes essays on grantmaking and grantseeking, as well as a chapter on the history of foundation funding of progressive social movements.

Viscusi, Margo. "Coming of Age." *Foundation News* 26, no. 3, May/June 1985, pp. 26–35.

Viscusi traces the development of the Council on Foundations' "Principles & Practices for Effective Grantmaking." Such principles, if adopted by individual foundations and the field as a whole, will result in better processes and more successful results for both grantmaker and grantseeker.

PROJECT VERSUS GENERAL SUPPORT GRANTS

Council on Foundations. *Indirect Costs* (Washington, DC: Council on Foundations, 1986). 60 pages.

Research report that clarifies the definitions and characterizes current policies and practices of foundations with regard to funding grantees' indirect costs. Makes recommendations that will help grantmakers to develop more informed policies and procedures.

Leonard, Jennifer. "Best Supporting Role." *Foundation News* 30, no. 5, September/October 1989, pp. 42–46.

Leonard outlines the trend over the past ten years of the growth of grantmaking to special projects over general support grants. She presents arguments of both grantmakers and grantees.

Russell, John M. *Giving and Taking Across the Foundation Desk* (New York: Teachers College Press, 1977). p. 39.

See Chapter 6, "Doing Its Thing," for a discussion of a wide variety of grant types with reasons and cautions for each.

THE GRANTMAKING PROCESS

Council on Foundations. *The Grantmaking Process: The Basics.*

See Section Three, "The Decision Making Process," for an assortment of articles, guidelines, and checklists relating to the entire grantmaking process.

Magat, Richard. "Decisions! Decisions!" *Foundation News* 24, no. 2, March/April 1983, pp. 24–31.

Magat stresses that the most important part of foundation work is evaluating proposals and selecting grantees, also known as the pregrant assessment process. This article is an excellent resource for establishing or refining this process. Part of the *Foundation News* "Hands On" series.

Odendahl, Teresa, and Boris, Elizabeth. "The Grantmaking Process." *Foundation News* 24, no. 5, September/October 1983, pp. 22–31.

This article is one of the most comprehensive works on the grantmaking process. Odendahl and Boris take the reader step by step through the process. The article effectively employs several models and applications of the grantmaking process. Part of the *Foundation News* "Hands On" series.

Schuman, Michael H. "A Grantee Bill of Rights." *Foundation News* 30, no. 2, March/April 1989, pp. 36–39.

Identifies 11 "rights" of grantees in seeking support from foundations. Schuman answers the questions, "How do foundations frustrate nonprofits?" and "What can be done about it?"

WORKING UP THE APPLICATION

Many private foundations include copies of their applications and descriptions of their funding process in their annual reports.

Andrews, F. Emerson. *Philanthropic Foundations* (New York: Russell Sage Foundation, 1956). p. 170.

See Chapter 7, "Application for Grants," for a discussion of the whole application process.

Goodwin, William M. "Proposal Reviews: 30 Financial Questions to Cut Funding Risks." *Foundation News* 17, no. 2, March/April 1976, pp. 30–39.

The controller of the Lilly Endowment provides a short summary of grantee budget review. He makes a case for exploring fiscal aspects of the grants as fully as the projected outcome of the grant project.

Gorman, Jim. "Adding the Human Dimension." *Foundation News* 26, no. 9, May/June 1987, pp. 32–37.

Gorman describes successful techniques for conducting site visits as part of evaluating grant proposals.

TYPES OF GRANTS

Council on Foundations. *How We Helped, 1986* (Washington, DC: Council on Foundations, 1987). 60 pages.

This booklet showcases interesting and successful grantmaking programs of selected foundations and corporate giving programs. The book covers the numerous and diverse ways foundations and corporate giving programs "provide for the common good."

Goodban, Nicholas. "Opportunity or Imposition?" *Foundation News* 24, no. 2, March/April 1983, pp. 36–39.

Goodban defines "challenge grants" and describes the general terms and conditions of this type of grant.

Hertz, Willard J., and Kurzig, Carol K. "A Grant for Every Purpose." *Foundation News* 24, no. 1, January/February 1983, pp. 26–31.

The article serves as a primer on grantmaking. The authors touch upon all the major elements and types of grants and the grantmaking process. Part of the *Foundation News* "Hands On" series.

Hopkins, Bruce. *The Law of Tax-Exempt Organizations*, 5th Ed. (New York: John Wiley and Sons, 1987). p. 537.

See Section 25.3 for a discussion of the regulations applicable to a "set-aside."

EXPENDITURE RESPONSIBILITY

Hopkins, Bruce. *The Law of Tax-Exempt Organizations*, 5th Ed., p. 574.

Explains the laws and procedures that foundations must follow to exercise expenditure responsibility.

INTERNATIONAL GRANTMAKING

Bolling, Landrum R., with Smith, Craig. *Private Foreign Aid: Philanthropy for Relief and Development* (Washington, DC: Council on Foundations, 1982). 283 pages.

A major work in the philanthropic field, this book provides a history and analysis of giving abroad by individual Americans, church groups, foundations, corporations, and international organizations.

Council on Foundations. *Educating Americans About International Affairs* (Washington, DC: Council on Foundations, 1987). 70 pages.

This resource for grantmakers discusses the presentations and conclusions drawn during a workshop for grantmakers interested in international education. It explores the opportunities for philanthropic involvement in international education at the precollegiate and undergraduate levels as well as in the community.

Council on Foundations. *Making Grants Overseas: A Resource for Foundations and Corporations Which Make Grants in Countries Outside of the United States* (Washington, DC: Council on Foundations, 1983). 60 pages.

This guide addresses legal and technical constraints encountered by U.S. foundations and corporations overseas. It defines *exempt purposes* and *expenditure responsibility* for overseas grantmaking.

Fox, Tom. "A Rising Tide?" *Foundation News* 26, no. 3, May/June 1985, pp. 56–57.

Fox charts growth and trends in grantmaking for international purposes.

Joseph, James. "Private Philanthropy & South Africa." *Foundation News* 29, no. 6, November/December 1988, p. 49.

Joseph presents ten points that serve as guidelines for grantmakers interested in funding programs in South Africa.

Knowles, Louis. "Tending South Africa's Wounds." *Foundation News* 28, no. 6, November/December 1987, pp. 16–23.

Discusses the scope of grantmaker involvement in South African programs and offers guidelines for funding.

Logan, David. *U.S. Corporate Grantmaking in a Global Age* (Washington: Council on Foundations, 1989). 105 pages.

The report strongly supports the extension of corporate giving overseas.

Williams, Roger. "Mobilizing Forces." *Foundation News* 29, no. 2, March/April 1988, pp. 31–37.

This article discusses the quickly expanding existence and influence in Central America of the U.S. nonprofit sector. It then focuses on the roles played by small foundations, mainline foundations, governmental grantmakers, nonsectarian nonprofits, sectarian nonprofits, watchdogs, and others in social and economic change in the region.

GRANTS TO INDIVIDUALS

Council of Michigan Foundations. *Establishing and Administering a Scholarship Program* (Grand Haven, MI: Council of Michigan Foundations, 1989). 125 pages.

This includes information on scholarship programs and rules governing them. It summarizes current tax law and includes sample forms.

Council on Foundations. *A Guide to the Making of Grants to Individuals by Private Foundations* (Washington, DC: Council on Foundations, 1987). 29 pages.

This paper explains the rules and shows the grantmaker how to set a grants program for individuals. An appendix includes a sample letter to the IRS seeking approval with a sample set of procedures.

Hopkins, Bruce. *The Law of Tax-Exempt Organizations*, 5th Ed. (New York: John Wiley and Sons, 1987). pp. 565–574.

Hopkins discusses grants to individuals by private foundations.

Treusch, Paul E. *Tax-Exempt Charitable Organizations*, 3rd Ed. (Philadelphia: American Law Institute, 1988). pp. 532–534.

Discusses a potential pitfall to making grants to individuals—when the foundation did not earmark the grant for the use of any specific individual.

Williams, Roger M. "To Each His Own." *Foundation News* 30, no. 3, May/June 1989, pp. 25–31.

Williams gives a brief history and addresses the recent trends in grants to individuals. He also investigates the policies and practices of foundations making grants to individuals.

LOANS AND PROGRAM-RELATED INVESTMENTS

Council on Foundations. *Program-Related Investment: A Primer* (Washington, DC: Council on Foundations, 1986). 120 pages.

Written by the Piton Foundation staff, this book explains the value of program-related investments (PRIs) as philanthropic tools and provides information foundation officers need to implement PRIs quickly and productively. The primer also includes a detailed discussion of the financial and legal issues surrounding PRIs. It contains several case studies based on both large and small foundations, lists of resource organizations, and examples of legal documents to use when making PRIs.

The Ford Foundation. *Program-Related Investments: A Different Approach to Philanthropy* (New York: The Ford Foundation, 1974). 23 pages.

This publication provides information in the Ford Foundation's Program-Related Investment Program while referring to the PRI programs of other foundations. It reviews the investment experience of the foundations as well. (An update is forthcoming.)

Marble, Melinda. *Social Investing and Private Foundations* (Washington, DC: Council on Foundations, 1989). 45 pages.

Based on interviews with numerous private foundations, this report celebrates the varied program-related investments made by private foundations. Foundations of many sizes are involved in different program areas using this technique. Marble also describes types of investments, possible problems, and solutions.

OPERATING PROGRAMS

Andrews, F. Emerson. *Philanthropic Foundations*, p. 151.

See Chapter 6, "The Operating Foundation," for a discussion of grant giving versus direct operating of programs. Emerson provides examples of operating foundations and their programs.

Operating programs are defined and the legal requirements discussed by the following:

Hopkins, Bruce. *The Law of Tax-Exempt Organizations.* 5th Ed. (New York: John Wiley and Sons, 1987). Chapter 22, "Types of Private Foundations," pp. 478–486.

Treusch, Paul E. *Tax-Exempt Charitable Organizations,* 3rd Ed. (Philadelphia: American Law Institute, 1988). Chapter 8, "Private Foundations: General Rules," pp. 453–460, and Chapter 9, "Private Foundations: Restriction on Operations," pp. 529–548.

THE BOARD MEETING

Nason, John. *Foundation Trusteeship: Service in the Public Interest.* (New York: The Foundation Center, 1989).
See Chapter 7, "Dynamics of an Effective Board."

ROCKS AND SHOALS

For an additional discussion of the topics, consult the following:
Hopkins, Bruce. *The Law of Tax-Exempt Organizations,* 5th Ed.
Treusch, Paul E. *Tax-Exempt Charitable Organizations,* 3rd Ed.

5

Relationships with Grantseekers and the Public

PARTNERS IN PHILANTHROPY

The grantor–grantee relationship should be a challenging and rewarding experience for both parties. It is essentially a partnership to which the grantor can bring more than money. Help with the preparation of the grant application, advice about other likely sources of funding, information on other agencies working in the same field—these are all part of the grantmaker's contribution to the partnership.

The prospective grantee typically brings to the relationship enthusiasm and dedication to a particular field of service or research and a knowledge of the subject that the foundation "generalist" can rarely match. In addition, the successful grantseeker becomes a working partner with the foundation, responsible for carrying out the agreed-upon charitable objective. Foundations can achieve their philanthropic purposes only through the work of their grantees. It is important that each partner understand at the outset this interdependence and that both state frankly their plans and expectations.[1]

Saying "No"

It is a fact of foundation life that for every "yes," there will be eight to ten rejected applications, not counting the form appeals. If role playing were a part of the educational process for grantmakers, each student should be required to play the part of a grant applicant who receives a declination. Only then would it be clear that how a foundation manager says "no" is as important as why that decision is reached. This chapter deals primarily with the "how."

Poor practices by some foundations lead to legitimate gripes among grantseekers: inordinately long delays in responding to requests, failure to respond at all, arrogance on the part of a foundation representative when an interview is granted, false hopes given to prospective grantees by too friendly grantmakers, and inappropriate intrusions into the grantee's operations after a grant is awarded.

There are remedies for many of these causes of friction. First, something can be done about the high percentage of disappointed applicants. Although it is hard for the "low-profile" foundation to believe, the effort a grantmaker expends in developing and publicizing its guidelines and areas of interest pays off in fewer "out-of-program" requests. Clear, frank statements of what a foundation does not do are as important as descriptions of its priorities and will save grantseekers the time and expense involved in submitting proposals that have no chance of success.

When foundations enter new program areas or wish to encourage work in a particular area, they may occasionally prepare and distribute to prospective grantees "requests for proposals" spelling out the foundation's intent, relevant conditions, and deadlines.[2] Such requirements should be clearly stated in guidelines and annual reports.

Even foundations with annual giving of $100,000 or less should prepare brief annual reports and one-page statements of purpose and criteria. These should also be supplied to the Foundation Center for inclusion in its directories or profiles and mailed to the public. They can be produced inexpensively, and the cost will be more than offset by the savings in the number of declination letters required. Such a communication effort should be thought of as an investment in the future of the field.

In the smaller foundation, whether staffed or managed solely by trustees, handling declinations is bound to be time consuming even with a routine and form letters. But philanthropy is a team operation. The grantmaker must rely on the integrity and ability of the grantee to carry out its charitable purposes, just as the grantee relies on foundations and other sources to provide the funds for its work. Responses to grantseekers, whether by mail, by phone, or in personal interviews, should be prompt and courteous and reflect the partnership concept. Too often this is not the case. Foundation managers are sometimes ac-

"Agreed. The foundation's annual report will be printed on paper recycled from the 2,400 proposals received last year."

cused of acting as if the funds they disburse were "their" money, rather than money they hold in trust for charitable purposes.

While each foundation has a style of its own, and the declination letters should reflect this, the samples included in Appendix 7 may be helpful. Many foundations develop such form letters on their computer systems and add individualized material as needed. Word processing has made it easier for staff or board members to provide prompt replies to inquiries.

Thus far, we have been concerned with the best way to say "no" when the request is clearly outside a foundation's program. Often, though, a request will appear to be within a foundation's area of interest, and further exploration will be needed before a decision can be reached. The question then arises whether the foundation should tell the applicant that the request is being considered or left until a decision is reached. If the inquiry process requires a site visit, or more information is needed from the applicant, the question answers itself. However, the foundation representative should try to avoid raising hopes unduly by stating that the odds are for a favorable decision.

If the foundation needs no additional information but anticipates a delay of a month or more before reaching a staff decision, then a brief response stating that the request is under consideration is in order. Give some indication of the date for a decision. If the expected delay is shorter than a month, it may suffice to notify the applicant immediately after the foundation has made a decision. However, many grantseekers would like to know that their proposal made it through the mail and that the foundation has received it. A postcard to that effect is a considerate response.

The reasons for a declination are sometimes easy to state: "outside our program interests," "not within our geographical area," or "we don't give to building funds." When a proposal has survived these initial hurdles and must still be turned down, a frank response may be difficult. Let us imagine that the project is clearly within the foundation's announced guidelines, but the investigations described in Chapter 4 have convinced the foundation managers that the leadership of the applicant organization is weak or that the proposal is unrealistic or duplicates other programs. To suggest such reasons in a declination letter could invite arguments and increase the likelihood of hard feelings on the part of the applicant.

While the use of phrases such as "with our limited resources, it is just not possible to respond favorably to all requests, no matter how worthy" may seem trite, they do convey an accurate and firm "no." They are probably more acceptable to the recipient than the famous, if cryptic, rejection letter attributed to an early executive of the Rockefeller Foundation: "We have nothing but praise for your project."

However, if a grantseeker is persistent and asks to know more about the reasons for the declination, or for suggestions of other funding sources, some program officers hold informal conversations where they try to provide more specific feedback. This is most workable in situations where the foundation representative has the time and experience to help the grantseeker find funding elsewhere or to provide some technical assistance, even though the foundation cannot provide dollars for the program.[3]

EVALUATION

Evaluation is crucial to a foundation's success in several ways. First, as discussed in Chapters 4 and 6, regular evaluations of a foundation's overall program and process help ensure that the foundation's priorities are appropriate and that its operations are fair and efficient. Second, careful evaluation of proposals is the essence of the grantmaking process. A third kind of evaluation, conducted either during the course of a grant or at its conclusion, is another important part of foundation management that deserves attention by the board and staff.

Some types of grants, such as general support for cultural institutions, seldom require evaluation. Others, such as demonstration projects in the social welfare field, may be almost a waste of money if an evaluation component is not built into the project design. The grantor and others will judge many grants that result in a report or a book only after the finished product is available.

Some students of the field draw a distinction between evaluation and monitoring and argue that both are necessary. Monitoring means simply keeping track of the grantee's fulfillment of certain commitments in the course of the grant: the filing of reports on schedule, the allocation of the grant monies to the purposes designated in the grant agreement, and carrying on the promised activities. Orderly monitoring can at times be very important in detecting managerial or fiscal accountability problems before they get out of hand. But those processes are no substitute for the assessment of results, which is evaluation.

When a funder evaluates a project, either as it progresses or at its conclusion, it is important that both the grantor and grantee have a clear understanding of their roles. The foundation should clearly indicate in the grant terms if it plans to use third-party evaluators so that the grantee is not taken by surprise. When the foundation manager or a consultant is to make site visits during the course of the grant, the funder should make this clear in advance as well.

A word of caution is in order: Problems have arisen when a representative of the grantor becomes deeply involved in the grantee's operations. Such involvement implies a degree of commitment to continuing support by the foundation that may not in fact be the case. Also, the foundation representative is unlikely to be so expert in the grantee's field of work that active involvement in the operation will be useful and welcome. While thorough monitoring or exercising expenditure responsibility may require the grantor to obtain detailed reports, the general warning against constantly looking over the grantee's shoulder is still valid.

Despite all these warning flags, evaluation should be a more important function for foundations than it usually is. Sometimes the cost and time that might be required to conduct a good evaluation causes foundation managers to shy away from this important aspect of grantmaking. However, without some organized effort in this regard by grantor and grantee, we may lose the lessons to be learned from many projects. When the project is successful, the possibilities of replication are increased if the results of evaluation are disseminated. Evaluations of unsuccessful projects may be useful in helping others to avoid similar mistakes, although reporting failures is a touchy business.[4]

Careful evaluation can also help the foundation determine how well it is doing its business. It has been said that if all grants are judged successful, perhaps the foundation is not taking enough risks. If many grants are judged to be failures, then perhaps the grant assessment process needs strengthening.[5]

Communication with the Public

In recent years the foundation field has devoted increased attention to the issue of accountability and communications. Thanks to leadership from the Foundation Center, the Council on Foundations, regional associations, the National Committee for Responsive Philanthropy, and the Communications Network in Philanthropy affinity group, foundations have learned about the importance of good communications. The good news is that an increasing number of foundations are regularly informing the public of their activities through published annual reports and other activities. The bad news is that a significant part of the field still fails to communicate adequately.

The IRS Form 990-PF is the most basic form of information sharing available to foundations. In fact, all private foundations are *required* to file Form 990-PF each year and to make it available for inspection at the foundation's office for 180 days after filing. Yet, the form is often filled out in a perfunctory manner. (Even well-known accounting firms have been known to make errors when preparing the forms on behalf of their clients.) Some foundations list grants only by name of recipient and amount despite the admonition in the regulations and instructions that the foundation include a "concise statement" of the purpose of each grant and that it classifies activities according to purpose.

When, on rare occasions, a member of the public asks to see the 990-PF of a foundation, there are often long delays while the law firm or accounting firm listed as the foundation's "principal office" tries to find the right form. Mail requests for copies of these forms are sometimes ignored or refused. So, while the 990-PF should serve as a tool for communicating basic information about the foundation, it is often not as useful as it could be.

Beyond the Legal Requirements

Most of the largest foundations publish annual reports. However, many smaller foundations do not publish annual reports or other materials. Yet, practitioners believe these materials to be among the best tools for communicating a foundation's activities.[6]

Reasons foundations give for this reluctance to tell their story include:

1. "Not enough people would be interested in our grants."
2. "We would rather spend the money on charitable activities."
3. "No one has the time to prepare the report."

Two underlying reasons are often influential in the foundation's decision not to publish information. One reflects the feeling that the money in the foundation is "ours" and that it is not anyone else's business how the money is invested or spent. This attitude has led to much of the hostility foundations have encountered both in the media and in the Congress. It is out of date and wrong: Assets transferred to a foundation are irrevocably dedicated to charitable purposes and cannot be taken back by the donor. Moreover, failure to draw the distinction clearly between the donor's assets and those of the foundation has at times produced apparent conflict-of-interest situations and self-dealing problems.

A second reason for not issuing reports is, "If we put out a report we'd be swamped with new requests, and we have too many now." The law requires that the 990-PF be made available for inspection by the public. Also, the Foundation Center and other sources, including the IRS, make this basic information available to the public. The more this information is amplified by a foundation's own description of what types of grants it will consider—and those it will not consider—the fewer grantseekers will waste their time and money by submitting inappropriate requests. Conversely, the grantmaker will spend less time answering inappropriate requests.

Why else would a foundation want to communicate regularly with grantees or other publics? Richard Magat, a long-time foundation executive and journalist, cites several reasons in an article written for *Foundation News*.[7] By communicating openly, a foundation can help dispel mystery and avoid public suspicion of its activities. Foundations' tax-exempt status depends on the public's confidence. Other reasons include:

1. calling attention to the role of philanthropy.
2. increasing understanding and advocating for action on fundamental issues facing society.

3. disseminating the results of foundation-supported programs in the hope that successful work in one place will be carried out or supported more widely.

4. eliciting evaluations and criticism of foundations' activities, thereby improving their work.

The board should state its goals and develop a policy on communications, just as it would for grantmaking, investments, personnel, and other areas. For what audiences does the foundation wish to provide information: grantseekers, public officials, members of a local community, its own board and staff? A communications plan can be simple—a low-cost annual report or brochure with basic information such as the foundation's mission, application procedures, financial summary, and examples of recent grants.[8] A more elaborate effort might involve publishing a newsletter, producing a video, or publishing special reports on specific grant programs and the impact of the work being funded by the foundation. Some foundations try to communicate their message in a more personal way, by sponsoring or participating in public meetings.[9]

In order to tell a specific story or highlight successes, a foundation can actively pursue relations with the media, using such tools as targeted press releases or press briefings. Foundations should also regularly provide information to the Foundation Center, which publishes lists of grants and financial and program information on foundations for the grantseeking and grantmaking communities as well as the general public.[10]

In summary, every foundation, no matter how small, must at least be prepared to furnish to the public copies of its Form 990-PF containing comprehensive information. Providing further information, particularly guidelines for prospective grantees and clear statements of program interests, can help—not hurt—the efficiency of the grantmaking process. Telling the foundation's story to other audiences can serve both the interests of the individual foundation and philanthropy as a whole.

CONCLUSION

One last word of advice to the reader fortunate enough to be associated with a foundation or other philanthropic grantmaker: Remember that most applicants believe deeply in the particular activity for which they are seeking support. Whether you agree with their priorities or not, respect their motivation, and be a good listener.[11] Humility is not a trait frequently associated with giving away money. It should be.

NOTES TO CHAPTER 5

1. The Council on Foundations' "Principles and Practices for Effective Grantmaking," in Appendix 12, stresses the importance of open communications.

2. See Appendix 7 for examples.

3. Assistance at the most basic level should include informing the grant applicant of the collection of resource materials available through the Foundation Center.

4. It is difficult for a grantmaker to be frank about unsuccessful grants without being unfair to the grantee. The project may have been underfunded; the timing may have been wrong, or the grantor may have encouraged the grantee to tackle something outside its experience.

5. Martha Butt, "Getting to Know You," *Foundation News* 26, no. 4, July/August, 1985, p. 33.

6. The twelfth edition of *The Foundation Directory* (New York: The Foundation Center, 1989) lists approximately 6,600 foundations that had assets of $1 million or more or gave away $100,000 or more in the latest year of record. Of these, 1,800 (27%) published annual reports. Ten years ago, only 463 foundations of that size published reports (Introduction, p. xv.).

7. Richard Magat, "Out of the Shadows," *Foundation News* 25, no. 4, July/August 1984, pp. 24–33.

8. See Appendix 14 for an example of a simple annual report.

9. Several regional associations of grantmakers (New York, Northern California, and Minnesota, among others) regularly schedule public meetings or "meet the grantmakers" sessions, where grantseekers and grantmakers discuss program interests, policies, and other issues. The Bush Foundation was one of the first foundations to sponsor such an event, over a decade ago. A more recent example was the Sierra Foundation's meeting, which served as an information-sharing session and skill-building workshop for grantseekers. The Foundation Center regularly sponsors meetings with foundations and regional associations.

10. See Appendix 19 for a description of the work of the Foundation Center.

11. "A philanthropoid is, first, a listener. Unless he is to deny the essential nature of the field and organization he serves, he must make himself available to hear the hopes and needs of those around him." (Merrimon Cuninggim, *Private Money and Public Service* (New York: McGraw-Hill Book Company, 1972), p. 187.

ANNOTATED BIBLIOGRAPHY–CHAPTER 5

PARTNERS IN PHILANTHROPY

Council on Foundations. "Taking the Lead With a Potential Grantee: How Much Is Too Much?" *Foundation News* 25, no. 2, March/April 1984, pp. 62–64.

Foundation News asks several experienced grantmakers to what extent foundations should become involved with potential grantseekers. Appears in the "Ethics" section of the magazine.

Council on Foundations. "Should Personality Play a Part?" *Foundation News* 25, no. 1, January/February 1984, pp. 60–63.

This article addresses the question of whether the personality of a grantseeker should be considered in addition to the merits of the organization's proposal. Appears in the "Ethics" section of the magazine.

Council on Foundations. "The Sins of Omission." *Foundation News* 30, no. 4, July/August 1989, pp. 50–52.

This article addresses the grantees who alter their proposals to fit different foundations' objectives. How do grantmakers respond to proposals that do not necessarily reflect the whole picture? Appears in the "Ethics" section of the magazine.

Council on Foundations. "When a Grantee Seeks Money for Project 'A', and You Know It's Really for Project 'B' . . ." *Foundation News* 24, no. 2, March/April 1983, pp. 56–58.

This article addresses the challenge grantmakers are faced with when they know the foundation's money will be going directly or indirectly to a purpose other than for what the grant was intended. Appears in the "Ethics" section of the magazine.

Council on Foundations. "When Fellow Grantmakers Ask to See Your Write-Ups . . ." *Foundation News* 24, no. 4, July/August 1983, pp. 52–54.

The article addresses how grantmakers respond to requests by other grantmakers for information on an applicant. Appears in the "Ethics" section of the magazine.

Eisenberg, Pablo. "Philanthropic Ethics from a Donee Perspective." *Foundation News* 24, no. 5, September/October 1983, pp. 49–51.

The author raises nine questions about grantmakers' practices and priorities.

Krieg, Iris. "Interactive Philanthropy." *Foundation News* 30, no. 6, November/December 1989, pp. 59–60.

Krieg describes the interactive approach to grantmaking that enables foundations to target resources while preserving flexibility within their grantmaking policies.

Schuman, Michael H. "A Grantee Bill of Rights." *Foundation News* 30, no. 2, March/April 1989, pp. 36–39.

Schuman identifies 11 "rights" of grantees in seeking support from foundations. He broaches the questions, "How do foundations frustrate nonprofits?" and "What can be done about it?"

EVALUATION

Butt, Martha G. "Getting To Know You." *Foundation News* 26, no. 4, July/August 1985, pp. 26–35.

Butt describes the requirements, types, and means needed to develop a formal evaluation process. The article includes references to processes already used by grantmakers, problems they have encountered, and options for solving them.

Brim, Orville G., Jr. "Do We Know What We Are Doing?" In *The Future of Foundations* (Englewood Cliffs, NJ: Prentice-Hall, 1973).

Fritz F. Heimann, ed., pp. 216–258. Brim looks at program evaluation and administrative decision making. He includes short bibliography on evaluation research.

Council on Foundations, Inc. *The Grantmaking Process: The Basics* (Washington, DC: Council on Foundations, 1988). 110 pages.

See Section 5, "Post-Grant Evaluation," for articles and examples of the postgrant evaluation process.

Doermann, Humphrey. "Staying on the Mark: A Review of Grant Evaluation." *Foundation News* 23, no. 3, May/June 1982, pp. 4–7.

Doermann reviews different post-grant evaluation processes.

The Foundation Center. *Conducting Evaluations: Three Perspectives*, (New York: The Foundation Center, 1980). 50 pages.

The Foundation Center looks at the evaluation process from three different perspectives: The professional evaluator, the grantee, and the grantor. It provides insights on when, why, and how such evaluations should be undertaken and includes an annotated bibliography.

Frehse, Robert M., Jr., "The Working Document That Works: FR-1." *Foundation News* 21, no. 2, March/April 1980, p. 28.

The Hearst Foundation and other grantmakers asked grantees to voluntarily fill out a document entitled FR-1 in an attempt to evaluate the costs of financing charitable enterprises. FR-1 is an indicator of the effectiveness of an agency's fundraising techniques.

Hans, Pat, and Cook, Wayne. "A Proper Upbringing." *Foundation News* 29, no. 3, May/June 1988, pp. 52–54.

The authors use analogies to explain the need for grantors to follow up on

the distribution of their grants. Also, they prescribe pre- and postgrant procedures to monitor the grants and prevent misuse.

Hutchinson, Peter C., and Wurtele, Margaret V. B. "Accountability: Ask Your
Stakeholders." *Foundation News* 25, no. 5, September/October 1984, pp. 81–
83.

The article shows how the Dayton Hudson Foundation initiated an evaluation process by inviting seven constituencies to evaluate its grantmaking
practices.

Mahoney, Margaret E. "As a Planning Tool: Evaluation Can Help Make the
Foundation Manager's Life Easier." *Foundation News* 17, no. 6, November/
December 1976, p. 29.

Mahoney encourages foundations to consider evaluation to help manage its
affairs. Evaluation can help foundations to define their programs, select
grantees, monitor grants, and assess outcomes.

University of California Center for the Study of Evaluation. *The Program Evaluation Kit* (Berkeley: University of California Press, 1989). Nine-volume collection.

This collection was designed to assist anyone who has decided to conduct an
evaluation. All are written in a straightforward, readable style with numerous examples, illustrations, and checklists.

Wing, William G. "It's Easier Said Than Done But Some Foundations Do Try."
Foundation News 14, no. 6, November/December 1973, pp. 42–48.

Wing discusses findings of an informal survey of middle-sized foundations'
program evaluations. He discusses the purpose of evaluation, specific evalu-
ative techniques used by various foundations, and ways scientific research
methods can be incorporated into foundation evaluation efforts. The article
includes an evaluation bibliography.

REPORTING TO THE PUBLIC

Gottleib, Leslie. "Reaching the Media." *Foundation News* 27, no. 1, January/
February 1986, pp. 32–39.

Gottleib explores strategies foundations can employ to develop good public
relations programs.

Magat, Richard. "Out of the Shadows." *Foundation News* 25, no. 4, July/August
1984, pp. 25–33.

Magat identifies the advantages and importance of informing the public and
provides a framework for good communication. Part of the *Foundation News*
"Hands On" series.

National Committee for Responsive Philanthropy. *Corporate Philanthropy and
Public Reporting: Sunshine or Shadow?* (Washington, DC: NCRP, 1990). 60
pages.

This is an assessment of the information 200 corporations routinely report to the public about their grantmaking.

National Committee for Responsive Philanthropy. *Foundations and Public Information: Sunshine or Shadow?* (Washington, DC: NCRP, 1980). 79 pages.

This is an evaluation of information the largest foundations report to the public. NCRP recommends 22 specific areas that should be disclosed.

Price, A. Rae, ed. *Increasing the Impact* (Battle Creek, MI: W. K. Kellogg Foundation, 1985). 234 pages.

This is a compilation of essays on communications and evaluation written by communications professionals in foundations and other nonprofits. It explores the use of a wide range of communications tools.

Viscusi, Margo. "Annual Reports: Making a Good Idea Better." *Foundation News* 26, no. 1, January/February 1985, pp. 30–35.

Viscusi explains the purpose and goals of publishing an annual report. She outlines requirements, formats, and styles of publishing and disseminating a foundation annual report.

6

Governance and Administration

Are foundations more innovative and responsive than government bureaucracies? As with other sectors of our society, it is hard to generalize. Certainly opportunities exist for foundations, regardless of size, to manage their affairs in ways that enable them to respond quickly to new challenges and to seek new approaches to unsolved problems. Much depends on the degree of interest the directors take in a foundation's programs and the range of experience they bring to the task. Of equal importance is the caliber of the staff or the trustees. In this chapter, we are concerned with these two essential ingredients and the interaction between them.

THE BOARD'S POLICY-MAKING ROLE

In 1973, Robert K. Greenleaf described a foundation as "essentially a group of trustees who manage a pool of uncommitted funds that can be used for a wide range of socially useful purposes."[1] The chief function of the board is to establish policy by selecting from within this wide range a set of purposes that fit the wishes of the donor, the resources available to the foundation, and the priorities of the foundation's constituencies. Few new foundations are encumbered with purposes so precisely stated that they make such policy deliberations unnecessary. Boards of existing foundations, faced with a fast-changing social and economic environment, have a responsibility to keep their programs relevant.

Determining or reviewing program policies need not be an expensive or time-consuming process. It may only require setting aside one board meeting every second year. Free of the necessity to make decisions on specific grants, board and staff can use this meeting to examine past experience and look ahead to new opportunities for service. Some foundations have found it desirable to have board-and-staff retreats, lasting a day or two, to examine issues in greater depth. At longer intervals, an outside consultant or a small team of experienced people may be asked to review the foundation's programs and make recommendations. Or a new executive director may be asked to perform a similar function as part of his or her "warm-up."[2]

A similar process, or a tool such as the Council on Foundations' *Self Study Guide for Foundation Boards* might be used to review overall board

Drawing by Charles Schulz; © *1959*
United Features Syndicate, Inc.

performance or to review other foundation policies, such as those relating to investments, personnel, or communications. These subjects are discussed in other parts of this book, but they are mentioned here as examples of additional policy areas that deserve periodic evaluation by the board.

BOARD SELECTION

As suggested in Chapter 3, it is important for the creator of a foundation to provide, early on, the machinery for selecting a board of directors and terms of service. This will encourage both continuity and gradual change in the board's composition. While the decision-making process works differently among foundations, the board is the ultimate policy-making body. What attributes should a nominating committee look for in new board members? John Nason's *Foundation Trusteeship* should be required reading for all nominating committees. In his chapter entitled "Selection, Education, and Renewal," he lists ten important qualities for trustees:

1. interest in and concern for the foundation and its fields of operation;
2. some understanding of the area of the special purpose foundation and some broad perspective on the problems of society for the general purpose foundation;
3. objectivity and impartiality;
4. special skills among the members in management, investments, budgets, and the law;
5. a capacity for arriving at and accepting group decisions;
6. willingness to give time and thought to the foundation's affairs;
7. practical wisdom—the ability to see the whole picture, recognize the validity of opposing arguments, temper the ideal with what is realistic;
8. commitment to the foundation as a whole and not to special interests or constituencies;
9. commitment to the field of private foundations; and
10. moral sensitivity to the act of giving and to the need for giving.

Nason recognizes the desirability of having some board members with specialized knowledge, particularly if a specialized program such as health care for premature infants is involved. Generally, he concludes, "Foundations will be better served by men and women of vision and imagination, people who can bring dispassionate, objective, and broadly based judgments to bear on foundation policies and issues."[4]

In a separate chapter on "Board Composition," Nason makes a strong case for greater race, gender, and age balance in the composition of boards. He argues that differences in viewpoint can lead to wider choices and better decisions. Such diversity should make foundations more accessible to the general public and less vulnerable to charges of elitism.[5] He also argues for a plan for board succession and renewal; both are important ways of obtaining fresh ideas or different experience in order to carry on the foundation's work.[6]

Board Orientation and Training

How to engage and train the next generation to be involved in the foundation is an issue of particular concern to family foundations. Convincing young people to continue in the tradition of family philanthropy, particularly by participating on a foundation board, can be a great challenge. Some families find themselves dealing with competition for board seats among numerous grandchildren or great-grandchildren. Others face the problem of a lack of interest. Some family foundations have established training programs or have encouraged younger family members to sit in on board meetings before actually joining the board. Others have asked younger family members to join outright. Over time, those most interested have been eager to continue the work of the foundation.[7]

New board members, family or not, should be educated about the foundation and the role of private philanthropy in society. The board chair, executive director, or other board member can help by providing some kind of organized orientation for those beginning their first term. An initial meeting with the chair (and the staff director, if there is one) allows new board members to ask questions and clarify what is expected of them. Written materials, such as John Nason's *Foundation Trusteeship*, can help them understand the special role of foundation trustees. A board handbook or other manual that includes copies of the foundation's articles of incorporation, bylaws, policies, and plans, financial statements, and other background material can serve both as an introduction to the foundation and as a useful reference.[8]

Many foundation trustees feel the need for some kind of ongoing training as well. By attending meetings of local regional associations of grantmakers and the Council on Foundations, trustees can hear new ideas and share experiences as well as learn more about specific program or policy issues. Closer to home, they can also gain new insights by going on site visits to potential or current grantees or by attending meetings with experienced nonprofit leaders. These can be arranged in conjunction with a regular board meeting.

Board Committees

There are varying perceptions of the roles that board committees should play in the operation of foundations. Some with small boards and limited assets make all board decisions together as a "committee of the whole." However, most foundations will want to have at least two or three committees of the board: a nominating committee and an investment or finance committee. The role of an investment committee in overseeing the management of the endowment is discussed in Chapter 8. A finance committee may take on investment oversight, but it has broader fiscal responsibilities. It typically selects and recommends the appointment of outside auditors, reviews their work, and monitors the foundation's budget.

Views differ on the need for an executive committee with power to act for the board between meetings. If the board is large and some members must travel long distances to attend meetings, an executive committee is usually formed—although the Carnegie Corporation did away with its executive committee in 1971, wishing to guard against its becoming "the 'in' group of the board, with a corresponding loss of interest and attention of other trustees."[9] Often the executive committee is empowered to make grant decisions between board meetings, particularly where time is a factor or the amount involved is small.

Some foundations have appointed grants committees or employ outside advisory panels charged with reviewing grant requests and either recommending action to the full board or making final decisions. Others have gone a step further and divided the screening function between two or more committees with responsibility for different parts of the giving program.[10] A significant number of foundation committees include people with expertise in certain program areas but who do not serve on the foundation's board. These outside advisors can help add diverse points of view or special knowledge to a foundation's deliberations. Yet, while such delegation of the full board's decision-making role may work well, particularly for unstaffed foundations, experience suggests that it may have a divisive effect. Unless carefully planned, it may leave some directors with nothing more than a rubber stamp function. Also, proliferation of committees of the board should be guarded against lest it absorb both staff and board members' time that might be better spent on policy and program decisions.

Staffing

Decisions on staffing are equally as important as determining program policies and perhaps the first priority for a new foundation. Is there need for full-time staff? If so, what should the qualifications be for the position or positions? If a full-time staff is not needed, how will the foundation's program be implemented?

One of the most convincing arguments for hiring staff states that for all but the smallest foundations, staff can help improve the efficiency and quality of foundation operations. Despite a widely held view in the field that the best-run foundation is the one with low overhead, many foundations find that the financial investment in staff pays off.

Let us see how overhead costs might break down in an imaginary situation. The Frugal Foundation has $5 million in assets. It has annual expenditures, in grants and overhead (excluding investment tax), of $250,000. It operates out of the family offices and pays no rent. Its fixed overhead for investment services, accounting, and preparation of IRS returns has been held down to $10,000. The board serves without compensation. A part-time secretary, at $2,500 a year, handles the correspondence. Each year, the foundation has about $237,500 to give away in about 50 grants of $5,000 each or less.

The board of the Frugal Foundation is active and interested and meets four times a year. At each meeting, the directors review 50 to 100 legitimate requests and act favorably on about a dozen. Through their own volunteer services and that of friends, the five board members have reasonably current information on half the agencies the foundation funds. They do not investigate or evaluate the other half except by reading their requests. Under these not so unusual circumstances, it is a safe bet that five of the 50 grantees would not have survived a careful look at their financial statements, the quality of their services, or the actual need for the project or program for which funds were requested. If not actually wasted, the $25,000 paid to them was at least not wise philanthropy.

Had the foundation employed a part-time consultant working the equivalent of ten days before each meeting and two days after it (at an annual cost of $7,500), these mistakes would probably have been avoided. The board's time would have been conserved, the mail would have been handled, and at least some of the applicant agencies might have been interviewed. The consultant might even have introduced some new ideas for the board's consideration, such as a matching grant to call forth support from others. There would still have been $230,000 to give away, and overhead as a percentage of grants would be 8.7 percent—on the low side for foundations of that size.

Another valid reason for staffing, as suggested in Chapter 1, is that staffed foundations frequently contribute more than money to the fields of their interest. Advice on the preparation of proposals, suggestions of other public and private funding sources, and ideas about management practices (such as putting prospective grantees in touch with sources of technical assistance) are all part of the day-to-day work of an effective staff.

One alternative to full-time staffing for smaller foundations is to share staff. Foundations have done this in different ways: through an independent service agency that performs program and administrative work, such as Grants Management Associates in Boston, Massachusetts; by joining with one or several other foundations to share staff and office space; through a formal merger, such as the one that resulted in the Southern Education Foundation in Atlanta; or by contracting with a local community foundation to handle administrative work.

Since the 1970s, in several cities groups of young donors have collaborated and channeled their giving. This has been done through staffed foundations created for that purpose, such as the Vanguard Public Foundation in San Francisco, California, and the Haymarket Foundation in Cambridge, Massachusetts. Another alternative is to hire part-time staff or consultants for one or more functions. Experts in a given program area can help the foundation board shape programs and review proposals. Part-time clerical staff can assist the active board that needs help sorting through mail and handling correspondence.

If a foundation expects to make a relatively small number of sizable grants to established institutions, its need for executive and support staff will be reduced. However, smaller grants in greater numbers, particularly to new agencies or to individuals, will increase the need for staff. Operating foundations that run an institution or program, by definition, will have greater personnel needs than those of grantmaking foundations with comparable endowments.

Staff Qualifications

What qualifications should one seek in the candidate for a foundation staff position? There is no one field of professional training from which foundation staff are usually selected. Current foundation executives previously worked in business, education, law, nonprofit management, and other fields. For the new executive of a small- or middle-sized foundation, some administrative experience is valuable, but personal qualities of integrity, intellectual curiosity, and imagination are more important. Another useful tool is writing ability, but sensitivity to the aspirations of others and the ability to listen are essential. The foundation executive must avoid the two occupationally hazardous O's: Omniscience and Omnipotence. But if the foundation's money is to be spent promptly and well, the executive must be willing and able to exercise judgment and make decisions.

When recruiting staff, a foundation should make the process an open one, and it should strive for diversity on its staff. To find qualified candidates, foundations can advertise the availability of positions locally, or through national resources such as *Foundation News* or the *Chronicle of Philanthropy*. Using established networks in the community or the foundation field itself can also yield results. The several affinity groups of grantmakers that serve as professional societies can make recommendations.[11] For the largest foundations, executive search firms are helping boards screen a national pool of top talent.

Board–Staff Relations

If the board decides to delegate part of the foundation's work to paid staff, careful thought should be given to how the board–staff relationship will function. Researchers Elizabeth Boris, Teresa Odendahl, and Arlene Kaplan Daniels identified several models in the foundation world in their book, *Working in Foundations*.[12] While many foundations share characteristics of each model, this scheme may help board members to sort out the possibilities.

The *administrator model* employs a staff office manager and perhaps also a clerical worker who handle inquiries, prepare board meeting materials, and manage the office routine. The board makes all policy and grant decisions and is often involved in the day-to-day management of the foundation. The program usually reflects the wishes of an active donor. The family serves on the board, and the foundation is generally small.

For the *director model*, the foundation employs an executive director who works with the board to help set goals and review programs. The director recommends grant proposals and turndowns. The board reviews and acts on the recommendations and decides fiscal and program policies. In addition to the director, other program and administrative staff may be employed. Foundations using this approach are often small- or medium-sized, and often still involve the donor or the donor's family.

The *presidential model* employs staff that exercise more discretion. A chief staff officer and other staff are employed to carry out many of the grantmaking and administrative functions. The CEO provides leadership to the staff and the board, and may have some discretionary authority to make grants without prior board approval. The board concentrates on setting policy and monitoring progress. It generally ratifies staff recommendations for most grants and denials, discussing only the largest or most controversial grant proposals in any detail. The larger foundations that often no longer have donor involvement are most likely to use this model.

As in other human relationships, good teamwork between foundation boards and staff depends on mutual respect, clearly defined areas of responsibility, and willingness to approach problems with an open mind. The presiding officer of the board and the chief staff executive play important roles in achieving this teamwork. Good rapport between them is essential.

The larger the foundation, the more important it is that the respective roles of board and staff be spelled out in an operating manual or similar internal document. But even in foundations with one professional staff member, it is vital that the board defines what that person's functions are and respect that role. For instance, it should be clearly spelled out that every proposal for a grant be processed by the staff before the board acts on it. A board member's natural inclination to argue for a proposal with which he or she is especially familiar should be resisted until staff has had an opportunity to check it out. Alert fundraisers are adept at identifying and contacting sympathetic board members, but end runs can be damaging both to staff morale and to the quality of the foundation's program.

Many boards delegate to staff the important task of screening initial applications. Staff can more efficiently decline the typically large percentage of requests that do not fit a foundation's stated program interests. The board may wish to review a list of such declinations at each meeting, but the lists have become so long that this is often a pro forma exercise. More important is staff recognition of a connection between the applicant agency and a board member. As a matter of courtesy, an informal conversation with the board member before sending a declination will often avoid embarrassment. In borderline situations, where staff is not enthusiastic, brief descriptions of proposals may be included in board dockets with indications that the staff does not recommend a grant. In such cases, declinations are not sent until after board consideration.

Scholarships and fellowships, when administered directly by the foundation after IRS approval of procedures, are often handled by staff with the advice of special committees. These may and often do include nonboard members. Occasionally, outside review panels may be asked to make final decisions concerning such awards. In-house research and other operating programs are, of course, administered by staff.

Legal, Accounting, and Investment Services

The Tax Reform Act of 1969 has been called, only partially in jest, the "Lawyers' and Accountants' Relief Act." Even before the act, these two professions performed important functions in the administration of larger foundations. Now foundations of all sizes use their services. The accountant's function is usually preparing the annual returns to file with federal and state authorities, since much of the material is drawn from their annual audit. (Federal returns are due four and a half months after the close of the foundation's fiscal year.) Review of these returns by the foundation's lawyer is also common practice, and both staffed and unstaffed foundations will want to consult their attorneys when confronted with issues such as those listed at the end of Chapter 4.[13]

There are also occasions when the IRS recognizes a written opinion of counsel as demonstrating a foundation manager's good faith and will thus relieve him or her of liability for a penalty tax. For example, foundation managers are not liable for penalty taxes under Section 4945 if they agreed to a "taxable expenditure" based on "reasonable cause." A "reasoned written legal opinion" that the proposed grant or other act would not be a taxable expenditure will provide reasonable cause and will ordinarily relieve the manager of liability for tax.[14]

As will be discussed more fully in Chapter 8, many foundations employ outside investment counsel to advise on the management of their endowments. Most foundations also use banks, trust companies, or brokerage houses as custodians of their securities. If representatives of these institutions or partners of the foundation's legal or accounting firms also serve on the foundation's board, potential instances of self-dealing under Section 4941 may arise (see the following discussion of conflict of interest). However, the exception in that section for personal services rendered to the foundation will cover most such situations. Foundations must exercise particular care where a bank serves as its trustee and is therefore a disqualified person with respect to the foundation. ("Disqualified person" is a broad category including contributors to the foundation, its managers, and certain public officials.) The foundation may make use of the bank's "general banking services" without self-dealing, but other kinds of transactions between the foundation and the bank may be taxable.[15]

Conflict of Interest

The self-dealing rules cover many possible conflict-of-interest situations. Where a foundation manager or other "disqualified person" (or their near relative—see Chapter 7) receives direct or indirect payments from the foundation, penalty taxes may be incurred unless the transaction comes under the exception for personal services rendered.[16] But there are other situations not necessarily within the scope of the federal self-dealing rules where foundation managers may appear to have a conflict of interest. The usual one occurs when a foundation considers a grant to an organization with a board member who is also a board member or manager of the foundation. Under such circumstances, the grant would not be considered self-dealing under Section 4941.[17] But the public, if made aware of the circumstances, might well feel that the grantee exerted undue influence in obtaining the grant.[18]

The guidelines of the Northwest Area Foundation express the importance of avoiding even the appearance of a conflict of interest:

> Private foundations must strive so far as possible to be above suspicion. It is not enough that the directors and the staff believe that they are operating from the highest motives, and that any particular action is innocent, regardless of its appearance. So far as possible, actions and relationships must avoid an appearance of impropriety which raises questions in the minds of the public. (See Appendix 2)

Several options are open to foundations seeking to avoid appearances of conflict of interest. Using the example of overlapping directorships, the most drastic would be to refuse to consider the agency's request, which imposes a harsh penalty on the agency. Almost equally drastic would be a requirement that no director or staff member have an affiliation with a potential grantee. (This requirement is occasionally discovered in foundations today). Most foundations recognize the importance of active involvement in civic affairs by board members and staff. Many have adopted written guidelines requiring full disclosure of all outside affiliations. Many also require directors with potential conflicts of interest to abstain from voting on issues where the conflict might arise. Board meeting minutes should clearly show that the board member has abstained.[19]

Administrative Expenses

Every good manager tries to run the organization in the most efficient manner possible. Board members, staff, and professional advisors all have a stake in ensuring that foundations accomplish this goal. What level of administrative expenses is reasonable for a private foundation? How does one foundation compare with another? In contemplating foundation administrative expenses, Council on Foundations' Director of Private Foundation Services Deborah Brody notes that administrative costs typically include salaries and benefits, legal and professional fees, interest/taxes/depreciation, occupancy, travel, printing, and other expenses. In comparing foundation expense levels, she makes the following observation:

> Comparing your foundation's administrative expenses with those of other grantmakers is difficult. Each organization's practices are affected by a number of factors, including (1) the purpose of the foundation; (2) activities other than grantmaking undertaken by the foundation (such as conducting research, managing conferences, or running other types of programs); (3) whether operations are local, regional, national, or international; (4) the size and number of grant recipients; (5) the size and number of grants; (6) the number of staff and consultants; (7) the existence of foundation-run scholarships, fellowships, or other award programs.[20]

She also notes that administrative costs are related to economies of scale. Large foundations typically have lower costs as a percentage of assets than smaller ones. However, in smaller foundations with few or no staff, the donor or donor's family may absorb most or all of the overhead costs.

A Council on Foundations study of 500 foundations during 1985 found that charitable administrative costs ranged from .14 to 10 percent of assets. The median was .35 percent. Foundations with assets over $50 million tended to have an expense ratio slightly below the median, while foundations with assets between $10 and $50 million show higher ratios. (Typically, these foundations are large enough to require staff but too small to take advantage of the economies of scale experienced by larger foundations.) Smaller foundations are very diverse, with some having virtually no expenses and others having a high ratio because they have a staff person. Higher expense ratios might result from several factors, such as one-time start up costs incurred by new foundations or staff-intensive programs (like scholarship or fellowship programs).[21]

Compensation of Board and Staff

The Internal Revenue Code permits foundations to pay reasonable compensation, including expenses, to board members and staff for personal services. This applies even if the recipients are substantial contributors to the foundation or otherwise within the definition of "disqualified person."[22] In practice, most foundations reimburse non-staff directors for their expenses only and pay no fee for services. Many of the largest foundations pay an honorarium to directors, often based on the number of board and committee meetings attended. As foundations gradually bring persons outside the business and professional establishment onto their boards, such compensation is being recognized as a way of encouraging board service by those who might otherwise not be able to afford the time.[23]

In 1989 the Council on Foundations issued a statement outlining the arguments for and against trustee compensation. The statement cautions foundations against paying excessive fees and urges foundation boards to consider carefully the time and effort contributed by trustees in determining whether to offer compensation and what might be a "reasonable" fee. (See Appendix 13 for the full text of the statement.)

Foundations established as charitable trusts are often more accustomed to paying trustees fees, sometimes in substantial amounts. There are several reasons for this. State laws often prescribe schedules of fees for charitable trusts based on assets or income. Banks are frequently named as cotrustees of such trusts and expect compensation; in some instances, the trust instrument mandates the fee. While it is argued that trustees have greater exposure to personal liability than directors of foundations in the corporate form, the very high fees paid to some trustees are still difficult to justify either for this reason or because of the time and work involved.[24] Furthermore, regardless of what state laws permit, such fees may not withstand scrutiny under federal law if challenged by the IRS.

Compensation of staff is often based on the individual's experience and salary level in prior employment. The Council on Foundations maintains figures on the compensation of staff of its members, grouped according to foundation size, in its biennial *Foundation Management Report*. The report includes statistics covering fringe benefits such as medical and group life insurance, retirement annuities, and tuition reimbursement. It also provides information on personnel policies such as vacation, parental leave, and severance pay. Note that Section 501(c)(3) charities, including foundations, are able to offer their employees tax-sheltered annuities under Section 403(b). These are less complex than the qualified annuity plans used by industry.[25]

Regardless of the salary or benefits offered by a foundation, it is important to develop an overall plan and written record outlining how personnel issues are handled. Many foundations have adopted formal wage and salary plans that include job descriptions for all employees together with procedures and criteria for regular performance evaluations. Another useful management tool is a policy manual that outlines benefits and personnel policies such as hiring, firing, and conflict of interest.

Directors' and Officers' Liability

During the 1980s, a liability insurance crisis hit the United States, causing the cost of premiums to skyrocket. This created much concern on nonprofit boards. There have been few past instances of lawsuits against foundations. Still, the increasing potential for such actions in today's litigious society has caused many foundation board members and staff to be more concerned about their responsibility in these situations. General liability insurance for personal injury or property damage is readily available to foundations and should be obtained early in the organizing process.

Directors' and officers' (D&O) liability insurance, which covers claims other than those involving injury or property damage, poses more difficult problems. Council on Foundations General Counsel John Edie provides a detailed examination of the issues involved in *Directors and Officers Liability Insurance and Indemnification.*

Edie points out that liabilities not usually covered by general insurance include libel, slander, breach of contract, conflict of interest, mismanagement of funds, and others from common law. Cases involving allegations of discrimination in employment are the most common. In addition, the foundation and its managers can be liable for violations of the Internal Revenue Code, failure to withhold and pay social security tax, failure to withhold and pay federal income tax, and other federal laws. Similarly, the foundation and managers could be liable for violations of state or local laws and codes. For private foundations, the Internal Revenue Code Chapter 42 provisions require that penalty taxes be paid if violations of these provisions are proved.

Although state laws differ in the specifics, they generally permit or require a foundation to indemnify its officers and directors—to cover the legal costs, expenses, judgments, and settlements incurred by the officers or directors on behalf of the foundation. Edie strongly recommends checking with the foundation's legal counsel for specifics on state requirements. He also advises that the foundation include a written statement of its intent to indemnify officers and directors in the foundation's articles of incorporation or bylaws or by another formal procedure.

D&O insurance can provide additional financial protection. When should a foundation consider purchasing insurance, rather than remaining "self-insured" (depending on indemnification only)? Edie says there are no easy answers:

> It is very hard to draw the line between the foundations which really should have D&O coverage and those which should not. Obviously, the

larger your offices, the more staff you have, the more grants you make, the more controversial your grants are, the more investments you have, the more contracts you enter into, the greater your exposure to potential claims. At the other end of the spectrum, there are small foundations with no office, no staff, no contracts, few grants and limited investments. In these circumstances, the chance of a claim may be so remote that the cost of D&O insurance may not be warranted.[26]

Few insurance companies write D&O policies because of the complexity of the rules and the lack of experience with this type of coverage. Those that do often charge extremely high rates, depending on the coverage elected. For those deciding to purchase insurance, Edie also cautions that some policies cover *only* directors and officers, leaving other staff, committee members, and even the foundation itself still vulnerable. A policy that covers all is preferable.[27]

Also, although an insurance company can pay the costs of defense of alleged violations of Chapter 42 of the Internal Revenue Code, it cannot cover the cost of the penalty tax itself. This ruling indicates that a private foundation must treat as compensation to the director or officer that part of the D&O insurance premium that covers the foundation manager *only* when he or she is either (1) unsuccessful in his or her defense, or (2) the preceding is terminated by settlement, and he or she has acted willfully and without reasonable cause with respect to his or her foundation duties. However, the Council on Foundations argues that no part of a premium is compensation. In this regard, the council has provided a legal submission to the IRS, which is currently under review.[28]

Accounting and Record Keeping

The accounting requirements of a foundation will, of course, vary in complexity depending on a foundation's size and mode of operation. The information returns required by the federal government are set up on a cash basis. The additional reporting required by some states is usually on a similar basis.

The accounting profession has recently developed guidelines for nonprofit organizations (including foundations) primarily based on the accrual method of accounting. These guidelines introduce modified functional accounting requirements. If the foundation is to receive an unqualified opinion from a certified public accountant in connection with an annual audit, conforming with these guidelines may be necessary.[29]

Many small- and middle-sized foundations "farm out" their day-to-day bookkeeping and payrolls to accounting firms. Custodians, such as banks, perform their investment recordkeeping. Under these circumstances, in-house bookkeeping can be limited to checkbook entries for grants, petty cash, and the like. Important records and files include minutes of board and committee actions, copies of reports filed with IRS and state governments, and correspondence with attorneys, accountants, and custodians.

The most voluminous and active records foundations must maintain concern grant applications. Given the large number of requests received, it is important to handle unsuccessful applications as simply as possible. If each application is kept on file for any length of time, the space problem will become acute. Thus, many foundations merely log such requests with date received, date of rejection letter, and perhaps some comment on the reason for rejection. They then destroy the incoming material unless there is a possibility of future funding. Others may mail the material back to the organizations, especially those that made elaborate presentations. Requests the foundation acts on favorably are typically retained in individual files. These may also contain all subsequent correspondence with the grantee, including evidence of the tax status of the grantee and reports received on the progress and at the completion of the grant. These "grant files" are important for all grants. They form the starting point for grant evaluations and record the foundation's past experience with each grantee. They are essential for "expenditure responsibility" grants or grants to individuals. They may be examined by IRS agents during an audit to determine that the appropriate reports have been received by the foundation.

For both financial and grant information functions, many foundations use computers. Personal computers are most popular, although other types are also used. Word processing has replaced the typewriter in most offices and has enabled foundation staff and board members to respond to grant inquiries more quickly and efficiently. Computerized grants management includes tracking applications, scheduling grant payments and grantee reports, and maintaining historical records. Some foundations have hired consultants to develop custom programs, while a growing number are using the specialized "off-the-shelf" programs available. Financial software includes the general ledger, accounts payable, accounts receivable, payroll, and other subsidiary journals. The Council on Foundations and some regional associations of grantmakers can provide information on foundation use of computers, software vendors, and computer training and information. Some organizations offer computer assistance to nonprofits, including foundations.

Finally, as research on philanthropy continues to grow, scholars find that access to individual foundations' historical records are crucial to their efforts to describe and evaluate the role of philanthropy in society. As researchers are urging foundations to consider archiving their records and making them available for study more and more foundations themselves want to preserve their history.[30]

Who Needs a Budget?

Businesses, big or small, find it essential to prepare an operating budget before the beginning of a fiscal year. Foundations would be reluctant to make grants to any operating charity that did not do likewise. Yet many small- and even some middle-sized foundations function from year to year with little more than the expectation that their expenditures will equal their income. The charitable payout requirements of Internal Revenue Code Section 4942 are, fortunately, sufficiently flexible so that shortfalls in expenditures for the current year can be made up in the following year. Overexpenditures can be carried forward for five years.[31]

The use of a simple, functional budget reviewed (if not formally approved) by the board at its last meeting of the fiscal year should serve several useful purposes in planning its program for the coming year. It will give the board a picture, not usually available until the foundation's audit is completed well along in the new year, of the relationship between administrative costs and grants. It should also be helpful in spotlighting the amount of uncommitted funds available for new grants, especially if the foundation has several multiyear grant commitments outstanding. It can provide a means of focusing attention on the relative weight to be given to different program interests of the foundation. Finally, it can help avoid end-of-the year pressures to reach a particular spending level by giving board and staff a target for the year's expenditures before the new year begins.

NOTES TO CHAPTER 6

1. Robert K. Greenleaf, "The Trustee: The Buck Stops Here." *Foundation News* 14, no. 4, July/August 1973, p. 31.

2. Susan Calhoun, "A Helpful Look Inward." *Foundation News* 28, no. 1, January/February 1987, pp. 63–64; Humphrey Doermann, "Long-Range Planning: Shaping Future Programs," *Foundation News* 27, no. 3, May/June 1986, pp. 56–57. These articles describe retreats where the board reviews program direction, investment policy, evaluation, and other issues. Information on retreats is sometimes published as part of a foundation's annual report. Foundations that have recently undergone extensive program or operations review include the Rosenberg Foundation, which did so on the occasion of its 50th anniversary; the Jessie Ball duPont Religious, Charitable, and Education Fund (with the advent of a new staff director); and the Robert Wood Johnson Foundation, which made program changes to reflect society's changing healthcare needs.

3. The self-study process involves using a questionnaire and discussion to enable board members to assess their knowledge and involvement in foundation activities. They must also address their performance as a group in areas such as mission and program, organization, management, grantmaking, and fiduciary responsibilities. Versions are available for family and nonfamily private foundations.

4. Nason, *Foundation Trusteeship: Service in the Public Interest* (New York: The Foundation Center, 1989). pp. 56–57.

5. *Ibid.*, pp. 42–45. See also the Filer Commission Report (note 3, Chapter 1), pp. 170–171.

6. *Ibid.*, pp. 60–62.

7. "Passing the Torch," *Foundation News* 30, no. 5, September/October 1989, pp. 50–52. This article offers four strategies employed by different foundations to teach new family board members their roles and responsibilities.

8. A listing of items to include in such a manual is part of the *Trustee Orientation Packet* (Washington, DC: Council on Foundations, 1991.)

9. Caryl P. Haskins, "A Foundation Looks at Itself." *Foundation News* 13, no. 2, March/April 1972, p. 9.

10. An even more extreme form of delegation, although usually limited to a small portion of a foundation's giving, occurs when individual board members are given discretion to make or recommend grants. Such delegation of the board's responsibility may lead to decision making by whim and to allegations of favoritism, if not self-dealing.

11. Professional associations in the grantmaking field that could be helpful in identifying candidates include the Association of Black Foundation Executives, Hispanics in Philanthropy, Asians and Pacific Islanders in Philanthropy, Native Americans in Philanthropy, and Women and Foundations/Corporate Philanthropy. The Council on Foundations can provide the current address and contact person at each of these organizations.

12. Teresa Jean Odendahl, Elizabeth Trocolli Boris, and Arlene Kaplan Daniels, *Working in Foundations: Career Patterns of Women and Men* (New York: The Foundation Center, 1985), p. 13. See also Odendahl and Boris, "A Delicate Balance: Board-Staff Relations." *Foundation News* 24, no. 3, May/June 1983, pp. 34–45.

13. There is also, however, an occupational hazard among attorneys, particularly those with limited experience in exempt organization law: excessive caution. This has led to unneeded forms and unwillingness to advise favorably on expenditure responsibility grants.

14. Regulation 53.4945–1(a)(2)(vi). Similar effect is given to advice of counsel on self-dealing questions, Regulation 53.4941(a)–1(b)(6), and jeopardy investments, Regulation 53.4944–1(b)(2)(v).

15. Regulation 53.4941(d)–2(c)(4) spells out the exception to the self-dealing rules for general banking services. See also example 3 of Regulation 53.4941 (d)–3(c)(2). Checking accounts are within the exception as long as the bank does not charge interest on amounts overdrawn, Revised Ruling 73–546, 1973–2 CB 384. Savings accounts are also permissible when the foundation may withdraw its funds on no more than 29 days notice without penalty, Revised Ruling 73–595, 1973–2 CB 384. Situations that may trigger penalty taxes include the purchase of a mortgage by the foundation from the bank, Revised Ruling 77–259, 1977–2 CB 387, and the foundation's purchase of the bank's certificate of deposit, Revised Ruling 77–288, 1977–2 CB 388.

16. Regulation 53.4941(d)–3(c).

17. Regulation 53.4941(d)(f)(2). Note, however, that if "control" exists, the grant may not be a qualifying distribution. See Chapter 4.

18. Sometimes the reverse of this situation can be troublesome, e.g., when a board member for some personal reason argues against a particular grant request.

19. For a discussion of practices see Frederick Willman, "Written Guidelines on Conflict of Interest." *Foundation News* 18, no. 3, May/June 1977, pp. 51–54. See also Appendix 2.

20. Deborah Brody, "Expense Management." *Foundation News* 30, no. 6, November/December 1989, pp. 66–68. This article summarizes research conducted by the Council on Foundations. Based on data from the 1985 Forms 990-PF of 500 foundations, 83 percent of foundation spending was for grants, 8 percent for investment expenses, and 9 percent for grant and other charitable administrative expenses.

21. *Ibid.*, p. 68.

22. Regulation 53.4941(d)–3(c).

23. For a full discussion of directors compensation see Nason, *Foundation Trusteeship*, Chapter 10. Also, the Council on Foundations' biennial *Foundation Management Report* includes statistics on trustee compensation.

24. After reviewing some of these fees, Nason concludes:

    There is no moral justification, whatever the law permits, for diverting more than a very modest sum from the proper beneficiaries of a foundation to the pockets of the trustees who are responsible for the charitable trust. Those who reject this position would do well to reflect on the ammunition that large payments to trustees can easily provide for the next populist attack on foundations. (*Foundation Trusteeship*, p. 105)

25. Most Section 403(b) annuity contracts are defined contribution plans that provide for an individual account for each participant and for benefits based solely on the amount contributed. These contracts can be purchased by a foundation for its employees from a number of different insurance companies. The employer's and employee's contributions are excludable from the employee's gross income to the extent of his or her allowance (which very roughly is 20 percent of income each year). One popular feature of the Section 403(b) annuity is that employees may agree with their employers to take a reduction in salary, which is used to increase the employer's con-

tribution to the employee's annuity. For further explanation of the federal tax rules for these annuities, see IRS Publication 571, *Tax-Sheltered Annuity Programs for Employees of Public Schools and Certain Tax-Exempt Organizations*. Section 403(b) plans must also comply with the requirements of the Employee Retirement Income Security Act (ERISA).

26. John A. Edie, *Directors and Officers Liability Insurance and Indemnification* (Washington, DC: Council on Foundations, 1990), p. 15.

27. Among the D&O insurance policies on the market is a plan endorsed by the Council on Foundations that addresses specific needs of grantmaking foundations. However, regardless of the plan chosen, foundation managers should take care to examine their foundation's own risks and needs before choosing to purchase any policy.

28. See IRS private letter ruling 8615076.

29. In August 1989, the Financial Accounting Standards Board (FASB) issued an invitation to comment on the form and content of financial statements of nonprofit organizations. They are reviewing these issues because current guidance is often confusing and contradictory, resulting in varying practices. The American Institute of Certified Public Accountants, which has issued audit guides and Statement of Position 78–10 (this includes information for private foundations) is assisting in this effort. FASB expects to deliberate the issues in 1990 and eventually issue standard reporting requirements.

30. The largest foundations have established in-house archives or participate in a combined archive center such as the Rockefeller Archive Center, which houses Rockefeller, Russell Sage, and Commonwealth foundation archives, among others. Some take advantage of a growing number of centers at universities and historical societies, such as the Western Reserve Historical Society in Cleveland, the Huntington Library at Stanford, the Rockefeller Archive Center, the Social Welfare Archives at the University of Minnesota, and the Wisconsin State Historical Society. For more information on this issue, see Darwin Stapleton, "Plumbing the Past," *Foundation News* 28, no. 6, November/December 1987, pp. 67–68, and Peter Dobkin Hall, "Taming the Archival Tiger," *Foundation News* 30, no. 6, November/December 1989, pp. 61–63.

31. Regulation 53.4942(a)–3(e).

ANNOTATED BIBLIOGRAPHY–CHAPTER 6

Gross, Susan. "The 10 Most Common Organizational Problems: Getting to Their Source." *Foundation News* 24, no. 1, January/February 1983, pp. 22–25.

Gross discusses the problems that foundations most often present to management consultants and offers suggestions for solving them.

O'Connell, Brian. *Non-Profit Management Series* (Washington, DC: Independent Sector, 1988). Nine Volumes.

O'Connell offers guidelines in nine nonprofit management areas. The volumes include: (1) *The Role of the Board and Board Members*; (2) *Finding, Developing, and Rewarding Good Board Members*; (3) *Operating Effective Committees*; (4) *Conducting Good Meetings*; (5) *The Roles and Relationships of the Chief Volunteer and Chief Staff Officers: Who Does What?*; (6) *Recruiting, Encouraging and Evaluating the Chief Staff Officer*; (7) *Fund Raising*; (8) *Budgeting and Financial Accountability*; and (9) *Evaluating Results*.

BOARD OF DIRECTORS

The primary reference for this section is John Nason's *Foundation Trusteeship: Service in the Public Interest* (New York: The Foundation Center, 1989). 173 pages.

This comprehensive book covers issues related to governing boards.

The Commission on Foundations and Private Philanthropy (Peterson Commission, 1970). *Foundations, Private Giving and Public Policy*.

See pp. 87–90, 137–139, and 249–250 for details on the role of trustees, frequency of board meetings, and other data collected from a survey of the trustees of 20 large foundations. The commission recommended increased diversity of trustees and more independent trustees.

Commission on Private Philanthropy and Public Needs (Filer Commission, 1977). *Giving in America*.

The commission recommended "that tax-exempt organizations, particularly funding organizations, recognize an obligation to be responsive to changing viewpoints and emerging needs and that they take steps such as broadening their boards and staffs to insure that they are responsive."

Council on Foundations. "Board Colleague's Conflict—Do You Tell?" *Foundation News* 27, no. 1, January/February 1986, pp. 64–66.

This article addresses the problem of potential conflicts of interest by members of foundation boards. Appears in the "Ethics" section of the magazine.

Council on Foundations. "When Trustees Cross the Line . . ." *Foundation News* 25, no. 4, July/August 1984, pp. 70–72.

The article addresses foundation trustees straying from the mission in the foundation charter. Appears in the "Ethics" section of the magazine.

Dayton, Kenneth N. *Governance is Governance* (Washington, DC: Independent Sector, 1987). 14 pages.

This is adapted from a keynote presentation by the author. He addresses the basics of effective management.

Greenleaf, Robert K. "Prudence and Creativity: A Trustee Responsibility." *Foundation News* 15, no. 3, May/June 1974, pp. 28–32.

Greenleaf defines three characteristics of foundations, which differentiate them from other institutions. He shows how these differences make foundation trusteeship unique.

Greenleaf, Robert K. *Trustees as Servants* (Cambridge, MA: Center for Applied Studies, 1974). 36 pages.

Greenleaf provides an overview of the role of governing boards. He delineates trustee roles from the those of staff administrators.

Houle, Cyril O. *Governing Boards* (Washington, DC: National Center for Non-Profit Boards, 1989). 223 pages.

The author provides comprehensive guidance on improving the effectiveness of governing boards in nonprofit and public organizations.

Joseph, James A. "Trusteeship in Transition: Challenges to Governance." *Foundation News* 27, no. 1, January/February 1986, pp. 53–55.

This is the text of a speech given by the President of the Council on Foundations in January 1986. Joseph points up the need for foundations to articulate their principles and to nurture the talent within their staff.

O'Connell, Brian. *The Board Member's Book* (New York: The Foundation Center, 1985). 208 pages.

This book is written for nonprofit board members. O'Connell has developed a practical guide to the essential functions of voluntary boards covering such areas as the legal responsibility of board members, the selection of board members, constructive planning for voluntary organizations, budgeting and financial accountability, the role of the president, hiring and working with a staff director, the relationship of board and staff, and evaluating results.

Park, Jane. "Caught in the Machinery." *Foundation News* 30, no. 2, March/April 1989, pp. 54–55, 59.

Park discusses some foundations' effectiveness or ineffectiveness in grant-making. She suggests that trustees must retool foundation operations.

Stevenson, J. John. "A Case Study: Lessons in Board Responsibility." *The Philanthropy Monthly* 13, no. 10, October 1980.

Stevenson points out the pitfalls of trusteeship. He explains the difference between a corporate director and a foundation trustee, and discusses ways to minimize trustee liability while improving performance.

THE BOARD'S POLICY-MAKING ROLE

Armbruster, Timothy D. "Foundation Policy Review." *The Philanthropy Monthly* 13, no. 4, April 1980, p. 15.

Armbruster discusses ways to involve foundation governing boards more directly in policy review and strategic planning.

Calhoun, Susan. "A Helpful Look Inward." *Foundation News* 28, no. 1, January/February 1987, pp. 63–64.

The author describes a self-study process that enables foundation trustees to evaluate and improve their performances. The *Self Study Guide for Foundation Boards* uses a questionnaire and discussion to help boards draw out issues of concern. The guide has been successfully used by private family and non-family foundations and is available through the Council on Foundations.

Greenleaf, Robert K. "The Trustee: The Buck Stops Here." *Foundation News* 14, no. 4, July/August 1973, p. 31.

Greenleaf cites the decisionmaking power of foundation trustees and their unusual obligations.

Nason, John W. *Foundation Trusteeship: Service in the Public Interest* (New York: The Foundation Center, 1989).

See Chapter 3, "Programs by Default or By Design."

BOARD SELECTION AND SUCCESSION

Nason, John W. *Foundation Trusteeship: Service in the Public Interest.*

See Chapter 5, "Board Composition," and Chapter 6, "Selection, Education, and Renewal."

Council on Foundations. "Passing the Torch." *Foundation News* 30, no. 5, September/October 1989, pp. 50–52.

This article proffers four strategies employed by different foundations to teach new family board members their roles and responsibilities.

BOARD ORIENTATION AND TRAINING

Council on Foundations. *Trustee Orientation Packet* (Washington, DC: Council on Foundations, 1990). 70 pages.

This resource is designed to provide new foundation trustees with a basic understanding of their role and responsibilities. It includes several publications of the council related to trusteeships and a suggested reading list.

Strauch, Carol. "Getting Oriented." *Foundation News* 31, no. 5, September/October 1990, pp. 28–33.

Strauch suggests techniques for orientation of new trustees and argues for continuing education and board development.

STAFFING

Boris, Elizabeth, and Brody, Deborah, et al. *1990 Foundation Management Report* (Washington, DC: Council on Foundations, 1990). 181 pages.

Produced biennially, the *Management Report* presents data on topics such as staff salaries, benefits, demographics, personnel policies, trustee compensation, terms of office, and other subjects for over 700 foundations.

Chicago Community Trust. "Evaluating Foundation Staff Performance." *Foundation News* 18, no. 5, September/October 1977, p. 7.

This is a report of a survey conducted by the Chicago Community Trust in 1975, designed to illustrate the trust's grantmaking activities through the eyes of its applicants. The trust asked grantees to evaluate its staff's performance and grant procedures.

Council on Foundations. *Developing Position Descriptions* (Washington, DC: Council on Foundations, 1987). 101 pages.

This is a resource for foundation administrators who are revising their personnel and salary plans or developing human resource programs for the first time. It introduces the subject and provides background articles and samples of actual foundation staff position descriptions for private, community, and corporate foundations. It also includes a bibliography and list of resources.

Foote, Joseph. "Stretching the Career Ladder." *Foundation News* 26, no. 1, January/February 1985, pp. 25–28.

Foote explains the causes of burnout among philanthropic professionals and the ways in which foundations have found to combat this via management training and personal enrichment. Part of the *Foundation News* "Hands On" series.

James, H. Thomas. "Perspectives on Internal Functioning of Foundations." In *The Future of Foundations*, Fritz F. Heimann, ed. (Englewood Cliffs, NJ: Prentice-Hall, for the American Assembly, 1973). pp. 192–215.

James discusses foundation trusteeship, staffing, program development, grants monitoring, foundation reporting, and other issues.

Menninger, Roy. "Foundation Work May be Hazardous to Your Mental Health" (Washington, DC: Council on Foundations, 1981).

Adapted from a speech given by Dr. Menninger, this piece outlines some of the occupational dangers of grantmaking and grant receiving.

Nason, John W. *Foundation Trusteeship: Service in the Public Interest.*
See Chapter 8, "To Staff or Not to Staff."

Odendahl, Teresa, Boris, Elizabeth, and Kaplan Daniels, Arlene. *Working in Foundations: Career Patterns of Women and Men* (New York: The Foundation Center, 1985). 115 pages.

This book is based on focused personal interviews with 60 foundation chief executives, program officers, and administrative assistants. The authors offer an in-depth look at the roles and responsibilities of foundation staff, and how gender, age, ethnicity, education, employment history, volunteer activities, and family responsibilities have affected their career opportunities.

Zurcher, Arnold J., and Dustan, Jane. *The Foundation Administrator: A Study of Those Who Manage America's Foundations* (New York: Russell Sage Foundation, 1972). 171 pages.

This study presents data on foundation administrators and trustees. Its focus is the selection and training of administrators, their professional satisfactions, and their opinions of foundation employment. Although the data are out of date, this landmark study contains some useful insights into foundation administration.

BOARD–STAFF RELATIONS

Dayton, Kenneth. "Define Your Roles." *Foundation News* 26, no. 3, May/June 1985, pp. 68–71.

The author recommends that nonprofits, including foundations, clearly outline the duties and responsibilities of the board and staff. He suggests what those roles can be and how they can complement each other and work together to achieve success.

Odendahl, Teresa, and Boris, Elizabeth. "A Delicate Balance: Foundation Board–Staff Relations." *Foundation News* 24, no. 3, May/June 1983, pp. 34–45.

According to this article, the most important factor for successful foundation management is board–staff relations. Odendahl and Boris offer a comprehensive guide to achieving and maintaining solid relations between the foundation board and staff.

Many of the books listed at the beginning of this chapter also contain sections on this topic.

LEGAL, ACCOUNTING, AND INVESTMENT SERVICES

Nason, John W. *Foundation Trusteeship: Service in the Public Interest.*
See Chapter 12, "What Doth the Law Require?" for a summary of the major legal and moral duties of the foundation trustee.

CONFLICT OF INTEREST

Council on Foundations. "How Close Is Too Close?" *Foundation News* 25, no. 3, May/June 1984, pp. 65–67.

The article addresses the issue of mixing professional and personal relationships in the "Ethics" section of the magazine.

Willman, Frederick. "Written Guidelines on Conflicts of Interest." *Foundation News* 18, no. 3, May/June 1977, pp. 51–54.

The article offers pros and cons to a written code of ethics for foundation personnel to help assure impartiality in grantmaking decisions.

COMPENSATION OF BOARD AND STAFF

Boris, Elizabeth, and Brody, Deborah, et al. *1990 Foundation Management Report.*

This includes extensive data on staff salaries, benefits, personnel policies, and trustee compensation.

Internal Revenue Service, Department of the Treasury. *Tax-Sheltered Annuity Programs for Employees of Public Schools and Certain Tax-Exempt Organizations.* Publication 571 (Washington, DC: Government Printing Office).

Nason, John W. *Foundation Trusteeship: Service in the Public Interest.*

See Chapter 10, "Compensation of Trustees," for a useful discussion on trustee compensation.

DIRECTORS AND OFFICERS INSURANCE

Council on Foundations. "Who Needs D&O Insurance?" *Foundation News* 29, no. 4, July/August 1988, pp. 52–54.

The article discusses directors' and officers' liability insurance and its costs and benefits to nonprofit organizations.

Edie, John. *Directors and Officers. Liability Insurance and Indemnification* (Washington, DC: Council on Foundations, 1989). 35 pages.

This resource is prepared in a question-and-answer format, designed as a basic introduction to directors and officers liability insurance and indemnification.

ACCOUNTING AND RECORD KEEPING

Accounting Advisory Committee. "Study of the Inadequacies of Present Financial Reporting by Philanthropic Organizations." In *Research Papers, Volume V* (Filer Commission). Part 1, p. 2869.

This summarizes accounting and reporting practices for eight categories of philanthropic institutions, including private foundations. The authors conclude that the diversity in practice is not justified and recommend that a single, uniform set of accounting principles be adopted and followed by all philanthropic organizations.

American Institute of Certified Public Accountants. *Statement of Position 78–10 Accounting Principles and Reporting Practices for Certain Nonprofit Organizations, December 31, 1978* (New York: AICPA, 1979). 117 pages.

This paper recommends financial accounting principles and reporting practices for nonprofit organizations not covered by existing guidelines.

Council of Michigan Foundations and Southeastern Council of Foundations. "When the IRS Comes Calling."

This is a guide to help foundations understand how an IRS audit works and how to prepare for it. It is reprinted in *Foundation News* 27, no. 5, September/October 1986, pp. 26–29, or available through the regional associations.

Gross, Malvern J., Jr., and Warshauer, William, Jr. *Financial and Accounting Guide for Nonprofit Organizations*, 3rd Ed. (New York: Ronald Press, 1979). 550 pages.

This is a guide to nonprofit accounting. The authors provide information on reporting, planning, and control of nonprofit organizations.

Hall, Peter Dobkin. "Taming the Archival Tiger." *Foundation News* 30, no. 6, November/December 1989, pp. 61–62.

Hall suggests that building a foundation's archival history takes planning, but it may also be an essential to efficient and effective operation.

Haller, Leon. *Financial Resource Management for Non-Profit Organizations* (Englewood Cliffs, NJ: Prentice-Hall, 1982). 191 pages.

This book looks at the role of financial management in small nonprofit organizations.

Stapleton, Darwin. "Plumbing the Past." *Foundation News* 28, no. 6, November/December 1987, pp. 67–68.

The author points out that foundation archives are becoming an invaluable resource for those seeking to understand philanthropy's role in society.

Stapleton, Darwin, and Rose, Kenneth, eds. *Establishing Foundation Archives* (Washington, DC: Council on Foundations, 1991). 70+ pages.

This is a compilation of papers presented at a conference cosponsored by the Council on Foundations and the Rockefeller Archive Center.

ADMINISTRATIVE EXPENSES

Brody, Deborah. "Expense Management." *Foundation News* 30, no. 6, November/December 1989, pp. 66–67.

This article provides foundations with a way to approach their administrative costs and some of the reasons costs differ from foundation to foundation.

Internal Revenue Service. *Private Foundation Grant-making Administrative Expense Study* (Washington, DC: Internal Revenue Service, January, 1990). 77 pages.

7

Government Regulation of Foundations

Federal Regulation

The logical place to begin any discussion of government regulation of foundations is with the Tax Reform Act of 1969. In this chapter, we summarize the provisions of the act relating to foundations, updated to reflect important amendments through 1989. Before dealing with substance, it may be helpful to glance briefly at the events that led up to the 1969 legislation.

Grantmaking foundations have been investigated by Congress on several occasions in the past but were not singled out for major legislative action until 1969. The late Congressman Wright Patman (D-Tex) held several hearings and published extensive reports critical of foundations in the late 1950s and early 1960s. This barrage of criticism, aimed in part at the Treasury and the IRS for failure to correct the abuses Patman alleged, resulted in a full and balanced Treasury study presented to the Congress in 1965. The study characterized the foundation field as an important and useful part of the voluntary sector but recommended general legislative changes. These changes would improve the accountability of foundations and give the IRS more effective regulatory authority. Neither Congress nor the foundation field acted upon these regulations until 1969.

Early in 1969, the House Ways and Means Committee, under the strong chairmanship of Congressman Wilbur Mills (D-Ark), launched a series of hearings aimed at tax reform. The 1965 Treasury Report provided readymade background reading, and Congressman Patman and others provided lively witnesses. Thus, "foundations" became the first topic for these hearings. Without any sizable "constituency," regarded as too "liberal" by some and too "conservative" by others, surrounded by an unfortunate aura of secrecy, and the symbol to populists of concentration of wealth and power in a few hands, foundations became fair game at the hearings. Some legislators even wanted to put them out of existence within a limited number of years. With such vigorous attacks and the lack of an organized constituency, it is remarkable that the legislative result was not more punitive. In general, the final compromise produced by the legislative process has proved to be a workable, if overly complex, regulatory framework.

The various major sections of the Internal Revenue Code added in 1969 (Sections 4940–4945) address one or more of the problem areas highlighted by the Patman reports, the Treasury report, and the 1969 hearings. A new system of sanctions for violations of the rules was central to this watershed legislation. Prior to 1969, the main enforcement tool available to the IRS was the authority to revoke the tax exempt status of a foundation. In short, no matter how large or small the infraction, terminating the organization was the only sanction.

For example, where the infractions were merely occasional or minor, the IRS had difficulty making a total revocation of tax status stand up in court. In addition, the penalty did not directly affect the person responsible but instead seriously handicapped the foundation. Therefore, acting on the 1965 Treasury recommendations, Congress installed a system of penalty taxes that could be levied against "private" foundations and—in certain cases—against the private foundation manager as well. In each case, these penalties are a percentage of the amount of money involved in the transaction. Revoking the tax status still remains as a backup sanction for particularly grievous and ongoing violations.

Appendix 1 provides a summary of the act and related statutory provisions.[1] The reader should keep in mind that changes in these laws occur quite often. For example, significant changes were added in 1984, 1986, 1987, and 1988.[2] An up-to-date version of Appendix 1 is available from the Council on Foundations.

At various points in this book, we discuss the practical application of the law. But because the 1969 legislation represents a very significant chapter in the relationship between government and philanthropy, we outline the general regulatory concepts here.

Section 4940—Excise Tax

The excise tax imposed by Section 4940 is a compromise between the "filing fee" suggested by the field and the Ways and Means Committee's belief that foundations should bear some share of the expense of government oversight of their activities.

Congress originally set the tax at the rate of 4 percent of net investment income (including interest, dividends, and net realized capital gains).[3] The Council on Foundations convinced Congress to reduce the tax to 2 percent as part of the Revenue Act of 1978. Even at the reduced 2-percent rate, effective for tax years beginning after September 1977, the revenues from the tax continued to exceed the annual budget of the exempt organizations branch of the IRS responsible for oversight of foundations. Moreover, they are part of the general revenues of the government.[4]

At Congressional hearings in 1983, the IRS testified that annual expenditures for the Exempt Organizations division were approximately $35 million. The excise tax was then collecting over $112 million per year. The Deficit Reduction Act of 1984 included amendments to Section 4940 once again reducing the tax. This time Congress permitted a reduction to 1 percent. But this only applied if a foundation could demonstrate that during the tax year its qualifying distributions as a percentage of the market value of its investments exceeded a five-year average by an amount equal to the tax saving. Congress hoped that in this way, any tax savings would be translated into increased charitable activities.

The formula is complicated and requires year-end estimates of portfolio values and investment income *before* year-end in order to make sufficient qualifying distributions. Perhaps for this reason, only about a quarter of private foundations have taken advantage of the opportunity to reduce the tax to 1 percent since 1984. Meanwhile, total collections from the excise tax skyrocketed to $217 million in 1986, $218 million in 1987, and $229 million in 1988.

The Tax Reform Act of 1986 included a change in the method of collection of the excise tax, which had been payable with the annual information return (Form 990-PF) four and one-half months after the end of a foundation's fiscal year. Since 1987, the tax has been payable quarterly as an estimated tax, using the same rules applicable to for-profit corporations.[5]

Section 4941—Self-Dealing

The stringent rules against self-dealing in Section 4941 reflect concern about the use of foundations for personal gain. They also reflect the difficulty the IRS had in determining whether transactions between foundations and their donors, directors, or managers were truly arms length as required under previous law. Self-dealing is defined to include almost all financial transactions between a foundation and "disqualified persons." This is a broad category including contributors to the foundation, its managers, and certain public officials. Thus, a sale of property or facilities to a foundation by its donor is considered to be self-dealing even if the transaction can be shown to benefit the foundation. Family members of disqualified persons are also disqualified, as are corporations and partnerships in which disqualified persons hold significant interests.

There are several important exceptions to the self-dealing rule: Foundations may pay reasonable compensation for personal services furnished by disqualified persons (except government officials); they may furnish goods, services, and facilities to such persons on a nonpreferential basis; and they may accept gifts and interest-free loans from them. These and other more technical exceptions are summarized in Appendix 1 (TRA as amended), as are applicable penalty taxes.

Section 4942—Required Distributions

Section 4942, the "payout" requirement, was intended to meet the problem of foundations sitting for years with relatively unproductive assets and making little substantial contribution to charity. Following several amendments to the original 1969 payout requirement, private nonoperating foundations must now pay out in "qualifying distributions" a minimum of 5 percent of the market value of that year's investment assets by the end of the following year.

Qualifying distributions include eligible grants to other organizations, charitable activities conducted directly by the foundation, assets acquired directly for the active conduct of exempt functions, and reasonable and necessary administrative expenses. Each foundation receives a credit toward meeting the payout minimum each year equal to the amount of taxes paid under Section 4940 (see earlier). Appendix 1 also describes the calculation of the payout, provisions for carry-forward of excess payments, and special rules for "set-asides" of amounts to be paid in future years.

In 1984, Congress added a new aspect to the payout requirement. The oversight hearings in June 1983 had noted reports of excessive trustee fees, and the California attorney general had called for a stiffer, more manageable definition of acceptable administrative costs. As Congress probed this area, it noted that a foundation might be able to meet the minimum payout requirement solely with administrative expenses. To forestall this possibility, Congress amended the law to limit the amount of *grant* administrative expenses that could be counted toward meeting the 5-percent minimum. The limit was .65 percent (.0065) of net investment assets.

Because this rule was passed despite a dearth of information on what actual foundation administrative expenses were, Congress commissioned the Treasury Department to study foundation administrative costs and submit a report by the end of 1989. The study included audited data from over 800 private foundations and concluded that private foundations were "in substantial compliance with the law." In fact, the .65-percent rule in no instance helped the IRS detect "abusive situations." Based on the Treasury Department's recommendation, the law expired at the end of 1990; however, it applies through 1991 to foundations whose 1990 fiscal year ends in 1991.

Section 4943—Excess Business Holdings

Section 4943 attacked another problem highlighted by the Patman and Treasury reports: control of businesses by foundations with opportunities for unfair competition, diversion of management attention from the foundations' charitable functions, and, in some cases, substantial losses to charity through concentration of investments in one company.

The basic requirement now is that a foundation and its disqualified persons together may not own more than 20 percent of the voting stock of a business corporation or equivalent interests in a business partnership.[6] Recognizing that the immediate enforcement of these rules could result in forced sales and substantial losses to charity, the drafters provided for gradual divestiture over periods as long as 35 years for assets held prior to the act. But they allowed only a five-year period for disposition of such assets received from donors after 1969.

A 1984 amendment permits a five-year extension of this divestiture requirement if the foundation can convince the Treasury secretary that it has met certain tests showing a good faith effort to divest. Failure to meet the divestiture requirements will subject the foundation to a penalty tax equal to a percentage of the value of the holdings that exceed the amount of ownership permitted.

Section 4944—Jeopardy Investments

The section dealing with speculative investments, Section 4944, stemmed more from the typical regulator's concern over prudent investment standards than any specific findings during the hearings. When investments are found to have jeopardized a foundation's purposes, penalty taxes, measured as a percentage of the amounts improperly invested, may be imposed on the foundation and its managers. The test to apply is whether managers used "ordinary business care and prudence" in making the investment. Hindsight is not required. Exceptions to these requirements and types of investment flagged for close scrutiny by IRS are described in Chapter 8.

Section 4945—Taxable Expenditures

Section 4945 prohibits, circumscribes, or regulates a number of foundation activities with which the 1969 hearings dealt at length. These include influencing legislation, intervening in political campaigns, making grants to individuals, and making grants to other private foundations and nonexempt organizations. The section imposes taxes on a foundation and its managers based on a percentage of the amount improperly expended, unless the payments fall within exceptions such as that permitting technical advice to government agencies on request.[7]

Observers initially believed these taxable expenditure provisions would materially restrict foundations' freedom to select their grantees and would have a chilling effect on support of possibly controversial projects or individuals. In fact, experience has shown that the rules affecting grantmaking, although sometimes requiring additional paperwork, still permit foundations to support a tremendously wide range of charitable activities. For example, grants to individuals for travel, study, or similar purposes are permissible. Grants to organizations not qualified as public charities may be made if the foundation exercises "expenditure responsibility." And it is even possible for foundations to support organizations whose activities include attempts to influence legislation, provided grantor and grantee understand and scrupulously observe the regulations.

Reporting

The reporting requirements enacted in 1969 (Section 6033) reflect concern voiced by critics and representatives of the field alike that not enough information was available on what foundations do with their money. The IRS expanded the annual information return (Form 990) required of all Section 501(c)(3) organizations and tailored it to fit the statutory requirements of Sections 4940–4945. It became the Form 990-PF. In addition, the foundation must make the form available for public inspection during normal business hours for 180 days after it is filed. The foundation must also publish a notice each year announcing the foundation's phone number and the availability of the return for public inspection. It must file copies with state authorities in the states where it is incorporated and maintains its principal office.

All Section 501(c)(3) organizations (including private foundations) must make available for public inspection a copy of the application for tax exempt status (Form 1023) and all supporting documents. This includes papers filed by the organization in support of the application and any letter or list of questions from the IRS about the application.

Deductibility of Contributions to Foundations[8]

Gifts of Cash. In any given tax year, an individual donor may contribute cash to a private foundation and treat the gift as a charitable contribution that is deductible in calculating his or her income tax. However, the annual deduction of cash is limited to 30 percent of the donor's adjusted gross income.

Gifts of Appreciated Property. Appreciated property is long-term capital-gain property such as stocks, bonds, or land. Here, if the recipient is a private foundation, the donor may deduct gifts up to 20 percent of adjusted gross income. The donor can only deduct the current fair market value of the gift of appreciated property if the gift is one of publicly traded stock (not closely held stock, not bonds, not land).[9] If the gift of appreciated property is not publicly traded stock, the donor may deduct *only* the cost (or basis) of the asset and none of the gain.

Carryover. If, in any year, the donor exceeds any of the limits noted above, he or she may apply (or carry over) the excess above these limits to tax returns due in the next five years.

Alternative Minimum Tax. Finally, as the result of the 1986 Tax Reform Act, the donor's deduction for gifts of appreciated property even of publicly traded stock may be limited to cost only (or basis) if he or she is subject to the alternative minimum tax.

ENFORCEMENT

Responsibility for enforcing the Tax Reform Act is theoretically split between the IRS and state authorities—usually the state attorney general. In practice, with notable exceptions in California, New York, and a few other states, enforcement occurs primarily through IRS audits. A full cycle of such audits, designed to cover every identifiable private foundation, took place between 1971 and 1975. It revealed a strikingly high degree of compliance with the act's complex requirements. Auditing since then has been done on a much more selective basis, using a list of "sensitive" foundations and modifications of the computer techniques used to choose individual returns for audit. On average, IRS audits about 3,000 private foundations each year. However, beginning in 1990 it reduced that number as a result of the high compliance record of private foundations.

In 1974, Congress provided for the "integration" of the tax-exempt organization responsibilities under a new assistant commissioner at IRS for exempt organizations and employee pension plans. The objective was to improve the quality and quantity of staffing of the Exempt Organization (EO) IRS branch. In the first year or two after this reorganization, the size of the exempt organization staff did not increase because the Employee Retirement Income Security Act (ERISA) demanded much of the new assistant commissioner's time and led to the borrowing of several hundred EO employees. More recently, the IRS has succeeded in developing more experienced staff at the EO Division. However, the areas of the division's enforcement activity have grown rapidly, and Congress has not responded with comparable increases in budget appropriations for this part of the IRS.

Despite the very detailed regulations issued by the Treasury, questions frequently arise regarding applying these rules to particular situations. For example, the law requires advance IRS approval of criteria for most grants to individuals and for set-asides that are to be used as qualifying distributions. Requests for these and other IRS actions are usually best handled by an attorney familiar with IRS procedures and exempt organization law, but the procedures are similar to those established for IRS actions on other types of tax matters.[10]

State Regulation

Federal regulation of foundations is the responsibility of the IRS, now armed with a detailed set of rules and penalty taxes. State regulation has typically been the concern of the state attorney general, who enforces provisions of the state not-for-profit corporation law as well as statutory and common law requirements governing charitable trustees. The states that have been active in this area have a much more flexible battery of enforcement powers available to them than the IRS. The attorney general can go to a state court and ask it to exercise its equity powers to protect the public interest in funds committed to charity.

These powers may include surcharge or removal of the foundation trustees, recision or reform of improper contracts, and a whole range of less drastic steps tailored to the particular situation.[11] The attorney general also can exercise a degree of discretion in reaching compromise settlements with foundation managers to correct alleged abuses of their fiduciary responsibilities. Thus, inadvertent missteps of foundation managers may be taken care of under state law without the imposition of fixed—and sometimes costly—federal penalty taxes on the managers and the foundation.

Congress designed the federal regulatory system to encourage more active state regulation. It incorporated provisions of Sections 4941–4945 of the Internal Revenue Code into the state charters of private foundations so that state authorities could enforce them. The reporting forms that foundations must file with the IRS must also be filed with appropriate state authorities. The IRS is required to report to state authorities any penalty taxes it assesses against foundations under that state's jurisdiction.

NOTES TO CHAPTER 7

1. The summary (reprinted as Appendix 1) attempts to put some 60 pages of law into understandable language. It has been revised to take into account changes in the law and the important new IRS regulations and rulings. More detailed treatment of each section of the law, including useful examples, will be found in the Treasury regulations and in IRS Publication 578. Most law firms and accounting firms have copies of the regulations. Or, a set may be obtained by contacting the legal services department of the Council on Foundations.

2. For a more thorough treatment of the development of legislation affecting foundations, see John A. Edie, *Congress and Private Foundations: An Historical Analysis* (Council on Foundations, September 1987).

3. See Chapter 8 for information related to computing net investment income.

4. Foundations can reduce the 2-percent tax on investment income by adjusting their levels of funding to a formula on Form 990-PF. For those who understand the concept but fear that in practice it will prove "expensive," I offer a suggestion—plan the foundation's giving budget so that the foundation meets the test for the reduction every other year. This practice can help the foundation avoid eroding its purchasing power while still reducing the amount paid to the government.

5. Unfortunately, the first quarter's estimated payment is due one month before the previous year's final tax return is due, and the fourth quarter's payment is due before the end of the tax year. Efforts are underway to make these dates more appropriate.

6. For purposes of Section 4943, the definition of *disqualified person* is expanded to include other private foundations under common control or with common contributors. Section 4946(a)(1)(H).

7. Under specified circumstances, Revenue Procedure 89–13 exempts a private foundation from penalty even though its grant to a charity may be so large as to "tip" it into private foundation status. See Chapter 4 for a full discussion of *tipping*.

8. Historically, Congress has provided an added incentive for the living donor to make a contribution to a public charity (church, school, medical institution, or publicly supported organization) rather than to a private foundation. Gifts to either type of organization at death are subject to no limitations. Congress established these preferences for gifts to public charities on the theory that these donations would be used more quickly to provide needed charitable services.

9. This exception for gifts of publicly traded stock to private foundations expires at the end of 1994.

10. Most of the procedural rules governing requests for IRS actions are found in 26 CFR 601 (Code of Federal Regulations).

11. The litigation over the $40 million estate of the artist Mark Rothko, which New York's attorney general entered on behalf of the ultimate beneficiaries of the Rothko Foundation, provides an example of the breadth of a state court's equity powers. After a long trial, the surrogate dismissed the three executors named in the will and cancelled contracts they had made with an art gallery to handle the sale of Rothko's pictures. Moreover, the surrogate held the executors liable to the estate for up to $9 million in damages for conflict of interest and negligence and appointed one of Rothko's children as sole administrator (*New York Times*, February 21, 1979).

ANNOTATED BIBLIOGRAPHY–CHAPTER 7

FEDERAL REGULATION

Commission on Foundations and Private Philanthropy (Peterson Commission). *Foundations, Private Giving and Public Policy* (Chicago: University of Chicago Press, 1970). 270 pages.

Chapter 19, "Federal Regulations of Foundations: Further Considerations and Summary," discusses which federal agency should oversee foundations and comments on provisions of the 1969 Tax Reform Act that are necessary as well as those it finds detrimental.

Council on Foundations. "Private Foundations and the 1969 Tax Reform Act." In *Research Paper Volume III* (Filer Commission, Dept. of Treasury, 1977), pp. 1557–1653.

See Part III, "The 1969 Tax Reform Act and Its Effects," for a discussion of the Tax Reform Act and its effect on foundations.

Cuninggim, Merrimon. *Private Money and Public Service: The Role of Foundations in American Society* (New York: McGraw-Hill Book Company, 1972). 267 pages.

Chapter V, "The Tax Reform Act of 1969," gives an overview of developments leading up to the passage of the act. Cuninggim discusses the positive effects as well as the problems associated with the act and its impact on foundations.

Edie, John. "Another Look at Lobbying." *Foundation News* 27, no. 6, November/December 1986, pp. 50–51.

Edie discusses the government regulations that apply to charitable dollars as they relate to lobbying.

Edie, John. *Congress and Private Foundations: An Historical Analysis* (Washington, DC: Council on Foundations, 1987). 35 pages.

This booklet is a chapter excerpted from *America's Wealthy and the Future of Foundations* cited earlier in this bibliography.

Edie, John. *Use of Fiscal Agents: A Trap for the Unwary* (Washington, DC: Council on Foundations, 1989). 13 pages.

Edie highlights circumstances when fiscal agents may be misused, explains the fundamental legal rules governing their use, and acquaints the reader with problems and penalties. He also illustrates several proper uses of the fiscal agent.

Fremont-Smith, Marion R. *Foundations and Government: State and Federal Law and Supervision* (New York: Russell Sage Foundation, 1965). 564 pages.

Chapter X, "Agencies for Federal Supervision," looks at the role of Congress, the Treasury Department, and the IRS in federal regulation of foundations. A short discussion of the litigation process and the appellate courts is also included as well as a section on federal–state cooperation.

Ginsberg, David, Marks, Lee R., and Wertheim, Ronald P. "Federal Oversight of Private Philanthropy." In *Research Papers Volume V* (Filer Commission), Part I, p. 2575.

This paper covers the relationship of the federal government and private philanthropy with a detailed examination of the IRS and the Internal Revenue Code. It rejects the suggestion that oversight activities should be transferred out of the IRS.

Jones, David R. "Tax Reform. Can Charity Make it?" *Foundation News* 25, no. 5, September/October 1986, pp. 20–25.

Jones outlines the major effects that the Tax Reform Act of 1986 had on foundations and nonprofits.

Magat, Richard. "The Big Chill: 20 Years Later." *Foundation News* 30, no. 6, November/December 1989, pp. 32–40.

Magat recounts the history of the Tax Reform Act of 1969 and the effects that it has had on the foundation field.

Nielsen, Waldemar A. *The Big Foundations* (New York: Columbia University Press, 1972). 475 pages.

Chapter 1, "Philanthropy Under Fire," traces the development of major criticisms against foundations. Chapters 19 and 20 describe the history, setting, and people involved in the 1969 hearing which led to the Tax Reform Act.

Stone, Lawrence M. "The Charitable Foundation: Its Governance." In *Research Papers Volume III* (Filer Commission), Part II, p. 1723.

Stone provides specific recommendations for policies and strategies for foundations to take to encourage appropriate government regulation and avoid inappropriate regulation.

Treasury Report on Private Foundations. Submitted to the Senate Committee on Finance and the House Committee on Ways and Means, February 2, 1965.

This document looks at foundation practices and recommends legislative correction of abuses. It provided the background for hearings leading to the Tax Reform Act of 1969.

PROVISIONS OF THE TAX REFORM ACT OF 1969

The following publications provide summaries of the provisions of the Tax Reform Act of 1969 that affect foundations:

Council on Foundations. "Summary of Provisions of the Tax Reform Act of 1969 Relating to Private Foundations" (as amended through 1989) (Washington, DC: Council on Foundations).

Reproduced in Appendix 1, this summary provides a clear and useful enumeration and explanation of the provisions of the Tax Reform Act of 1969 that relate to foundations.

Internal Revenue Service, Department of the Treasury. *Tax Information for Private Foundation Managers*. Publication 578 (Washington, DC: Government Printing Office, November 1989). 75+ pages.

This covers the tax regulations that apply to foundations. Topics include determination of status, filing requirements, termination, tax on net investment income, disqualified persons, taxable expenditures, failure to distribute income, self-dealing, jeopardy investments, and excess business holdings.

The following books provide clearly written, detailed coverage of federal foundation regulations with examples and explanations.

Hopkins, Bruce R. *The Law of Tax-Exempt Organizations*, 5th Ed. (New York: John Wiley and Sons, 1987). 949 pages.

Treusch, Paul E. *Tax-Exempt Charitable Organizations*, 3rd Ed. (Philadelphia: American Law Institute, 1988). 705 pages.

The following publications discuss specific aspects of federal regulations:

Sugarman, Norman A. "Penalties on Foundations and Foundation Managers: How to Avoid Them." *New York University Proceedings of the Eleventh Biennial Conference on Charitable Foundations*, Volume 11 (New York: New York University Press, 1973), pp. 235–257.

Sugarman tells how to avoid the penalty taxes imposed on foundations for certain activities. He discusses record keeping, use of professional services, and ruling procedures.

Troyer, Thomas A. "Charities, Law-Making and the Constitution: The Validity of Restriction on Influencing Legislation." *New York University Journal, 31st Annual Institute on Federal Taxation* (New York: New York University Press, 1973).

Troyer traces the history behind the limitation on the legislative activities of charities and provides a detailed analysis of the restrictions governing private foundations' attempts to influence legislation.

STATE REGULATION

Fremont-Smith, Marion R. "Impact of the Tax Reform Act of 1969 on State Supervision of Charities." *Harvard Journal on Legislation* 8, no. 537, 1971, pp. 537–569.

Fremont-Smith discusses the various ways the Tax Reform Act of 1969 caused the states to enforce private foundation rules.

Office of the Ohio Attorney General. "The Status of State Regulation of Charitable Trusts, Foundations and Solicitations." *Research Papers, Volume V* (Filer Commission), Part 1, p. 2705.

This document surveys state charitable trust and foundation statutes and other state laws regulating the solicitation of funds for charitable purposes. It finds that supervision by state attorneys general is most effective and that close cooperation between state authorities and the IRS is desirable.

SECTION 4941—SELF-DEALING

Council on Foundations. *Company Foundations and the Self-Dealing Rules* (Washington, DC: Council on Foundations, 1987). 28 pages.

This publication explores the problems caused by the self-dealing rules for company foundations. It includes guidelines for what is acceptable, an executive summary, and a 14-page technical analysis of the self-dealing rule.

Geske, Alvin. "Indirect Self-Dealing and Foundations: Transfers for the Use or Benefit of Disqualified Persons." *Houston Law Review* 12, no. 2, January 1975.

Geske provides a technical discussion of Section 4941 on acts of self-dealing involving private foundations and disqualified persons. Defines *indirect self-dealing.*

Hopkins, Bruce R., and Beckwith, Edward J., and DeSirgh, Jana. *Company Foundations and the Self-Dealing Rules* (Washington, DC: Council on Foundations, 1987). 40 pages.

The authors provide a technical analysis of private foundation self-dealing rules.

The following publications provide regular updates on the legal and tax matters concerning foundations:

Commerce Clearing House, Inc. *Federal Estate and Gift Tax Reporter* (Riverwoods, IL). 3-volume set. Looseleaf service.

This contains information needed for handling federal, estate, gift, and generation-skipping transfer tax problems. Weekly reports on new developments to keep the reader informed of current law.

Commerce Clearing House, Inc. *Private Foundation Reporter* (Riverwoods, IL). 2-volume set. Looseleaf service.

This describes state and federal legal requirements for private foundations. Updated biweekly.

Prentice-Hall. *Tax-Exempt Organizations* (Washington, DC). 2-volume set. Looseleaf service.

This describes federal legal requirements for tax-exempt organizations. Updated monthly.

Weithorn, Stanley S. *Tax Techniques for Foundations and Other Exempt Organizations,* 7 volumes (New York: Matthew Bender). Looseleaf service.

This describes the law of federal income, gift, estate, and excise tax as it affects all nonprofit organizations. It looks at problems from contributor, donor, and nonprofit points of view. It is updated annually.

8

Managing Foundation Assets

Investing assets wisely is one of the most important challenges for a private foundation's board and staff. While some foundations receive regular gifts from donors that are quickly "passed through" the foundation and on to charity, most foundations rely on income from their endowments to meet their charitable objectives. If a foundation plans to operate far into the future, its managers must invest with an eye toward both meeting charitable requirements and allowing the financial base to grow at least enough to keep pace with inflation.

Since the first edition of this handbook was published, two events have occurred that are of great interest to those concerned with foundation investments. First, as described in the preceding chapter, Congress revised the distribution requirements of Section 4942 in 1981 to require foundations to distribute annually an amount equal to 5 percent of their investment assets. (Prior to 1981, foundations were required to pay out either this amount or all earned income, whichever was greater.) Second, in 1989 a report was completed for the Council on Foundations by Lester Salamon and Kenneth Voytek that provides a wealth of information on how the investment function is currently performed.

As this report, *Managing Foundation Assets*, points out, a significant number of foundations establish formal objectives and pursue an active, well-managed investment policy. However, many foundations do not give this area sufficient attention.[1] While foundations may adopt different strategies (depending on individual program goals, donor wishes, and other factors), all foundation boards should establish a plan that provides for responsible oversight of this part of foundation administration.

After analysis of a survey completed by 478 foundations and financial data on all foundations with assets in excess of $10 million, Salamon and Voytek distinguished two patterns of foundation investment management: active involvement of the foundation board and a focus on "total return" (income plus appreciation) and a more "hands-off" style with emphasis on maximizing current income. For the period 1979–1985, the larger foundations, most of them practicing the active style, achieved "superior performance." Small foundations, while producing higher income yield, failed to achieve sufficient growth in asset value to keep up with inflation. The report found a "need to focus more attention on the investment function of foundations."[2]

BOARD RESPONSIBILITY

Legal requirements and practical management considerations place the responsibility for setting investment objectives on the foundation's board. Decisions on the long-range future of the foundation, the board's major responsibility, should help to determine investment policy. For example, if the board decides, or is required by the foundation's charter, to spend the foundation's assets as well as its income in a limited period of time, the investment policy will probably stress high yield and liquidity. If the board decides to maintain the purchasing power of the foundation's assets for future charitable needs, the investment policy will stress growth in the value of the portfolio. Current giving may be limited to an amount close to the statutory requirement.[3]

While the final responsibility for a foundation's investment management is the board's, specific tasks are frequently delegated to an investment committee of the board. This committee may in turn delegate day-to-day investment decisions to one or more outside investment managers while maintaining general supervision over their activities. It is usual among the largest foundations to develop in-house capability to monitor the performance of outside investment managers. Some foundations also employ investment counselors to help evaluate the performances of their managers. A limited number of foundations manage part or all of the portfolio in-house.[4] Regardless of the system established for day-to-day management, the board should set the policy and evaluate investment performance on a regular basis.

In setting policy, the board establishes the investment objectives and forms the overall strategy for achieving them. One of the first discussions might explore the level of risk the board is willing to accept. Foundations are prohibited by law from making investments that might jeopardize their charitable status (see page 137). But within the "Prudent Man" rule under which it must operate, a foundation has many alternatives from which to choose.

Once the board has established the objectives, it can work on its own, with investment counsel, or with staff to outline the strategies it will use to achieve its goals. What "style" of management should the foundation pursue? How often will performance be reviewed, and will that regular oversight be handled by the full board or a committee reporting to it? An active investment strategy might call for reviews on a quarterly or monthly basis.[5]

How will the portfolio be composed? What types of assets (stocks, bonds, cash equivalents, real estate, etc.) and what proportion of each type of asset should be included? Many foundations decide on a maximum and minimum allowable proportion of each asset class.

Day-to-Day Management

To implement its strategies, the board must also decide whether to hire outside investment managers or handle daily investment operations in-house. In selecting outside managers, the board or its investment committee may do its own research and evaluation or hire a specialized firm or consultant to help in the selection. Large foundations use several outside managers, often specializing in different types of assets. They may also develop in-house capability to handle part of the portfolio or to select and monitor a group of mutual funds. In either case, the managers should be given guidelines and judged on their ability to generate competitive rates of return. Smaller foundations may obtain satisfactory results from a single manager.[6]

Payout Requirement

As outlined in Chapter 7, foundations are required by law to pay out in qualifying distributions (including reasonable administrative expenses) an amount equivalent to 5 percent of investment assets. As mentioned earlier, between 1969 and 1981 foundations were required to pay out the equivalent of their adjusted net income if greater than the applicable percentage of assets. This alternative was removed in 1981 in response to protests that, in periods of high interest rates, foundations were being constrained in their investment choices and losing ground to inflation. Preliminary indications of investment results since 1981 suggest that removal of the income payout requirement has in fact improved foundation investment performance.[7]

Valuation Rules

This brings us to another aspect of foundation investments: their valuation for payout purposes and for determining capital gains or losses. Briefly, foundations must calculate the market value of investment assets under Section 4942 of the Internal Revenue Code to determine whether they are meeting the 5-percent payout requirement. For securities for which market quotations are available, this market value is determined by averaging monthly values obtained by any reasonable method consistently followed. Cash on hand is to be similarly averaged. But an amount equal to 1.5 percent of all investment assets may be excluded from the calculation as cash held for the foundation's charitable activities. Assets for which market values are not readily available must be determined annually, except that a valuation of real property, if established by a certified independent appraisal, may be used for five years.[8]

Another valuation rule of particular interest to foundations holding large blocks of stock in a single company is "blockage." Under a 1976 amendment to the Tax Reform Act, the application of a discount in valuing such large blocks (an accepted practice in estate valuation) is permitted but only up to 10 percent of market price.[9]

While these valuation rules sound complicated, they should pose few problems for the typical foundation and are routinely handled by trust departments or accounting firms charged with preparing foundations' Forms 990-PF for the IRS. In fact, the IRS will accept financial institutions' computer pricing systems in obtaining market value figures, if such systems have been approved for estate tax purposes.[10]

Capital Gains and Losses

Also, rules concerning capital gains and losses are of day-to-day interest to managers of foundation investment portfolios. In general, these follow the rules that apply to individual investors and have been changed each time the holding periods and rates for individual investors have been changed. There are three important differences to note. First, the only tax on such gains is the 2-percent (or 1-percent in certain cases) excise tax levied on "net investment income" including net capital gains, short- or long-term.[11] Property and securities held by a foundation on December 31, 1969, have a basis for determining such gain, not less than market price on that date. Second, net capital losses are not deductible from other income and may not be carried forward into future years.

These differences mean that while there is some "saving" in tax available by balancing out realized gains and losses each year, it is not likely to have a significant impact on the foundation's overall financial picture. The manager need not feel "locked in" by tax considerations when considering sale of a particular security which appreciated in value. However, foundations seeking to meet the formula for reducing their excise tax to 1 percent should be alert to the impact of sizeable gains realized toward the end of the fiscal year.[12]

Jeopardy Investments

Despite the admonition in Section 4944 of the Internal Revenue Code against investments that jeopardize the carrying out of their purposes, foundations have considerable latitude in their investment alternatives. Penalties may be incurred under the federal law only if it is determined that the managers, in making an investment, have "failed to exercise

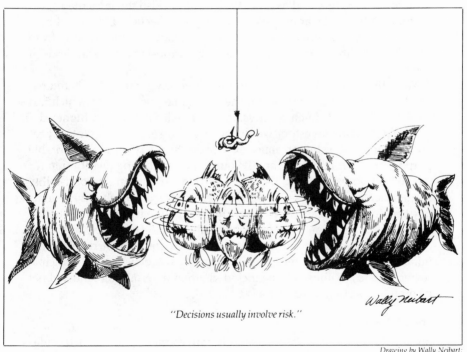

"Decisions usually involve risk."

Drawing by Wally Neibart;
© Johns Hopkins Magazine

ordinary business care and prudence. This is based on the facts and circumstances prevailing at the time of the investment in providing for the long- and short-term financial needs of the foundation to carry out its exempt purposes."[13]

The regulations describe the factors to be considered in exercising this standard, including "the need for diversification within the investment portfolio." While "no category of investments shall be treated as a per se violation of Section 4944," certain types and methods are flagged in the regulations as subject to close scrutiny: margin trading, commodity futures, working interests in oil and gas wells, "puts," "calls," "straddles," warrants, and selling short.

There are three important exceptions to these general rules concerning jeopardy investments: investments made prior to January 1, 1970, those received by gift and program-related investments. Investments made prior to January 1, 1970, and those received by gift are exempted from the provisions of Section 4944, unless after December 31, 1969, the foundation changes the form or terms of such investments. Note, however, that this safe haven applies only to the federal law. Applicable state common or statutory law may well indicate that fiduciary responsibility goes further and may require that when speculative investments are received as gifts, they be sold. Also the laws may specify that portfolios be appropriately diversified. Section 4944 states specifically that its provisions do not exempt a foundation from compliance with other federal or state laws imposing other standards of conduct.

The third exception is the program-related investment. In Chapter 4, we discuss its characteristics and the charitable purposes for which it is particularly suited. Such an investment usually involves a higher degree of risk than investors would normally take. Like a grant, a program-related investment must be made to carry out a charitable purpose of the foundation, and it counts as a qualifying distribution for payout purposes. It must also meet certain expenditure responsibility requirements. Interest or dividends received from such investments must be included in gross investment income when computing the excise tax under Section 4940 (although gain or loss from their sale is excluded). The value of the investment is not counted in determining minimum investment return, but interest, dividends, and principal (when repaid), will usually be included when determining adjusted net income for Section 4942 purposes.[14]

Social Responsibility

Social responsibility, as it relates to the investment policies of foundations, is another topic much discussed in the foundation world. For the past two decades or more, institutional investors have been taking an active interest in the social impact of companies in which they invest. Foundations have been involved in two ways: through grants to organizations that monitor corporate activities and as investors.

In 1972, several foundations joined a group of colleges and universities in establishing the Investor Responsibility Research Center, which analyzes the issues presented for stockholder vote at annual meetings of major corporations. Armed with this information or similar material available from other organizations that monitor corporate social responsibility, committees of directors of several foundations regularly advise their boards on whether to vote for or against management on such issues as defense production, environmental pollution, and South African operations.[15] On occasion, some foundations have withheld their proxies and written corporate management, expressing concern or requesting additional information on corporate policies. This exercise of the stockholder ballot by institutions has not been limited to large holdings of stock.

Foundations may also pursue social investments in other ways. Some make deposits or purchase financial services from minority banks or institutions with stated commitments to community development. Others invest in mutual funds or money market funds that select investments using social guidelines, such as the Pax World Fund, New Alternatives Fund, Calvert Social Investment Funds, Working Assets, and others. For example, some funds do not invest in tobacco companies, weapon manufacturers, or companies with poor environmental records. The performance of these funds demonstrates that "ethical investing" and reasonable return on investments can both be achieved.[16]

One-stock Portfolios

In this chapter, we have discussed investment responsibilities, problems, and strategies as they relate to balanced and diversified portfolios. Many large and small foundations have been established by gifts or bequests of large blocks of stock in one company. Some of these, notably the Ford Foundation and Kresge Foundation among the largest, have aggressively diversified their portfolios. Others funded before 1969 have taken advantage of the liberal transition periods permitted them under Section 4943 of the Internal Revenue Code to retain such holdings, selling only enough shares to meet their liquidity requirements under the payout rules.[17]

Understandably, there are sharp differences of opinion over the practice of holding large blocks of one company's stock in a foundation's portfolio. Some foundations in this category point out that over the years, such holdings have outperformed diversified portfolios in terms of both current return and appreciation. On the other hand, examples can be cited of foundations that have all but disappeared because their investments were not diversified.

These "one-stock" portfolios pose special problems for foundation managers. If the stock is a volatile one, changes in its market price may cause sizeable fluctuations in the amount the foundation is required to pay out. If the company itself is in a cyclical industry or encounters serious financial reverses, the "see-saw" effect on the foundation's giving program may be even more unsettling. Where the combined holdings of the foundation and "disqualified persons" approach 20 percent of the company's voting stock, the complicated rules of Section 4943 must be closely followed to avoid inadvertent penalty tax situations.[18]

With these problems in mind, the managers of some large foundations have taken the precaution of limiting their purchases of stock in any one company to less than the two percent *de minimis* holding permitted under Section 4943.[19] Others have recognized that diversification or divestiture may be achieved by a number of different methods. Some have made occasional large grants in stock rather than cash. Others have adopted a gradual diversification program over a period of years.

NOTES TO CHAPTER 8

1. Lester Salamon and Kenneth Voytek, *Managing Foundation Assets: An Analysis of Foundation Investment and Payout Procedures and Performance* (New York: The Foundation Center, 1989), p. 55. Appendix 11 contains a *Foundation News* article summarizing this report. Also see: Salamon, Lester, *Foundation Investment and Payout Performance: An Update* (Washington, DC: Council on Foundations, 1991).

2. *Ibid.*, pp. 2–3.

3. See Donald W. Trotter, *Payout Policies and Investment Planning for Foundations* (Washington, DC: Council on Foundations, 1990); or Donald W. Trotter, "Mixing It Up," *Foundation News* 31, no. 4, July/August 1990, pp. 62–64 (Appendix 11).

4. See Charles Rooks, "Managing the Trust's Investment Portfolio," *Meyer Memorial Trust Annual Report*, 1989; David Frazer, "Investing Your Foundation's Assets," *Foundation News* 26, no. 1, January/February 1985, pp. 119–122; and Humphrey Doermann, "Facing Realities in Portfolio Management," *Foundation News* 27, no. 2, March/April 1986, pp. 111–113. These three articles show different approaches to investment management and oversight, as instituted by the Meyer Memorial Trust, Flinn Foundation, and the Bush Foundation, respectively. Additionally, the Council on Foundations regularly collects information on foundation financial policies and practices and reports on these topics in the biennial *Foundation Management Report*.

5. Salamon and Voytek, p. 26.

6. Early in 1989, legislation had been proposed in Congress to permit foundations to pool their assets for investment purposes in a "common fund." If approved, this common fund should benefit foundations of all sizes; it will be of particular interest to small foundations that find it difficult to take advantage of professional investment management on their own. For more information, please contact the government affairs office of the Council on Foundations or a local regional association of grantmakers.

7. Salamon and Voytek, pp. 47, 50, 51.

8. Regulation 53.4942(a)-(2)(c)(4).

9. This discount is also available, if the foundation establishes its reasonableness, for securities in closely held companies and for securities, the sale of which would result in a forced or distress sale. Section 4942(e)(2)(B) and Regulations 53.4942(a)-2(c)(4)(i)(c) and (iv)(a).

10. Regulation 53.4942(a)-(2)(c)(4)(i)(d).

11. As the term suggests, *net investment income* is calculated by subtracting from gross investment income the costs of administering the portfolio. Such costs, in addition to the fees and expenses of investment counsel and the commissions of stockbrokers, may include an allocable share of the fees of outside accountants, lawyers, and custodian banks, and the foundation's office overhead and staff salaries when staff members perform both program and investment functions. Regulation 53.4940–1(c), (d) and (e); *Julia R. & Estelle J. Foundation, Inc.*, F. 2d (2d Cir. 1979); Revised Ruling 75–410, 1975–2 CB 446. Foundation managers should take care in making such allocations, since they are frequently challenged by the IRS in connection with the computation of the 4940 tax.

12. See Chapter 7, discussion of Section 4940—Excise Tax.

13. Regulation 53.4944–1(a)(2)(i).

14. Regulation 53.4942(a)–(2)(d)(2)(iii)(a). A program-related investment may also be treated as a distribution from corpus, in which case repayment will not be included in income. Revised Ruling 77–252, 1977–2 CB 390.

15. Such organizations include the Council on Economic Priorities (New York), the Interfaith Center on Corporate Responsibility (New York), and the Social Investment Forum (Minneapolis/St. Paul).

16. Louis Knowles, "Alternative Investments: Helping Communities the Old Fashioned Way," *Foundation News* 26, no. 3, May/June, 1985, pp. 18–21; David Jones, "Coming of Age," *Foundation News* 28, no. 4, July/August, 1987, pp. 16–21.

17. For foundations created since 1969, the requirements of Section 4943 are more limiting, since the IRS only allows five years for divestiture instead of the 10–30-year transition periods it allows for pre-1969 holdings. However, in 1984 Congress amended the law to permit the Treasury secretary to extend the divestiture period an additional five years, provided the foundation demonstrates a good faith effort to divest.

18. Regulations 53.4943–3. See Appendix 1 for summary of Section 4943.

19. Under Section 4943(c)(2)(C), a private foundation is not treated as having excess business holdings in any corporation in which it owns not more than 2 percent of the voting stock and not more than 2 percent in value of all outstanding shares of all classes of stock [Regulation 53.4943–3(b)(4)]. So long as a foundation's holding in one stock is within this limit, it will not be affected by and need not keep track of the holdings of disqualified persons in that stock. This *de minimis* rule applies also to partnerships and other similar business enterprises, but not to proprietorships, for which there are no permitted holdings.

ANNOTATED BIBLIOGRAPHY–CHAPTER 8

Reilly, Raymond, and Skadden, Donald. *Private Foundations: The Payout Requirement and Its Effect on Investment and Spending Policies* (Ann Arbor, MI: University of Michigan, 1981). 50 pages.

This study was sponsored by the Council of Michigan Foundations. It investigates foundation investment practices and the effect of the foundation payout requirement. Includes results of a survey of Michigan Foundations.

Salamon, Lester, and Voytek, Kenneth P. *Managing Foundation Assets: An Analysis of Foundation Investment Payout Procedures and Performance* (New York: The Foundation Center, 1989). 89 pages.

In this collaborative report commissioned by the Council on Foundations, the authors examine issues relating to foundation investment management, including rates of return and payout rates.

Salamon, Lester. *Foundation Investment and Payout Performance: An Update* (Washington, DC: Council on Foundations, 1991). 29 pages.

This is an update to Salamon and Voytek's earlier work. Analyzing foundations by asset size, Salamon reveals differences in performance and investment strategy.

BOARD RESPONSIBILITY

Byrd, John W. "Who Minds Your Money?" *Foundation News* 28, no. 5, September/October 1987, pp. 56–57.

The author believes the most prudent and profitable way for trustees to manage endowments is through a money manager.

Commission on Foundations and Private Philanthropy (Peterson Commission). *Foundations, Private Giving and Public Policy.* pp. 72–76.

See Chapter 8, "Foundation Funds: Sources, Investment, Performance and Amount of Payout," for a presentation of survey results on ways to create a foundation endowment. Criticizes the investment performances of foundations and foundation payout figures.

Craig, John. "The Treasurer's Report," *The Commonwealth Fund Annual Report* (New York: The Commonwealth Fund, 1989), pp. 82–97.

Doermann, Humphrey. "Facing Realities in Portfolio Management." *Foundation News* 27, no. 2, March/April 1986, pp. 64–66.

Doermann describes how foundations can link investment targets with long-range grantmaking goals and reorganize their portfolios to accommodate this linkage. He uses the Bush Foundation as an example.

Frazer, David R. "Investing Your Foundation's Assets." *Foundation News* 26, no. 1, January/February 1985, pp. 46–49.

Frazer outlines the elements involved in effective investment decisions.

Larochelle, Wayne. "Take Custody of Your Assets." *Foundation News* 27, no. 4, July/August 1986, pp. 61–63, 76.

The article explains how automated and centralized custodian maintenance of investments could benefit nonprofit organizations and foundations.

Ross, Loren D. "Selecting an Investment Manager." *Foundation News* 13, no. 5, September/October 1972, pp. 20–26.

Ross considers investment philosophy, the number of investment managers to use, and whether or not to give the managers full operating discretion.

Trotter, Donald. *Payout Policies and Investment Planning for Foundations* (Washington, DC: Council on Foundations, 1990). 45 pages.

Trotter examines how payout policy and asset mix are interrelated and ways foundations might determine specific mixes to meet specific foundation requirements.

Trotter, Donald. "Mixing It Up." *Foundation News* 31, no. 4, July/August 1990, pp. 62–64.

Trotter summarizes the study, "Payout Policies and Investment Planning for Foundations."

SOCIAL RESPONSIBILITY

Jones, David. "Coming of Age." *Foundation News* 28, no. 4, July/August 1987, pp. 16–21.

Jones discusses the concept of socially responsible investing (SRI) and its potential for growth in the future.

Knowles, Louis. "Alternative Investments: Helping Communities the Old Fashioned Way." *Foundation News* 26, no. 3, May/June 1985, pp. 18–21.

Knowles describes various ways beyond grantmaking that foundations and other donors can use their dollars to help solve community problems.

Knowles, Louis. "Helping Apartheid Out." *Foundation News* 26, no. 6, November/December 1985, pp. 35–43.

Knowles offers strategies for investing and grantmaking to battle apartheid in South Africa.

Simon, John G., Powers, Charles W., and Gunnemann, Jon P. *The Ethical Investor* (New Haven, CT: Yale University Press, 1972). 208 pages.

The authors discuss corporate social responsibility and the role that institutional investors play. The book includes a discussion of legal issues and suggested guidelines for investing.

PAYOUT REQUIREMENT

Boris, Elizabeth T. "Paying for Keeps." *Foundation News* 29, no. 2, March/April 1988, pp. 69–71.

The article discusses the concern among foundations about their long-term ability to generate and give grant dollars within the restrictions of the payout rule.

For a discussion of the payout requirement see the following:

Hopkins, Bruce. *The Law of Tax-Exempt Organizations,* 5th Ed. (New York: John Wiley and Sons, 1987). 949 pages.

Treusch, Paul E. *Tax-Exempt Charitable Organizations,* 3rd Ed. (Philadelphia: American Law Institute, 1988). 705 pages.

This subject is also discussed at length in the Reilly and Salamon reports cited at the beginning of this chapter.

JEOPARDY INVESTMENTS, VALUATION RULES, AND ONE-STOCK PORTFOLIOS

Cormey, John, and Luchini, Larry. "Protecting Against Inflation." *Foundation News* 29, no. 6, November/December 1988, pp. 55–57.

The authors discuss foundation objectives and investment goals as they relate to IRS requirements for private foundations and inflationary trends.

Hopkins, Bruce. *The Law of Tax-Exempt Organizations,* 5th Ed., pp. 553–558.

See Chapter 27, "Jeopardizing Investments," for a discussion of the rules and sanctions involved. Also see pp. 539–541 for a discussion of "Valuation of Assets," with references. Chapter 26, "Excess Business Holdings," pp. 544–553, discusses the rules and sanctions for excess business holdings.

9

Sources of Information and Assistance

THE COUNCIL ON FOUNDATIONS

A wealth of information and experience is available for the asking from the Council on Foundations. Through telephone information and referral services, publications, and educational programs, Council staff regularly assist new and experienced trustees and staff of grantmaking foundations. The Council also serves the field as an advocate for laws and regulations favorable to foundations. It also regularly interprets organized philanthropy to the media. Staff can offer assistance in many of the areas covered in this book, and some of the resources available are cited throughout the preceding chapters. Appendix 16 provides a more complete description of the Council's services.

One of the Council's most useful roles is that of convener. Its annual conference and other educational programs provide opportunities for grantmakers of every type to exchange information, learn about new developments in philanthropy, and refresh their understanding of good practices and procedures. Attendance at such meetings is often open to all grantmakers, whether or not they are members of the Council. The registration fees and travel expenses for foundation board members or staff to attend such meetings are appropriate administrative expenses for a private foundation. Each year more grantmakers find such continuing education a good investment.

"By God, gentlemen, I believe we've found it—the Fountain of Funding!"

One of the best ways to learn the ropes in the grantmaking world is, of course, to talk with experienced practitioners. Although the field is relatively small, at least in terms of staffed foundations, the Council can suggest knowledgeable people with whom to consult in most parts of the country. Several newly appointed foundation executives have found it useful to set aside time to visit a number of foundations, not only to pick up how-to-do-it pointers, but also to establish lines of informal communication. These may be invaluable when grant requests are being reviewed, particularly in program areas with which the new executive may not be familiar. And if the new foundation is to have a fairly narrow focus, such as giving to educational institutions in its region, contacts with national and local foundations at work in that field will be a "must."

Regional Associations

Another source of information, advice, and contacts that may be closer for new foundation managers is the regional or local association of grantmakers. The emergence of regional associations of grantmakers was one of the most significant developments in philanthropy in the 1970s.

Although a few grantmaking groups existed earlier (the Conference of Southwest Foundations was holding annual meetings as early as 1948), most of the associations were created in the aftermath of the Tax Reform Act of 1969. Many foundations felt isolated from other grant-making institutions. Concern about further legislation and the need to comply with new regulations motivated foundations to create these associations. Many trustees felt the need for better communication among grantmakers in order to be more effective in their work. Members of the associations come together to examine and improve their operations, share ideas, analyze current and future needs, engage in joint projects, and find ways to become more easily accessible to grantees and the general public.

In 1970, there were eight associations. By 1990, there were over 30 formally organized city, state, or regional membership organizations with programs. The associations, like the grantmaking organizations they comprise, vary greatly in size, geographic scope, and function. Some of the associations draw their members from a single metropolitan area, such as the Coordinating Council for Foundations in Hartford, Connecticut, and the Donors Forum of Chicago. Others cover one state, like the Indiana Donors Alliance. Still others cover a wider territory, such as the Southeastern Council of Foundations, with members in eleven states.

Program and service offerings vary as well. For instance, the Metropolitan Association for Philanthropy in St. Louis prepares reports on nonprofit organizations and on program areas for its members. The Minnesota Council on Foundations sponsors an annual public meeting where grantors and grantseekers come together to discuss areas of common concern. The Council of Michigan Foundations has developed a program to encourage development of the state's community foundations. The Northern California Grantmakers coordinates members' joint ventures.

Yet, despite this diversity, the associations have a number of common traits. Most regional associations disseminate information and sponsor training programs for the grantmaking community. Most associations organize workshops or annual meetings. Some publish newsletters, directories, and special reports. Many also provide liaison between the philanthropic community and legislative bodies at state and national levels. Most regional associations have staff to assist members and others with their needs. See Appendix 17 for a list of regional associations that exist at the time of publication. Check with the Council on Foundations for the most current list of associations.

Affinity Groups

Foundation and corporate grantmakers have formed over 20 "affinity groups" of grantmakers to provide forums for learning the newest trends in program areas and maintaining networks with other grantmakers with programs in those areas. Like regional associations, affinity groups differ in the scope of their activities. Some, like Grantmakers in Health or the Precollegiate Education Group, are formal, staffed organizations that provide regular programs and publications. Others are less formal but also hold regular meetings developed by active volunteers. In addition to providing services and a forum for meeting with other grantmakers, affinity groups often serve as advocates for their interests, urging other grantmakers to consider funding in these areas. Funders Concerned About AIDS, for instance, has helped to increase foundation funding of programs that assist people with AIDS and research the prevention and cure of the disease.

Some affinity groups serve primarily as professional societies for their members. Examples include Women and Foundations/Corporate Philanthropy, Hispanics in Philanthropy, the Association of Black Foundation Executives, Asians and Pacific Islanders in Philanthropy, Native Americans in Philanthropy, and the Communications Network in Philanthropy. These organizations can also be good resources for a foundation looking for candidates for its board or staff. Appendix 18 lists affinity groups, but check with the Council on Foundations for the most up-to-date listing.

Some philanthropic organizations advocate specific philosophies of grantmaking and foundations' role in society. For example, the Philanthropic Roundtable provides services and programs for foundation and corporate grantmakers who want to explore a "conservative" approach to grantmaking. The roundtable offers an information clearinghouse, a project development service, a bimonthly newsletter, and regular conferences that cover a wide variety of topics. The National Network of Grantmakers also provides regular programs and publications and is a membership association of grantmakers who advocate for "progressive" actions by foundations to bring about social change.

The Foundation Center

Funded in part by foundations, the Foundation Center serves the general public by publishing a wide variety of material on foundations and corporate giving programs. In its own public libraries, field offices, and nearly 200 regional collections around the country (housed in other public libraries), the Foundation Center maintains reference works on philanthropy and unrivaled compilations of information on foundation grants. The foundation manager can find computer printouts of recent grants in many different areas of giving as well as useful profiles of individual foundations. These will provide leads to the foundations most worth a visit or call. The Foundation Center's collections should also be used if the manager wants to determine current trends in giving activity in particular fields as a way of helping the board to set its program priorities.

Helpful resources include *Benchmark Studies* and *Comsearch Broad Topics*, which provide detailed information on foundation grants made in a specific area. Also helpful are the many books on philanthropic topics, such as John Nason's *Foundation Trusteeship*, cited earlier in this book, which was published by the Foundation Center. Funders may also refer grantees to the Foundation Center to locate other sources of support.[1]

Independent Sector

National foundations, corporations, and voluntary agencies come together through the Independent Sector to learn how to improve their performance and effectiveness and to work together to improve the national climate for philanthropy and voluntarism. Staff and volunteers organize an annual meeting each year, maintain effective government relations, conduct and encourage research on the nonprofit sector, and develop programs that help increase giving and the effectiveness of nonprofit management.[2]

Consultants

When donors form a new foundation or an existing foundation experiences sudden growth or wants to change program direction, the foundation may have difficulty undertaking the research and other homework necessary to chart a new course. One solution is to employ a consultant to gather information and report to the foundation board and staff.

Choosing the right consultant is not easy. Eminent researchers or practitioners in a field that the foundation is considering as an area of interest may have difficulty being objective. Management consultants experienced in analyzing problems for corporate clients may not be knowledgeable about the voluntary sector. A better approach is to identify a person with at least some experience in nonprofit management, preferably in grantmaking, who can undertake the assignment.

There are numerous individual consultants and consulting firms that can be helpful, and they can be identified in a number of ways. Phone calls to some of the resource organizations mentioned so far can lead to foundations that have recently dealt with similar issues. Subsequent calls to these foundations may yield referrals to consultants and insight into how those foundations handled these situations. *Foundation News* and the *Chronicle of Philanthropy* publish classified advertisements from consultants. *Foundation News* also publishes an annual guide to consultants. Locally there may be other foundations, nonprofit technical assistance centers, or other nonprofits that can recommend or provide good consultant help.

Research on Foundations

Efforts of the Council on Foundations, the Foundation Center, Independent Sector, and major universities have all contributed to an increase in research being conducted on organized philanthropy and the nonprofit sector. A foundation board or staff member, journalist, or academic researcher can now find a solid body of statistical, theoretical, and practical research being conducted by these organizations. Among university programs conducting research are Yale's Program on Nonprofit Organizations, the Center for the Study of Philanthropy at the City University of New York, Duke's Center for the Study of Philanthropy and Voluntarism, the Center on Philanthropy at Indiana University, the Mandel Center for Nonprofit Organizations at Case Western Reserve University, and the Institute for Nonprofit Organization Management at the University of San Francisco.

Historical information about specific foundations is sometimes compiled in published reports celebrating significant anniversary dates and also in the writings of foundation executives. The historical files or archives of foundations can also provide valuable information to researchers.

Information on Grantees

There are two organizations that review the fundraising costs and other aspects of the work of several hundred national operating charities. They are the National Charities Information Bureau and the Philanthropic Advisory Service of the Council of Better Business Bureaus. Each organization reviews financial and program information from operating charities against a set of published standards. (Their standards are listed in Appendix 15.)

The National Charities Information Bureau, funded by contributions from foundations, corporations, chambers of commerce, and individuals, supplies its contributors and the public with detailed reports on the agencies it reviews. It also publishes *Wise Giving Guide* three times a year and occasional reports on topics such as evaluating charities, useful to both donors and grantees alike. The Philanthropic Advisory Service, funded by the Council of Better Business Bureaus, supplies a similar reporting service. It also publishes periodic reports on topics of interest in nonprofit operations and *Give . . . But Give Wisely*, which lists the agencies that meet its standards and those that do not or have not responded to inquiries.[3]

IRS Publications and Other Legal Information

The IRS provides a number of useful publications. These include the *Cumulative List* (Publication 78), a list of organizations recognized by the IRS as having charitable status under Code Section 501(c)(3) as well as how-to booklets on applying for tax-exempt status (Publication 557) and on complying with the laws and filling out the forms required of private foundations (Publication 578). Of these, the *Cumulative List* is the most useful in the day-to-day operation of foundations, since it provides essential information as to the tax status of prospective grantees.

The IRS publishes revenue rulings and procedures in its monthly *Bulletin*. This and other useful federal tax information is published in the commercial periodical *Tax Notes*.[4] The *Washington Update* newsletter of the Council on Foundations contains news of pending legislation, regulations, and other legal news. The Council sends it regularly to its members. Other useful references on legal matters are included in the text and notes of Chapter 7.

Periodicals

As the footnotes throughout this book have suggested, the Council on Foundations' bimonthly publication *Foundation News* contains a wealth of information useful to board members and staff of foundations. Other publications of interest, although directed to somewhat different audiences, include the *Chronicle of Philanthropy*, *Chronicle of Higher Education*, *Nonprofit Times*, and *Philanthropy Monthly*. Some regional associations, such as the Minnesota Council on Foundations and the Donors Forum of Chicago, also publish periodicals.

NOTES TO CHAPTER 9

1. The Foundation Center's headquarters is located at 79 Fifth Avenue, 8th Floor, New York, NY 10003–3050. Telephone 212/620–4230 or 800/424–9836.

2. Independent Sector is located at 1828 L Street N.W., Washington, DC 20036. Telephone 202/223–8100.

3. For more information, write to National Charities Information Bureau, 19 Union Square West, New York, NY 10003–3395, or call 212/929–6300 and Council of Better Business Bureaus, Philanthropic Advisory Service, 4200 Wilson Boulevard, Arlington, VA 22203–1804. Telephone 703/247–9323.

4. *Tax Notes* is published weekly by Tax Analysts, 6830 Fairfax Drive, Arlington, VA 22213. Telephone 703/532–1850. Also Prentice Hall's *Tax Exempt Organizations* and Commerce Clearinghouse's *Exempt Organization Reports* are available and used by attorneys in the field. Both are comprehensive binders containing laws, regulations, revenue rulings, and other information. Subscribers receive regular updates. When none of these services provides an adequate answer to a question, it may be appropriate to ask your local IRS office for technical advice or a ruling, although this is frequently a slow and frustrating process and may cost several hundred dollars.

ANNOTATED BIBLIOGRAPHY–CHAPTER 9

Foundations' annual reports provide a wealth of detail about the activities, programs, and priorities of foundations in the United States. The Foundation Center libraries have extensive collections of annual reports for reference purposes.

Annual Report of the Council on Foundations (Council on Foundations) 1828 L Street, N.W., Washington, DC 20036.
> This report presents an overview of the activities of the council and lists member foundations.

The Regional Associations of Grantmakers (RAGs) are another source of information and assistance for those interested in foundation activities. RAGs offers a variety of publications, from newsletters to annual reports. Two particularly useful publications are the following:

Forum. Steven McGuire, Director of Publications. 53 West Jackson Blvd., Suite 426, Chicago, IL 60604. The Donors Forum of Chicago. Bimonthly.

Giving Forum. 425 Peavey Bldg., Minneapolis, MN 55402. Minnesota Council on Foundations. Bimonthly.

Two excellent articles written about RAGs are the following:

Foote, Joseph. "For RAGs It's Riches." *Foundation News* 27, no. 4, July/August 1986, pp. 22–27.
> Foote reports on the emergence of Regional Associations of Grantmakers as a significant force in philanthropy.

Foote, Joseph. "Glad RAGs." *Foundation News* 31, no. 1, January/February 1990, pp. 17–21.
> Foote explains why Regional Associations of Grantmakers have multiplied faster than any other sector of philanthropy. He discusses the potential of this growing source.

The Council on Foundations publishes an updated list of Regional Associations of Grantmakers. Copies of these may be obtained by writing to the Council on Foundations.

The following periodicals provide current information on activities, issues, and topics in the philanthropic field:

Chronicle of Higher Education. Corbin Gwaltney, ed. (Washington, DC: Chronicle of Higher Education). Weekly.

Chronicle of Philanthropy. Philip Semas, ed. (Washington, DC: Chronicle of Philanthropy). Biweekly.

Council Columns. Robin Hettleman, ed. (Washington, DC: Council on Foundations). Biweekly.

The newsletter features coverage of events and activities of the council and its members, plus updates on legislative activities of Congress. Special columns focus on trustees, corporate giving, community foundations, research, publications, and other news.

Foundation News. Arlie Schardt, ed. (Washington, DC: Council on Foundations). Bimonthly.

Long recognized as the journal of philanthropy, *Foundation News* provides comprehensive coverage of current philanthropic activities and issues. It includes regular features on private and community foundations, corporate giving, nonprofit programs, legislation and regulations, international programs, books, and the views of foundation leaders.

Nonprofit & Voluntary Sector Quarterly. Jon Van Til, ed. (San Francisco: Jossey-Bass). Quarterly.

This journal of the Association of Voluntary Action Scholars includes papers, book reviews, and commentary on nonprofit issues.

The Philanthropy Monthly. Henry C. Suhrke, ed. (New Milford, CT: Non-Profit Report, Inc.). Monthly.

This is a monthly magazine for foundation executives and for nonprofit organizations and the individuals who support them. It contains articles written by experts in the field and editorials on topics of current interest.

Philanthropy. Leslie Lenkowsky, publisher (Indianapolis, IN: Philanthropic Roundtable). Bimonthly.

This periodical is a publication of the Philanthropic Roundtable and presents current issues and topics of interest to those in the philanthropic field.

Information about foundations, their activities, and their grants can be found in the following books which are updated annually:

The Foundation Grants Index, 19th Ed. (New York: The Foundation Center, 1990.)

National Databook of Foundations, 15th Ed. (New York: The Foundation Center, 1991).

Source Book Profiles (New York: The Foundation Center, 1991).

The Foundation Directory, 13th Ed. (New York: The Foundation Center, 1990).

In addition, the *National Data Book* lists state and local directories of foundations. Some are published by regional associations of grantmakers.

The following publications provide information about grantees. The Philanthropic Advisory Service and National Charities Information Bureau reports are often helpful in evaluating the status of grantee organizations as well:

Internal Revenue Service, Department of the Treasury. *Cumulative List of Organizations.* Publication 78 (Washington, DC: Government Printing Office).

This is an annual with three cumulative supplements; it lists organizations to which contributions are tax deductible with key numbers, indicating category (e.g., private foundation, public charity).

Give But Give Wisely. Philanthropic Advisory Services (PAS), Council of Better Business Bureaus, 4200 Wilson Boulevard, Arlington, VA 22203–1804.

This is a quarterly rating list of the most active 360 nonprofit organizations that do or do not meet PAS charitable standards. PAS maintains records and provides reports on about 10,000 national organizations that conduct national and international fundraising activities. The PAS reports include information on the subjects' background, management policies, financial condition, fundraising activities, tax status, and program activities as well as a statement of compliance or noncompliance with Better Business Bureau standards.

Wise Giving Guide. National Charities Information Bureau (NCIB), 19 Union Square West, New York, NY 10003–3395.

This is a triannual rating list of over 400 national nonprofit organizations monitored by the NCIB. It reports whether the organizations meet NCIB charitable standards. NCIB also publishes reports on these organizations that are usually three to eight pages in length and contain a brief statement of the agency's origin and purpose, a description of its program activities, a listing of controlling board and paid staff head, an analysis of the agency's financial statement, and information on its tax-deductibility status, salary ranges, and current budget.

The following periodicals provide technical tax and estate information:

Internal Revenue Bulletin. Internal Revenue Service, Department of the Treasury (Washington, DC: Government Printing Office). Weekly.

IRS vehicle for announcing official rulings and procedures for publishing Treasury decisions, executive orders, tax conventions, relevant legislation, court decisions, and other tax items of general interest.

The Journal of Taxation (Boston, MA: Warren, Gorham, and Lamont for Tax Research Group, Ltd.). Monthly.

Provides current news for tax practitioners and summarizes tax decisions, court actions, and revenue rulings.

Tax Exempt News (Washington, DC: Capitol Publications, Inc.). Monthly.

Provides current information on philanthropic issues in Congress and developments relating to the IRS. Also lists private letter rulings and U.S. Tax Court decisions.

Tax Notes (Arlington, VA: Tax Analysts). Weekly.

Reports on current tax legislation, IRS decisions, and trends in tax policy.

Trusts and Estates (Atlanta: Communication Channels). Monthly.
Publishes articles on estate planning and administration.

Taxwise Giving. Conrad Teitell, ed. (Greenwich, CT). Monthly.
Reports on revenue rulings and letter rulings that apply to charitable foundations.

RESEARCH ON FOUNDATIONS

The following are some valuable publications concerning research on foundations:

Derrickson, Margaret Chandler, ed. *The Literature of the Nonprofit Sector: A Bibliography with Abstracts*. Volumes I & II (New York: The Foundation Center, 1989 and 1990). 403 pages and 332 pages.

Hodgkinson, Virginia A. *Academic Centers and Research Institutes Focusing on the Study of Philanthropy, Voluntarism, and Not-for-Profit Activity* (Washington, DC: Independent Sector, 1988). 74 pages.
This publication is the result of a survey of 20 academic centers that study some aspect of the nonprofit field. The survey covers (1) programs and founding dates; (2) program characteristics; (3) program descriptions and activities; (4) functions, objectives, and disciplinary features of the centers; and (5) faculty, management, and budgeting.

Independent Sector. *Research-in-Progress* (Washington, DC: Independent Sector). Updated annually.
This volume is a compiled list of hundreds of research projects on philanthropy, voluntary action, and not-for-profit activity. Individual listings are complete with project description and information on the researchers.

Layton, Daphne Niobe. *Philanthropy and Voluntarism: An Annotated Bibliography* (New York: The Foundation Center, 1987). 308 pages.
A valuable source for independent research on philanthropy and its many aspects, this book includes sections on "The Concept of Philanthropy," "Manifestations of Philanthropy," "Functional Areas," and "Periodicals, References, and Organizational Resources."

Powell, Walter W., ed. *The Non-Profit Sector: A Research Handbook* (New Haven, CT: Yale University Press, 1987). 464 pages.
This book is a collective review and assessment of scholarly research on the nonprofit sector. This volume was compiled in association with the Program on Non-Profit Organizations at Yale University. The authors present a thorough and realistic appraisal of current knowledge in the field; moreover, they provide integrative frameworks that will help readers interpret previous research on the subject. The handbook is organized into 6 parts and 24 chapters.

Research Reports (Program on Non-Profit Organizations, Institute for Social and Policy Studies, New Haven, CT: Yale University Press). Occasional.

These are reports on the progress or results of program-sponsored research related to the nonprofit sector. They include updates on the program's working papers series.

Several books written or edited by the late F. Emerson Andrews provide reference information on the foundation field:

Foundation Watcher (Lancaster, PA: Franklin and Marshall College, 1973) (Now available from the Foundation Center).

Foundations: 20 Viewpoints (New York: Russell Sage Foundation, 1965).

Legal Instruments of Foundations (New York: Russell Sage Foundation, 1958).

Philanthropic Foundations (New York: Russell Sage Foundation, 1956).

Appendixes

Summary of Provisions of the Tax Reform Act of 1969 Relating to Private Foundations (as Amended Through 1989)

DEFINITION OF PRIVATE FOUNDATION (SECTION 509)

Private foundations are defined as all organizations, including foreign organizations, described by Section 501(c)(3), except:

1. organizations described in Section 170(b)(1)(A)(i) through (vi)—churches, schools, hospitals, certain organizations affiliated with colleges or universities, publicly supported organizations, and government units.
2. organizations that meet a double "support" test:
   a. They must not normally receive more than a third of their support from investment income.
   b. They must normally receive more than a third of their support from: (1) gifts, grants, contributions, membership fees, and (2) sales, or the furnishing of services or facilities in an activity that is not an unrelated business.
3. supporting organizations.
4. organizations testing for public safety.

EXCISE TAX BASED ON INVESTMENT INCOME (SECTION 4940)

Private foundations must annually pay a 2-percent excise tax on their net investment income. Net investment income is the excess of gross investment income over deductions stemming from the production or collection of such income. Gross investment income includes interest, dividends, rents and royalties, and net capital gains from the sale of property held for the production of income. For purposes of computing capital gains, the basis of property held on December 31, 1969, is no less than fair market value on that date. Unrelated business income separately taxed under Section 511 is not subject to the tax on investment income.

The rate of the Section 4940 tax can be reduced from 2 percent to 1 percent if the amount of qualifying distributions made by the foundation during that taxable year equals or exceeds the sum of:

1. an amount equal to the foundation's net investment assets for such taxable year multiplied by the average percentage payout for the previous five years; and

2. one percent of the foundation's net investment income for such taxable year.

The foundation's percentage payout is computed for any given year by dividing the amount of qualifying distributions made by the foundation in the taxable year by the foundation's net investment assets for the taxable year. A special adjustment rule is provided to prevent the general computation formula described earlier from requiring continually higher payout rates in order to qualify for the reduction in the 2-percent tax. Under this special rule, if the amount of the excise tax for any taxable year in the five-year base period is reduced to 1 percent by reason of the formula set out above, the amount of qualifying distributions made by the foundation during such year is to be reduced for purposes of this formula computation by the amount of such reduction in tax.

A newly formed foundation has no base period and, therefore, no reduction is available in its first year. For foundations in existence less than five years, the base period is the taxable years during which the foundation has been in existence.

The reduction to 1 percent is not available for a given year if, at any time during the five-year base period, the foundation has incurred a penalty for failure to meet the minimum payout requirement (Section 4942).

The Tax Reform Act of 1984 created a new, hybrid classification called an "exempt operating foundation" (see discussion of private operating foundation under Section 4941). An exempt operating foundation may avoid the Section 4940 excise tax and the requirement that other private foundations must exercise expenditure responsibility (see discussion of Section 4945) for grants made to it.

A Section 501(c)(3) organization may qualify as an exempt operating foundation with respect to any taxable year if:

1. the organization either: (1) had private operating status on January 1, 1983; (2) qualified as an operating foundation for its last taxable year

ending before January 1, 1983; or (3) had been publicly supported under Section 170(b)(1)(A)(vi) or 509(a)(2) for at least ten years prior to the taxable year.

2. the governing body of the organization, at all times during the taxable year, consists of individuals at least 75 percent of whom are not disqualified individuals.

3. the governing body of the organization, at all times during the taxable year, is broadly representative of the general public.

4. no officer of the organization, is at any time during the taxable year, a disqualified individual.

A disqualified individual is a person who is:

1. a substantial contributor to the foundation;

2. an owner of more than 20 percent of the total combined voting power of a corporation, the profits interest of a partnership, or the beneficial interest of a trust or unincorporated enterprise, which corporation, partnership, or enterprise is a substantial contributor to the foundation; or

3. a member of the family of an individual described in 1 or 2 above.

For purposes of these requirements, persons such as public officials, individuals appointed to the governing body by public officials and community leaders (such as educators, civic leaders, or clergy) who (considered together) represent a broad cross section of the views and interests of the general public are considered to be broadly representative of the general public.

ESTIMATED TAX PAYMENTS REQUIRED

A private foundation is required to pay its tax on net investment income as estimated taxes in four installments. The rules governing such estimated payments are governed by the same rules applicable to for-profit corporations under sections 6154, 6655, and 6656.

The estimated payments are due on the fifteenth days of the fourth, sixth, ninth, and twelfth months of the taxable year of the foundation and must be paid into an institution that has been authorized as a depository for federal taxes.

If the payment is late or not filed with an authorized depository, there is a 10 percent penalty on the amount due. If the amount paid is too small, the penalty imposed is the amount of the underpayment times a specified underpayment tax rate for the period of the underpayment.

Generally, for each estimated payment, the foundation must pay one-quarter of the year-end tax due based on "annualized" estimates of the total taxable income expected. Depending on the size of the foundation, certain "safe harbor" rules apply to such payments in order to avoid penalties.

SELF-DEALING (SECTION 4941)

With the exceptions listed below, direct or indirect transactions between private foundations and "disqualified persons" (defined in Section 4946) and actions by private foundations for the benefit of such persons are taxed as self-dealing. "Disqualified persons" (individuals, corporations, and other entities) are:

1. "substantial contributors"—those whose total donations to a foundation at any given time exceed the greater of $5,000 or 2 percent of all contributions to the foundation up to that time. Contributions by spouses are aggregated for this purpose. All contributions made on or before October 9, 1969, are treated as if made on that date. Once attained, substantial contributor status will cease only if, at the close of the taxable year of the private foundation, each of three requirements are satisfied:
   a. neither the substantial contributor nor any related person made a contribution to the foundation at any time within the ten-year period ending at the close of the taxable year.
   b. neither the substantial contributor nor any related person was a foundation manager of the private foundation during the ten-year period.
   c. the aggregate contributions (adjusted for appreciation on such contributions while held by the foundation) made by the substantial contributor and all related persons are determined by the IRS to be insignificant when compared to the aggregate amount of contributions to that foundation by one other person. Although not specified in the law, congressional intent for the meaning of "insignificant" is less than 1 percent.
2. foundation managers—officers, directors, trustees, and employees with similar powers and responsibilities.
3. a person owning more than 20 percent of:
   a. the voting power of a corporation;
   b. the profits interest of a partnership; or
   c. the beneficial interest of a trust or unincorporated enterprise, which is a substantial contributor to the foundation.
4. for purposes of the self-dealing section, only, certain government officials defined in Section 4946(c):

a. federal officials elected to office, appointed by the president, or occupying positions listed in Schedule C of Rule VI of the Civil Service rules receiving not less than certain minimum compensation;

b. congressional employees earning more than $15,000 per year;

c. equivalent state and local officials earning more than $20,000 per year; and

d. personal assistants and secretaries of the foregoing.

Family members (spouse, lineal descendants and their spouses, and ancestors) of disqualified persons are themselves disqualified persons. Beginning January 1, 1985, the definition of "lineal descendant" of a disqualified person is limited to the individual's children, grandchildren, and great-grandchildren, and the spouses of such descendants. Where disqualified persons own more than a 35-percent voting interest in a corporation (or more than a 35-percent profit or beneficial interest in a partnership, trust, or estate), that entity is also a disqualified person.

Section 4941 imposes an initial tax of 5 percent on the amount involved on the self-dealer and $2\frac{1}{2}$ percent (maximum $10,000) on foundation managers participating with knowledge. Additional taxes of 200 percent and 50 percent (maximum $10,000) respectively are imposed if the self-dealing act is not corrected within a prescribed period.

Exceptions

Private foundations may:

1. pay reasonable compensation to disqualified persons (except government officials) for personal services necessary to accomplish exempt purposes.

2. furnish goods, services and facilities to a disqualified person only on a nonpreferential basis.

3. borrow money and accept goods, services or facilities from a disqualified person if these transactions are without interest or other charge and the proceeds are used for exempt purposes.

4. continue joint use of property with a disqualified person if the interests of both were acquired prior to October 9, 1969.

5. accept a transfer of encumbered property (real or personal) from a disqualified person if the foundation does not assume the encumbrance and a disqualified person has not placed an encumbrance on the property for at least ten years before the transfer.

6. enter into transactions (with certain limitations) with a disqualified corporation either: (a) under terms of securities acquired before May 27, 1969; or (b) pursuant to corporate reorganizations on nonprefer-

ential terms, provided the foundation receives at least fair market value.

7. sell for fair market value property owned by the foundation on May 26, 1969, to a disqualified person to avoid the excess business holding tax. This rule also applies to excess business holdings acquired under trusts irrevocable as of, or wills executed on or before May 26, 1969, but otherwise does not apply to subsequently acquired business interests. The Tax Reform Act of 1976 briefly extended the time within which certain other business interests and certain leaseholds could be sold to disqualified persons.

8. agree to employ a government official after the termination of his government service, but not prior to 90 days before such termination.

9. make certain payments to government officials including:
   a. domestic travel expenses, not to exceed 125 percent of U.S. Government allowances;
   b. tax exempt Section 117(a) scholarships and fellowships for study at educational institutions described by Section 170(b)(1)(A)(ii);
   c. annuities under certain qualified retirement plans;
   d. contributions of services or facilities whose aggregate value is not more than $25 per year; and
   e. prizes and awards subject to the provisions of Section 74(b) if the recipients are selected from the general public.

REQUIRED DISTRIBUTIONS (SECTION 4942)

Private foundations that are not "operating foundations" or do not operate "extended care facilities" as defined below must annually distribute their "minimum investment return" in "qualifying distributions" by the end of the year following the close of the current tax year. Any federal income taxes and the 2-percent excise tax (or 1 percent, if applicable) are, in effect, credited against the amount required to be distributed.

Minimum investment return is 5 percent of the market value of investment assets (less acquisition indebtedness) for accounting years beginning in 1976 and thereafter increased by:

1. repayments to the foundation of amounts previously treated as qualifying distributions (e.g., scholarship loans),
2. amounts received on disposition or sale of assets previously treated as qualifying distributions, and
3. amounts previously set aside for a charitable project but not so used.

In calculating minimum investment return, the market value of a stock may, in limited circumstances, be reduced up to 10 percent for "blockage" (where the foundation owns a large block of stock that cannot be sold in a reasonable period without depressing its price).

"Qualifying distributions" are the following: (a) grants and other payments (including necessary and reasonable administrative expenses) to accomplish exempt purposes, including contributions to other private nonoperating foundations and "controlled" organizations where the recipient foundation makes certain "qualifying distributions" of an equal amount (in addition to distributions otherwise required of the recipient foundation) within the year following receipts; (b) payments to acquire assets used in carrying out exempt purposes; (c) set asides; and (d) program-related investments (see Section 4944). Qualifying distributions that exceed the minimum payout may be carried forward and applied to future years (up to five years).

"Operating foundations" are private foundations that make "qualifying distributions" of a required amount (see later) directly for the active conduct of the activities for which they are organized and operated, and do one of the following:

1. **Assets Test.** Devote substantially more than half of their assets directly to such activities, or to functionally related business activities, or both.

2. **Expenditure Test.** Normally make qualifying distributions, directly for the active conduct of such activities, equaling at least two-thirds of their "minimum investment return" (now $3\frac{1}{3}$ percent of net investment assets).

3. **Support Test.** Normally receive 85 percent of their support excluding investment income from five or more unrelated exempt organizations (not more than 25 percent from one organization) or the general public, and do not normally receive more than half of their support from investment income.

The required distributions, or payout requirements, for operating foundations were amended by the Economic Recovery Tax Act of 1981. For taxable years beginning *after* December 31, 1981, an operating foundation must make "qualifying distributions" directly for the active conduct of the activities for which it is organized and operated *equal to* "*substantially all*" *(85 percent) of the lesser of:* (1) its adjusted net income, or (2) its minimum investment return (5 percent of the market value of its investment assets).

In more general terms, in order to satisfy the distribution requirements of Section 4942, the 1981 Tax Act requires an operating foundation to pay out annually 85 percent of its net investment income, and even if that amount is less than 85 percent of its minimum investment return (4.25 percent of net investment assets), it has still satisfied the payout requirement. However, if it must also satisfy the "Expenditure Test" (see discussion earlier), the payout requirement of 3⅓ percent of investment assets must still be met.

Finally, the 1981 amendments created an additional requirement for an operating foundation if it decides to distribute *more* than the minimum investment return (5 percent). In such a case, the operating foundation must make sure that 85 percent of the amounts paid out, including those in excess of the minimum investment return, are for the active conduct of its charitable activities. This requirement precludes any attempt by a nonoperating foundation to qualify for operating foundation status while continuing to fund substantial grant programs out of distributions in excess of the minimum requirements.

Under legislation enacted in 1978, private foundations that have, since at least May 26, 1969, operated "extended care facilities"—those providing long-term care for the permanently disabled, the elderly, needy widows or children—will meet minimum distribution requirements of Section 4942 if they meet the two-thirds minimum investment return provisions described earlier.

Qualifying distributions can include funds "set aside" by a foundation for a specific purpose or project if the Treasury is satisfied in advance that: (a) grants under the project will be paid out in five years, and (b) the project can better be accomplished by a set-aside than by immediate payment. The five-year period may be extended by the Treasury in appropriate circumstances. The 1976 Act added an alternate set-aside procedure. Under the alternate, (b) above does not apply, but (a) must be met (extensions are not permitted), and the foundation must also comply with the following statutory formula regarding its distributions: By the later of its 1976 accounting year or the fifth year of its existence, cash distributions by the foundation for exempt purposes must at least equal its then current "distributable amount," and cumulative cash distributions over the four preceding years must at least equal the sum of stated percentages of each year's minimum distribution requirements (20 percent of year one, 40 percent of year two, 60 percent of year three, 80 percent of year four).

Excess distributions in the five preceding years (not earlier than 1970) offset the required distributable amount (but past excess distributions are not taken into account in applying the fifth year requirement under the alternate set-aside rules).

The law imposes an excise tax of 15 percent on amounts not distributed as required, with an additional 100 percent tax if distribution is not made within a defined correction period. The initial tax is waived if deficiencies are subsequently distributed and are caused by incorrect valuation of assets due to reasonable cause.

EXCESS BUSINESS HOLDINGS (SECTION 4943)

Private foundations and disqualified persons (including, for this purpose, certain related foundations) [Section 4946(a)(1)(H)] together may not own more than 20 percent (35 percent if a third person has effective control) of the voting stock in a business corporation, except as provided later for May 26, 1969, holdings.

Holdings in excess of permitted limits acquired by post-May 26, 1969, gifts or bequests to a foundation or a disqualified person must be disposed of within five years from their acquisition. Post-May 26, 1969, purchases of stock by a foundation or a disqualified person that create or increase an aggregate holding beyond permitted limits do not qualify for the five-year disposition period, and may produce immediate tax effects for the foundation. Where disqualified persons own more than 20 percent (or 35 percent) of voting stock of a corporation, nonvoting stock held by the foundation is treated as impermissible.

For post-1969 acquisitions, the Tax Reform Act of 1984 gives the IRS discretionary authority to grant, in certain limited circumstances, one extension for an additional five years, of the original five-year divestiture period for acquisitions obtained by gift or bequest (not purchase). The extension is applicable only in the case of an unusually large gift or bequest of either diverse business holdings or holdings with complex corporate structures, and if the foundation meets other detailed planning and reporting requirements.

A general *de minimis* rule permits a foundation (together with related foundations) to hold not more than 2 percent of the voting stock and 2 percent of the value of all outstanding stock of a corporation. Holdings in a "functionally related business" or a business deriving 95 percent of its gross income from "passive sources" (both defined terms) do not constitute excess business holdings. Similar rules apply to interests in partnerships and other unincorporated businesses. Holdings in proprietorships are prohibited.

Where a foundation does not reduce its business holdings to the maximum permissible limits within the required period of time, an annual initial tax of 5 percent is imposed on the value of the excess holdings. If the holdings are not reduced appropriately within a defined correction period, an additional tax of 200 percent is imposed.

SPECIAL RULES FOR MAY 26, 1969 HOLDINGS

A two-phase set of divestiture requirements applies where the business holdings of a foundation (or a foundation and disqualified persons) exceeded the 20 percent or 35 percent limits on May 26, 1969. Under the first phase of these special rules, transition periods of 10, 15, or 20 years are provided for the reduction of foundation/disqualified person holdings to: (1) 50 percent of the voting stock of the corporation, or, if less; (2) 50 percent of the value of all outstanding shares. These rules do not permit an increase of aggregate foundation disqualified person holdings beyond the level held on May 26, 1969; if there is a subsequent reduction, any future aggregate increase above the percentage established by such reduction thereafter becomes an excess business holding if the total exceeds the 20-percent or 35-percent limits. However, under a revised "downward ratchet" rule, the decrease in the percentage holdings of a private foundation in a business enterprise is disregarded if:

1. the decrease was attributable solely to issuances of stock (or to issuances of stock coupled with subsequent redemptions of stock) in the business enterprise,
2. the net percentage decrease did not exceed two percent, and
3. the number of shares held by the private foundation is not affected by any such issuance of stock.

The first phase reduction periods are: 20 years where a foundation and disqualified persons hold more than 95 percent of the voting stock of the corporation, 15 years where the foundation and disqualified person hold aggregate interests exceeding 75 percent, and 10 years where the aggregate foundation/disqualified persons holdings exceed 50 percent.

After the expiration of the first phase reduction period, a fifteen-year second-phase set of divestiture requirements become operative. If, during phase two, disqualified persons never own more than 2 percent of the voting stock of the business enterprise, the voting stock held by the foundation must be reduced to not more than 35 percent by the end of the fifteen-year period. However, if disqualified persons own more than 2 percent at any time during the second phase, the voting stock held by the foundation must be reduced to 25 percent. The third phase of reduction is unlimited in time, and again the limit of voting stock that may be held by the foundation is 35 percent *unless* disqualified persons acquire more than 2 percent ownership of the business enterprise, and then the foundation must reduce its holdings to 25 percent.

The 1984 Tax Reform Act modified the application of the rules for the second and third phases for pre-1969 holdings. Prior to this modification, the law did not provide any time period for the foundation to reduce its percentage holdings below 25 percent when disqualified persons acquired more than 2 percent. Beginning July 18, 1984, a private foundation faced with this requirement has a five-year period beginning on the date of such acquisition to divest its holdings in excess of the 25-percent limit. The IRS does not have discretion to extend this initial five-year disposition period by an additional five years.

Where May 26, 1969, aggregate holdings do not exceed 50 percent but exceed the 20-percent or 35-percent limits, no further decrease is required if foundation holdings never exceed 25 percent.

These special rules apply to holdings acquired under trusts irrevocable, or certain wills executed by May 26, 1969. Within certain limitations, corporate redemptions of existing excess foundation business holdings will not result in the imposition of the accumulated earnings tax on the corporation or be treated as dividends to the foundation or other stockholders.

For pre-1969 holdings, the 1984 Tax Reform Act excludes from the definition of disqualified persons any employee stock ownership plan (ESOP) described in Section 4975(e)(7), but only for the purposes of these limitations on excess business holdings.

SPECULATIVE INVESTMENTS (SECTION 4944)

Foundations may not invest funds so as to jeopardize the carrying out of their exempt purposes. A tax of 5 percent of amounts improperly invested is imposed on the foundation, and 5 percent (maximum $5,000) on foundation managers participating with knowledge. Additional taxes of 25 percent are assessed against the foundation if improper investments are not corrected within a defined correction period, and 5 percent (maximum $10,000) against foundation managers refusing to correct the situations. Program-related investments do not jeopardize exempt purposes (Section 4944(c)).

TAXABLE EXPENDITURES (SECTION 4945)

Certain activities by private foundations are considered taxable expenditures and are punishable by penalty tax. An initial tax of 10 percent of the amount of the expenditure may be imposed on any foundation, and a tax of $2\frac{1}{2}$ percent (maximum $5,000) may be imposed on any foundation manager agreeing to such expenditure knowing it to be taxable. Additional taxes of 100 percent on the foundation and 50 percent on the foundation manager (maximum $10,000) may be imposed if the action is not corrected within a defined correction period. Taxable expenditures are:

1. any payments to carry on propaganda or otherwise to attempt to influence legislation by: (a) attempting to affect public opinion, or (b)

communicating with any legislator, legislative employee, or other government officials or employees participating in the formulation of legislation. Exceptions: A foundation may provide technical advice or assistance to a governmental body, or subdivision thereof, if requested in writing; may make available the results of nonpartisan analysis, study or research; and may communicate with or appear before a legislative body concerning matters affecting its own existence, powers or duties, tax-exempt status, or the deductibility of contributions to it.

2. payments to influence any specific election or to carry on, directly or indirectly, any voter registration drive, except grants to a 501(c)(3) organization:

   a. that receives substantially all its support (other than investment income) from the general public, governmental units, and exempt organizations, not more than 25 percent of such support being received from any one exempt organization and not more than 50 percent of total support from gross investment income (support is determined over a five-year period, including the year in question, but excluding years before 1970);

   b. whose activities are nonpartisan, not confined to one election period, and carried on in five or more states,

   c. substantially all of the income of which is spent directly for the active conduct of its activities; and

   d. contributions to which for voter registration drives are not restricted geographically or to a specific election period; "Expenditure responsibility" (see no. 4 below) is not required for grants to organizations meeting these tests.

3. individual grants (but not contracts for services), unless the award is objective and nondiscriminatory, the Treasury has approved the granting procedure in advance, and is satisfied that the proposed grants will constitute: tax-exempt scholarships or fellowships at educational institutions (Section 117); prizes or awards open to the public (Section 74(b)); or payments intended to achieve a special objective, produce a report, or enhance literary, artistic, musical, scientific, teaching, or similar talents.

4. grants to other private foundations, private operating foundations (except exempt operating foundations—see discussion of Section 4940), organizations exempt under paragraphs of Section 501 other than (c)(3), (e.g., social welfare organizations), and nonexempt organizations, unless the grantor assumes "expenditure responsibility" with respect to the grant. Expenditure responsibility requires the granting foundation to exert all reasonable efforts and establish adequate procedures to see that the grant is spent solely for the purpose for which made, obtain full reports from the grantee, and make detailed reports on the grant to the Treasury.

5. any activity not within the purposes of Section 170(c)(2)(B).

ABATEMENT OF FIRST-TIER PENALTY TAXES

As indicated earlier, violations of the private foundation rules (sections 4941–4945) result in the imposition of an initial excise tax on the foundation. In cases of self-dealing, jeopardy investments, or taxable expenditures, a tax may be imposed on the foundation manager as well. The taxes under Section 4941 (self-dealing) and Section 4944 (jeopardy investments) continue to be imposed in each year beginning when the prohibited act occurs and ending only when the IRS issues a deficiency notice or assesses a tax on the act, or when the act is corrected.

If the violation of the foundation rules is not corrected within a specified period, an additional second-tier tax is imposed on the foundation and, where applicable, on the foundation manager.

With the exception of the Section 4941 tax on self-dealing, the 1984 Tax Reform Act provides discretionary authority to the IRS not to assess, to abate, or to refund any initial (first-tier) tax if the foundation or foundation manager establishes to the satisfaction of the IRS that the violation of the foundation rules:

1. was due to reasonable cause;

2. was not due to willful neglect; and

3. has been corrected in the manner required by the particular statutory provision (in order to avoid any second-tier tax) within the appropriate correction period.

A violation that was due to ignorance of the law cannot qualify for such abatement. This abatement provision is available for taxable events occurring after December 31, 1984.

SPECIAL RULES (SECTIONS 507, 508, AND 4947)

Governing instruments of private foundations organized before January 1, 1970, had to be amended (by state law or otherwise) to require compliance with the new statute's provisions on self-dealing, required distributions, excess business holdings, investments, and program activities (sections 4941–4945), or judicial proceedings had to have been initiated prior to January 1, 1972, to require or excuse such compliance. Governing documents of private foundations organized after December 31, 1969, must require such compliance to attain exempt status. (Most states have enacted laws reflecting these rules.)

Rules under which charitable organizations establish their classification or status as private foundations, private operating foundations, or "public charities," as the case may be, are provided by Section 508. The Tax Reform Act of 1976 provides that charitable organizations may obtain court review of adverse or long-delayed IRS decisions as to their exempt status and classification (Section 7428).

Under Section 507, private foundations may give up that status, or that status may be terminated by the IRS for willful and repeated violations of the law. Termination of exemption may create tax liability equal to the lower of (1) the aggregate income, estate, and gift tax benefits to the foundation and all substantial contributors; or (2) the foundation's net assets. This tax is not imposed if the foundation either (1) operates for a continuous 60-month period (only 12 months if so operated in its first fiscal year after December 31, 1969) as an organization excluded from the private foundation definition by paragraph 1, 2, or 3 of Section 509(a)—in which case it will not be treated as a private foundation during that period; or (2) distributes its assets to certain public charities. Mergers and consolidations by private foundations are also permitted without tax.

With variations and subject to special rules, certain nonexempt charitable trusts are made subject to the private foundation rules (Section 4947).

RETURNS, PENALTIES, AND PUBLICITY OF INFORMATION

For accounting years beginning after December 31, 1980, all private foundations must annually file reports with the IRS (Section 6033) showing name and address of the foundation; foundation income and other receipts, expenses, disbursements, and details on grants made or authorized (including grant purposes); a balance sheet with accompanying details (including book and market values of securities and other assets); names and addresses of substantial contributors; names, addresses, and compensation of all foundation managers and highly paid employees; and, where a foundation owns a 10-percent or larger business interest, a list of foundation managers with a 10-percent or larger interest in that business. The report must be made available at the foundation office to any person requesting it within 180 days after a required notice of the report's availability has been published in a newspaper of general circulation. Notice must be published not later than the return filing date, and proof of notice must be filed with the report.

Beginning January 1, 1985, any required notice must include the telephone number for the foundation's principal office. If the foundation does not have a principal office, or does not have a telephone at its principal office, then the notice must include the telephone number either for the person to whom applications for grants from the foundation must be submitted or, if there is no such person, for the person having custody of the foundation's books.

The Omnibus Reconciliation Act of 1987 added a similar requirement for exemption applications. Effective December 22, 1987, private foundations are required to make available for public inspection during regular business hours a copy of their application for tax exemption (Form 1023) including a copy of any papers submitted with the application and any determination letters or other documents issued by the IRS in response to the application. A private foundation that submitted its application on or before July 15, 1987, is not required to comply with this inspection unless it had a copy of the application on hand on July 15, 1987.

The penalty for failure to file the required Form 990-PF is $10 per day with a maximum of $5,000 (Section 6652). The penalty is imposed on the foundation and/or the manager unless he or she had reasonable cause for failure to comply. Copies of private foundation returns must also be filed with appropriate state officials.

Also under Section 6652, the penalty for failure to permit inspection of the annual return (Form 990-PF) is the same: $10 per day ($5,000 maximum). The penalty is imposed on "the person failing to meet such requirement." The penalty for failure to permit inspection of the application for tax exemption (and related documents) is also $10 per day but there is no maximum. Here again, the penalty is imposed on "the person failing to meet such requirements." Also, with respect to failure to permit inspection of the application for exemption, any person required to comply is subject to an additional penalty of $1,000 if such failure is willful (Section 6685).

CHARITABLE CONTRIBUTIONS

Percentage Limitations

Contributions of cash or ordinary-income property by an individual to public charities or private operating foundations are deductible up to 50 percent of the donor's adjusted gross income. The 50-percent limitation applies to contributions of cash or ordinary-income property made by individuals to a private *nonoperating* (grantmaking) foundation *only* if the donee either redistributes all contributions within a specified period after receipt (conduit foundation) or qualifies as a "pooled-fund" foundation. For gifts of cash or ordinary-income property to all other private nonoperating foundations the limit is 30 percent for gifts made after July 18, 1984.

For gifts of appreciated property (or capital gain property), the percentage limitation is 30 percent for gifts to public charities, private operating foundations, and the conduit foundation and pooled-fund

MR. MERGENDEILER? THIS IS MR. BLANDLY OF THE FINK FOUNDATION. WE HAVE RECEIVED YOUR APPLICATION FOR AN ENDOWMENT AND WOULD LIKE A FEW FURTHER DETAILS.

AS YOU KNOW MR. MERGENDEILER, THE FINK FOUNDATION IS AUTHORIZED TO GIVE FINANCIAL GRANTS TO UNWORTHY CAUSES. CAN YOU PROVE THAT YOU QUALIFY?

THEN YOU **DO** HAVE REFERENCES. GOOD. YOUR MOTHER - ALL YOUR TEACHERS - YOUR PAST EMPLOYERS. WONDERFUL. NO, MR. MERGENDEILER, I DON'T THINK WE'D NEED THE NAMES OF GIRL FRIENDS.

NOW, IN THE EVENT YOU **DID** RECEIVE A GRANT, WHAT WOULD YOU DO WITH THE MONEY? I SEE. YOU'D FRITTER IT AWAY. FINE. FINE.

IN WHAT MANNER MAY I ASK? YOU'D LIE IN BED ALL DAY AND READ MYSTERIES. PERFECTLY DELIGHTFUL, MR. MERGENDEILER.

ONE LAST QUESTION, MR. MERGENDEILER. IF YOU **WERE** AWARDED A GRANT FOR THIS PROJECT HOW WOULD YOU FEEL? YOU'D FEEL GUILTY. **SPLENDID!**

YOU SHALL RECEIVE YOUR CHECK IN THE MORNING.

foundation mentioned above. For gifts of appreciated property to all other private nonoperating foundations, the limit is 20 percent of adjusted gross income. The limitation for all types of gifts by corporations is 10 percent.

Carryover of Excess Contributions

Charitable contributions by individuals or corporations that exceed the limits noted earlier may be carried forward and deducted over the following five years, subject to applicable percentage limitations in those years.

Value of Contributions of Appreciated Property

In the case of charitable contributions of appreciated property to public charities, private operating foundations, conduit foundations, and pooled income fund foundations, the amount deductible equals the fair market value of the asset at the time of the contribution (see discussion of alternative minimum tax later). As the result of the Tax Reform Act of 1986, the value of donations by living individuals of appreciated property to all other private nonoperating foundations is limited to the cost or basis of the asset.

The 1984 Tax Reform Act creates an exception to these reductions from fair market value for gifts of certain publicly traded stock. Effective July 18, 1984, the amount of deduction allowable for charitable contributions to private nonoperating foundations of certain qualified appreciated stock is the full fair market value of the stock on the date of contribution.

The term *qualified appreciated stock* is defined to mean any stock of a corporation for which market quotations are readily available on an established securities market and that is capital-gain property. This exception does not apply to gifts of bonds, notes, warrants, options, or partnership interests, and the exception expires (sunsets) on December 31, 1994. Finally, the nonreduced deduction for gifts of such qualified appreciated stock applies only to the extent that the cumulative aggregate amount of donations (including donations made prior to July 19, 1984) made by the donor and any member of his or her family of stock in a particular corporation does not exceed 10 percent in value of all the outstanding stock of that corporation.

The Tax Reform Act of 1986 also stiffened the alternative minimum tax. After December 31, 1986, the value of any contribution of appreciated property to any public charity or private foundation by a taxpayer who is subject to the alternative minimum tax is limited to the cost or basis of the property.

Sample Conflict of Interest Policies

Code of Conduct

Northwest Area Foundation, W-975 First National Bank Building, Saint Paul, MN 55101

PREAMBLE

This is a revision of the code of conduct originally adopted by the Board of the Northwest Area Foundation in 1971 (then the Louis W. and Maud Hill Family Foundation).

The purpose for the foundation having a "code of conduct" is twofold:

1. Private foundations must strive so far as possible to be above suspicion. It is not enough that the directors and the staff *believe* that they are operating from the highest motives and that any particular action is innocent, regardless of its appearance. So far as possible, actions and relationships must avoid an appearance of impropriety that raises questions in the minds of the public.

2. It is desirable that directors and staff have a practical guide to use in conducting the affairs of the foundation.

In general, this code of conduct deals with problems in the area commonly called "conflict of interest," which extends to possible charges of "undue influence," "conspiracy," or "favoritism." Actions, or decisions not to act, taken by the foundation should be defensible as having been based upon the best, unbiased judgment of the individuals involved.

The touchstone of this code is "complete disclosure." When connections, no matter how remote, of the individual or individuals who participate in decisions are fully disclosed, this avoids any misunderstanding or later charges of concealment. This code is also intended to cover those cases where the disclosure of a connection or past connection may indicate that the individual involved should abstain from participating in the decision-making process.

The principles stated below as to disclosure and abstention do not apply to cases where the grant application is rejected by staff in accordance with established policy of the foundation and such rejection is ratified by the board of directors.

BOARD OF DIRECTORS

Disclosure

Each director shall inform the foundation and fellow directors of any position presently held or held in the past, of any investment, and of any business or avocational activity that may result in a possible conflict of interest or bias for or against a particular grantee, action, or policy at the time such grant, action, or policy is under consideration by the board of directors. Each director shall file with the personnel committee a list of investments (without disclosing number of shares or amounts invested), as well as offices and directorships held in other charitable and business organizations, each year.

Abstention

Directors of the foundation shall abstain from voting on any action that has a direct or indirect financial interest.

Example 1. An officer or other paid employee of a bank or other financial institution who is also a director of the foundation shall abstain from voting on the employment, retention, or dismissal of the bank or financial institution as the fiscal agent of the foundation.

Example 2. An attorney serving as a director of the foundation shall abstain from voting on employment, reemployment, or dismissal of said attorney's law firm as legal counsel for the foundation, or on the question of continuing or discontinuing (or settling) a lawsuit or other proceedings in which said attorney's law firm is acting as counsel for the foundation.

Example 3. A director of the foundation who also is a paid officer or an employee of an institution (or formerly was a paid employee of such an institution) to which a grant is proposed shall abstain from voting on the motion for or against the grant. A director of the foundation who also is a nonpaid director or officer of the proposed grantee is *technically free to vote on the question (after disclosing the connection), but abstention is preferred.*

Example 4. A director of the foundation who is a substantial investor in a business concern that may be affected favorably or adversely by a grant shall abstain from voting on the motion for or against the grant. A director of the foundation who is an investor, but not in substantial amount, in such a business is free to vote on the question (after disclosing the connection), and shall decide individually whether or not to do so in light of all the circumstances.

STAFF MEMBERS

Volunteer Service with Other Organizations

Members of the paid staff of the foundation are free to serve as primarily unpaid volunteers, officers, board members, or advisors to local or national charitable organizations and government or quasigovernmental units, such as school boards, mayor's or governor's commissions, etc. *However, staff shall inform the president of the intention to accept an appointment or to be a candidate for office. The president shall similarly inform the personnel committee of the president's own intentions.*

It should be recognized by staff that if they serve in an official capacity with another organization, they will be from time to time placed in the position of "wearing two hats," that is, serving as an officer or board member of the charity or governmental unit seeking a grant or grants from their employing foundation, and then later being involved in participating in the evaluation of the proposal—or under the paragraph headed "Abstention" below, being required to abstain. Staff serving as a director or as an officer of a charitable organization should exercise care to avoid giving the impression that this service to the outside organization is an endorsement by the foundation of the organization, or is prima facie evidence that favorable action will be taken on a proposal by the organization to the foundation.

Staff should also report to the president any "per diem," or "expense reimbursement" or similar emoluments received from the charitable organization or governmental body with which staff is associated.

It is suggested that if staff serve on a board of directors (or other governing body) of a charitable organization, or on a public body such as a school board, mayor's or governor's commission, etc., terms should be limited to not more than five years (in most cases, one term, if a term is more than a year). This amount of time should provide staff with sufficient experience to understand the problems of the organization and gain knowledge of the field in which that organization is engaged, while avoiding the inference that staff has a strong bias in favor of a particular organization.

Service for Compensation to Other Organizations

Foundation policy permits staff to serve as consultants for compensation. Staff so serving should exercise extreme caution in connection with any suggestion of funding by Northwest Area Foundation of projects supported by such outside organizations.

If during the course of service by staff as consultants to another organization, it becomes apparent that a project the other organization is interested in cannot or will not be funded solely by the other organization, staff may suggest that Northwest Area Foundation join with the outside organization in support of the project, if the project is judged worthwhile. Suggestions such as this are acceptable according to foundation policy, but the proposal must then be handled on behalf of Northwest Area Foundation by other staff.

Staff are encouraged to undertake speaking engagements and to write articles, provided the time involved in doing so does not detract from the time necessary to accomplish foundation work. Staff shall not accept payments, royalties, or honoraria for speaking engagements or articles that are based on staff's foundation employment. Such compensation may be accepted when the speaking engagement or article is on a topic that is not within the scope of staff's regular foundation duties.

Disclosure

In all cases, staff are responsible for informing the president of any continuing relationship staff have with any charitable organization or governmental body, whether it be as a consultant, officer, or director, and the amount of time spent in work for each such organization. The president should also be informed of long-standing past connections with a charitable organization, even if staff are no longer serving that organization.

Staff shall also inform the president of any personal or immediate family investments or of any business or avocational activity that may result in a possible conflict of interest or ruling against a particular grantee, action, or policy at the time such grant, action, or policy is under consideration by staff or by the board of directors.

Abstention

Staff shall abstain from acting as program officer on any grant application from an organization for which staff serve as paid or nonpaid officer or board member. Staff shall likewise abstain if staff serve the applicant as a consultant or as a consultant on the particular project for which the grant is sought—in both cases, whether paid or unpaid.

Duties of President

The president shall be responsible for the application and interpretation of the above principles relating to staff. At least annually, the president shall inform the personnel committee of the consulting work being performed by staff, whether for compensation or on a volunteer basis, and of offices held (including directorships) in various organizations by staff.

The president shall report to the personnel committee any case that has occurred that might involve a violation of the foregoing principles. The president may bring before the personnel committee any instance that is perceived as requiring committee guidance.

At the time that a grant application is being considered by the board of directors, the president shall see that the staff memorandum on the proposal informs the board of directors of any current or past connection between the applicant and foundation staff of which the president is aware.

ADVISORY COMMITTEES

While it is recognized that the advice of local or regional experts is important to evaluate proposals effectively, the membership of advisory committees should, to the extent possible, include a majority of members who are not affiliated with organizations that are eligible for foundation funds. Thus, to the extent possible, the foundation will avoid placing on advisory committees that are to evaluate a grant proposal or proposals, or to evaluate performance of a grantee, any person who may have an interest—financial or as an unpaid officer or board member—in any organization that has submitted a proposal, or which foundation staff have reason to believe may submit a proposal.

If it develops that a member of an advisory committee has an interest in an organization that is submitting a proposal to be considered by the committee, the member shall:

1. be disqualified from participating in any way in the consideration of the proposal by the committee.
2. not communicate further with other members of the committee on the subject of the proposal.
3. not communicate further with foundation staff on the subject, unless foundation staff shall ask for information about the proposal.

If, after consideration of such a proposal by other members of the advisory committee, they recommend to the foundation board that a grant be made, they or foundation staff shall clearly inform the board of the nature of the relationship between the organization and the disqualified member of the advisory committee at the time the foundation board is considering the proposal.

Approved by the Board of Directors, August 12, 1971

Amended by the Board of Directors, September 5, 1975

Amended by the Board of Directors, April 18, 1982

Revised May 31, 1990

Conflict of Interest Policy

The Wallace Alexander Gerbode Foundation

The board and staff members of the Wallace Alexander Gerbode Foundation are encouraged to play active roles in their communities by serving as board members or otherwise being involved with a wide spectrum of nonprofit organizations. This means that, from time to time, potential conflicts of interest or the appearance of such conflicts will inevitably arise. It is the foundation's policy to deal with such conflicts in as open and appropriate a way as possible.

Conflicting involvements include but are not limited to the following: foundation board members serving as board members of applicant organizations, immediate family members of foundation board members serving as board members of applicant organizations, foundation board members or their immediate family members being employed by or doing business with applicant organizations.

In case of such conflicts or the appearance thereof, foundation board members and/or staff are expected to disclose the conflict prior to making any related grant decisions. Once such a disclosure has been made, the remaining board members will determine whether or not there is a potential conflict of interest. Should it be so considered, the board member involved shall abstain from voting and shall not participate in the discussion of the applicant organization other than to answer specific questions that may be raised by other board members.

In cases where the foundation's board of trustees decides to award a grant to an organization and one or more of the foundation's board members has abstained from voting as the result of a conflict or the appearance thereof, such grants and board members shall be identified in the foundation's annual report.

January 23, 1990

Legal Checklist for Managers of Private Foundations

No checklist is ever totally complete, and new changes in the law and regulations occur on a frequent basis. This checklist was prepared by combining earlier versions drafted by the Council on Foundations and by individual attorneys.[1] The documents described and the issues raised in this checklist are ones with which you should be intimately familiar. You should refer to them from time to time to refresh your recollection of their contents in order to ensure that the management of your foundation is in accordance with all legal requirements and in order to determine whether any modifications to the documents or to your procedures are necessary.

I. ORGANIZATIONAL AND OPERATIONAL DOCUMENTS

A. Articles of incorporation or declaration of trust. This document is the "constitution" of your foundation, its formative document. The following issues should be reviewed:

1. Are the foundation's activities authorized by the purposes set forth in the articles or declaration?

2. Is the actual number of your foundation's directors or trustees in accordance with the number required in the articles or declaration?

3. Are the registered agent and registered office that are named in the articles of incorporation still appropriate, or should the foundation notify the appropriate state office (secretary of state or attorney general) of its current registered agent/or office?

---

[1] This checklist was revised in October 1990 by John A. Edie, General Counsel at the Council on Foundations. He drew heavily from earlier Council versions drafted by David F. Freeman and Edward G. Thompson and from an excellent list prepared by Ann E. Ward, attorney with Jackson & Walker (Dallas, Texas), which was first presented to the Conference of Southwest Foundations (May 11, 1989).

4. If the articles contain a provision authorizing the foundation to indemnify directors, officers, and/or employees for costs or expenses arising out of an actual or threatened legal proceeding arising out of actions or inactions on the part of the director, officer, or employee in the course of his or her service to the foundation, are such provisions consistent with current law? Many states have revised their laws regarding indemnification.

B. Bylaws. State laws governing not-for-profit corporations require bylaws. For foundations in the corporate form, bylaws are the rules that govern day-to-day operations, meetings, the election of officers and directors or trustees, and other ongoing activities and issues. The following issues should be reviewed:

1. Are meetings of directors or trustees held at the times and in the places required by the bylaws? Is an annual meeting required by state law?

2. Are notices of meetings given (or appropriate waivers obtained) in accordance with the notice requirements in the bylaws?

3. Are the activities of each officer of your foundation consistent with the activities prescribed for such office in the bylaws?

4. Does your foundation have all of the officers that its bylaws require it to have?

5. Do the bylaws require the existence of an advisory committee or any other such group? If so, does your foundation have such a committee or group, and are its actions in accordance with the rules set forth in the bylaws?

6. Are your foundation's procedures for naming new and substitute directors and officers carried out as directed in the bylaws?

7. Are additional bylaws desirable to govern activities of your foundation or its managers that are not fully delineated in the current bylaws?

8. Do the bylaws authorize such things as the holding of meetings by telephone, or action by the directors by unanimous written consent instead of the holding of a regular meeting?

9. If the bylaws contain indemnity provisions as described earlier, are such provisions consistent with current law?

10. If the bylaws require use of a corporate seal, does your foundation have such a seal, and is it used regularly?

11. Do the bylaws require certain financial accounting activities, and, if so, are your foundation's actual activities in accordance with these requirements?

12. Does anything in the bylaws conflict with statements made on your foundation's application for its federal tax exemption?

II. DOCUMENTS RELATING TO FEDERAL TAX EXEMPTION

You should also be familiar with the following documents relating to your foundation's exemption from federal income tax and be sure they are kept in a safe place:

A. Form 1023, the application for recognition by the IRS as a tax-exempt organization.

B. Form SS-4, the application for employee identification number.

C. The IRS's favorable determination letter certifying that your foundation is exempt from income tax and specifying that it is a private foundation or a private operating foundation.

D. IRS Publication 78, *The Cumulative List of Organizations Contributions to Which Are Deductible Under Section 170(c)*, should be checked to be certain that your foundation is listed accurately. Private foundations are indicated by a footnote 4 and operating foundations by a footnote 3.

E. If applicable, the IRS letter approving your foundation's grant-making procedures. Such a letter is normally required for grants to individuals for study or travel, or for set-asides (see later).

F. Any other official correspondence from the IRS concerning the status or operations of the foundation including private letter rulings or audit findings.

III. DOCUMENTS RELATING TO STATE TAX EXEMPTION

You should also be familiar with any documents granting or denying your foundation's exemption from state income, sales, property, or franchise taxes and be sure they are kept in a safe place.

IV. SPECIAL PRIVATE FOUNDATION RULES (CHAPTER 42)

A. Section 4940 imposes a tax on net investment income that is due on the fifteenth day of the fifth month after the close of the foundation's tax year; however, estimated taxes must be paid during the year based on the same rules applicable to for-profit corporations. The tax is 2 percent and may be reduced to 1 percent if the foundation meets certain maintenance-of-effort tests. You should be familiar with these tests so that you can advise the foundation about designing a system to determine when meeting these tests might be most advisable. You should be familiar with the definition of *net investment income* and be certain that adequate record-keeping procedures are in place to keep track of all expenses that can be attributed to the production of investment income. Allocating investment expenses from charitable purpose expenditures is a favorite target of IRS audits.

B. Section 4941 prohibits all acts of self-dealing involving financial transactions with disqualified persons using foundation funds. Understand the definition of disqualified person as set out in Section 4946, and review arrangements for payments for personal services, offices and facilities, transportation, and the like that involve disqualified persons. Review banking and investment dealings with banks that are disqualified persons to be sure they fit within the very narrow exceptions from the self-dealing rules for general banking services [Regulation 53.4941(d)-2(c)(4)]. Note special rules on indemnification and liability insurance for directors and officers [Regulation 53.4941(d)-2(f)(1) and (3)]. Note also restrictions on direct or indirect payments to "government officials." Review all compensation of employees and trustees to be certain they are necessary and reasonable.

C. Section 4942 imposes a minimum payout requirement for private foundations. This payout is roughly the equivalent of 5 percent of net investment assets. You should be familiar with how this payout requirement is calculated, paying particular attention to the definition of *qualifying distributions*. Assets are measured using a monthly average formula; certain assets such as real estate must be valued on the basis of a qualified appraisal that is no more than five years old. There is a credit for any investment income taxes paid, and qualifying distributions that exceed the minimum required may be carried over and applied to later years (up to five). The payout must be met no later than twelve months after the end of the tax year in question; in other words, payments in the following year may be applied retroactively to make up any shortfall. Accounting and record-keeping procedures should be well designed to provide accurate and reliable information for these calculations. Payout usually consists of grants, necessary and reasonable administrative expenses to accomplish the grant program and other direct charitable activities, assets acquired for charitable purposes, program-related investments, and set-asides.

D. Section 4943 prohibits a foundation *in conjunction with all of its disqualified persons* from having excess business holdings (a controlling interest in a for-profit company, partnership, etc.). Determine whether any such holdings exist or whether they might be created by additional purchases by disqualified persons. Plan for any required divestiture and design a method for keeping track of the holdings of all disqualified persons. Regardless of the percentage owned by disqualified persons, the foundation need not divest if its holdings are less than 2 percent. Excess holdings acquired after 1969 must be divested within five years, although an additional five years may be granted by the IRS commissioner under limited circumstances.

E. Section 4944 imposes a penalty on the foundation and its managers for any investment that might jeopardize the carrying out of any of the foundation's exempt purposes. No type of investment is per se a jeopardy investment, but certain types are subject to special scrutiny (commodities futures, trading on margins, working interests in oil and gas wells, "puts" and "calls," etc.). Be familiar with the definition of "program-related investment," which is an exception to the jeopardy investment rules. For example, a below-market interest loan to a minority low-income housing development company could meet the definition, avoid the jeopardy investment prohibition, and count in meeting the minimum payout requirement.

F. Section 4945 provides a list of various kinds of grantmaking or expenditures that can subject a private foundation and its managers to penalty. Spending funds on a political campaign or for a noncharitable purpose are prohibited. Lobbying is also prohibited, although there are several exceptions including self-defense legislation, written requests from legislative committees, and nonpartisan analysis, study or research (*note:* detailed final regulations on lobbying were issued by the Treasury on August 31, 1990). Grants or expenditures for voter registration or education are permitted, but only if certain very strict rules are followed. Grants to individuals for study or travel (scholarships, fellowships, prizes, awards) are permitted only upon having the procedures to be used by the foundation approved *in advance* by the IRS. Grants to noncharities (trade associations, chambers of commerce, social welfare organizations, labor unions, for-profit companies, etc.) are subject to penalty unless the foundation "exercises expenditure responsibility." More foundations are finding that expenditure responsibility is not that onerous once normal grantmaking procedures are in place. Key foundation managers should understand when expenditure responsibility is required.

V. ADMINISTRATIVE REPORTING AND PUBLIC ACCOUNTABILITY

A. Establish procedures to supply information required for completing various notice and filing requirements such as:
   1. Annual IRS information return, Form 990-PF.

2. Annual filings required by state law.
3. SEC annual information returns for very large holdings (over $100 million).
4. For staffed foundations, reporting requirements as to fringe benefits under the Employees' Retirement Income Security Act of 1974; FICA; federal and state withholding; unemployment insurance (FUTA and any state requirements); Form 1099 for consultants, professional fees, director, or trustee fees; etc.
5. Special IRS notice requirements for reporting a dissolution or substantial contraction of a foundation (Section 6043, and see Section 507).
6. Foundations with unrelated business income must file Form 990-T (income from debt financed investment property and certain publicly traded partnerships are examples). Form 990-PF also has a section on income-producing activities.
7. Any transfers to and transactions and relationships with noncharitable exempt organizations (such as trade associations, or social welfare organizations) must also be reported on Form 990-PF (such as loans, rental of facilities, performance of services, etc.).

B. Each foundation is required to make certain information available to the public for inspection:
1. For 180 days after filing Form 990-PF, this document complete with all attachments must be available for public inspection during normal business hours; foundations are required to publish by the due date for filing the return in a newspaper of general circulation a notice that the return is so available.
2. Form 1023, any IRS responses, and all relevant correspondence relating to exempt status must also be available for public inspection.

VI. GRANT PROGRAMS AND POLICIES

A. If contributions of appreciated property are made to the foundation, and the donor wishes to take maximum income tax deductions, plan sufficient distributions to meet "flow-through" requirements under Section 170(b)(1)(E). Note also the need to maintain records and show that such distributions are made out of "corpus" on Form 990-PF.

B. Review grant programs in the light of the self-dealing rules, paying special attention to conflict of interest situations. Treasury regulations warn that it is an act of self-dealing for a private foundation to satisfy a legally enforceable personal pledge made by a disqualified person (e.g., an individual, spouse, or corporate donor to the foundation) to an independent charity [Regulation 53.4941(d)-2(f)(1)].

C. Determine status of recipient organizations as private foundations, private operating foundations, publicly supported charitable organizations, or "other." IRS Publication 78 is coded to indicate the status of over 300,000 charitable organizations. Organizations listed with no code number following their name are "public charities," grants to which do not require "expenditure responsibility" under Code Section 4945. Some well-known nonprofit organizations, such as the League of Women Voters and the NAACP, are *not* themselves charities, but their Section 501(c)(3) affiliates *are* listed in Publication 78 as public charities. Note also, however, that federal law permits grants to "noncharitable" organizations for charitable purposes, provided requirements for expenditure responsibility are met (see later). Unless a notice to the contrary has been published in the *Internal Revenue Bulletin,* foundations may generally rely on Publication 78, although it is common practice for foundations to ask for a copy of the grantee's IRS tax determination letter for its file.

D. Large grants to small publicly supported charities may "tip" them out of public charity status and force them to be reclassified as private foundations. This "tipping" problem was resolved in most instances for private foundations by Revenue Procedure 89–23.

E. Develop procedures and wording for grant letters, especially where expenditure responsibility provisions may apply [Section 4945(d)(4) and (h)], or where the grantee must expend the grant in the year following its receipt [Section 4942(g)(3)].

F. Don't be intimidated by the expenditure responsibility rules under Internal Revenue Code Section 4945. IRS data and the Council on Foundations' experience indicate that a significant number of Council members make expenditure responsibility grants as a matter of course. These foundations report that the expenditure responsibility rules are not burdensome, are generally consistent with their own grantmaking procedures, and are also an effective means of dealing with somewhat esoteric tax law questions that can arise, e.g., as to whether a particular grantee is a "publicly supported" organization. The Council has collected a variety of materials, including outlines, summaries of the expenditure responsibility rules, sample grant agreements, and the like, all of which are readily available on request.

G. Note especially limitations on types of grants (Section 4945), such as restrictions on direct or indirect payments to "government officials" [Section 4941(d)(1)(F) and (2)(G), Section 4946(c)].

VII. OTHER ISSUES

A. *Insurance.* Does your foundation wish to indemnify directors, officers, and employees for legal liabilities that may be incurred while performing their duties? Are the foundation's indemnification provisions up to date with state law? Is the general liability insurance that covers personal injury and property damage adequate? Approximately 62 percent of all foundations over $10 million in assets obtain directors' and officers' liability insurance (which covers liabilities that do not involve personal injury or property damage); does such insurance make sense for your foundation?

B. *Contracts.* Are all contracts or agreements recorded in written, signed documents, in order to avoid disputes about the terms of the agreements? Is the foundation in compliance with all contracts to which it is a party? Is there a written policy for completion of contracts with clear direction from the governing body as to what foundation managers may obligate the foundation?

C. *Real estate and other property.* Are all of your foundation's documents of title to real, personal, and intangible property located in a safe place and in the control of the proper persons?

D. *Employment.* Should the foundation have employment contracts with any of its employees? Is there a clear employment policies and procedures manual? Are the foundation's employment practices discriminatory? (*Note:* Wrongful termination suits are the claims most often filed under directors and officers liability policies).

E. *Pension.* Do the foundation's pension plans conform with the Employee Retirement Income Security Act of 1974 (ERISA)?

F. *Permits, licenses, and copyright.* If the foundation raises funds, does it need a charitable solicitation permit in the state in which it is raising the funds? Does the foundation need any other licenses or permits? Is the foundation qualified to do business in every state in which it conducts activities for which such qualification is required?

G. *Sales tax.* Should your foundation be collecting and paying state or local sales tax?

H. *Minutes.* Is the corporate minute book up to date and complete? Are the minutes kept in a safe place?

APPENDIX 4

Excerpts from
First Steps in Starting a Foundation

John A. Edie
Vice President and General Counsel
Council on Foundations

The book *First Steps in Starting a Foundation* was designed to help answer the questions that arise when a donor is considering alternative ways of organizing his or her charitable giving. What are the options? What are the benefits, tax implications, and drawbacks of starting a private foundation? An operating foundation? Or creating a fund in a community foundation?

Starting a grantmaking foundation means different things to different people. Not surprisingly, there are several different types of foundations one can create. Even though the term *foundation* by itself has no precise meaning, every donor who creates a foundation is interested in two major tax advantages: (1) they want the foundation to be tax exempt, and (2) they want donors to be able to treat their donations as tax deductible *charitable* contributions.

First Steps in Starting a Foundation provides an introduction to these issues. This appendix includes selected material to illustrate points made in Chapters 2–3 of this *Handbook*. The material is described in depth in *First Steps*. Also included is the book's table of contents, designed as an overview of issues covered. Readers interested in this subject are encouraged to obtain a copy of *First Steps in Starting a Foundation* from the Council on Foundations.

TABLE OF CONTENTS

PUBLIC v. PRIVATE: Effects on Donor

	Public Charity	Private Foundation
Gifts of Cash	50% limit	30% limit
Gifts of Appreciated Property	30% limit*	20% limit
Carryover	5 years	5 years
Value of Appreciated Property That Can Be Deducted**	100% of fair market value for all types	100% of fair market value for gifts only of publicly traded stock***
		Cost only for all other types of appreciated property

*When making gifts of appreciated property, the donor may take advantage of the higher 50% limit if he or she is willing to deduct only cost plus zero percent of the gain.

**After December 31, 1986, if the taxpayer is subject to the alternative minimum tax, the amount deductible may be limited to the cost or basis of the property.

***Barring action by Congress, this special treatment of gifts of publicly traded stock will expire in 1994.

NOTE: The above limitations apply *only* to income tax deductions. They do *not* apply to estate taxes. Bequests to "public" or "private" foundations are not subject to any of these limitations.

PUBLIC FOUNDATIONS
EFFECTS OF SELECTED TAX LAWS

LAWS AFFECTING LIVING DONORS	TRADITIONAL CHARITY	GROSS RECEIPTS CHARITY	SUPPORTING ORGANIZATION	COMMUNITY FOUNDATION
CASH GIFT	50% AGI	50% AGI	50% AGI	50% AGI
APPRECIATED PROPERTY*	30% AGI	30% AGI	30% AGI	30% AGI
CARRYOVER AVAILABLE	5 years	5 years	5 years	5 years
VALUE OF APPRECIATED PROPERTY*	Fair Market Value	Fair Market Value	Fair Market Value	Fair Market Value

LAWS AFFECTING DECEASED DONORS

ALL GIFTS	No Limits	No Limits	No Limits	No Limits

LAWS AFFECTING ORGANIZATION

INVESTMENT TAX	NO	NO	NO	NO
SELF-DEALING TAX	NO	NO	NO	NO
PAYOUT REQUIREMENT	NO	NO	NO	NO
TAX ON EXCESS HOLDINGS	NO	NO	NO	NO
JEOPARDY INVESTMENT TAX	NO	NO	NO	NO
TAX ON CERTAIN GRANTS**	NO	NO	NO	NO
PUBLIC SUPPORT TEST	YES	YES	NO	YES

*If the donor is subject to the alternative minimum tax, the value of the gift may be limited to cost.
*Effective December 22, 1987, political campaign expenditures by any public foundation are subject to penalty tax.

AGI = Adjusted Gross Income

PRIVATE FOUNDATIONS
EFFECTS OF SELECTED TAX LAWS

	INDEPENDENT FOUNDATION	COMPANY FOUNDATION	CONDUIT FOUNDATION	POOLED COMMON FUND	OPERATING FOUNDATION	EXEMPT OPERATING FOUNDATION
LAWS AFFECTING LIVING DONORS						
CASH GIFTS	30% AGI	10% Taxable Income (Corp.) 30% AGI (Ind.)	50% AGI	50% AGI	50% AGI	50% AGI
APPRECIATED PROPERTY	20% AGI	10% Taxable Income (Corp.) 20% AGI (Ind.)	30% AGI	30% AGI	30% AGI	30% AGI
CARRYOVER AVAILABLE	5 years	5 years	5 years	5 years	5 years	5 years
VALUE OF APPRECIATED PROPERTY*	FMV for publicly traded stock, otherwise cost only	FMV for publicly traded stock, otherwise cost only	Fair Market Value	Fair Market Value	Fair Market Value	Fair Market Value
LAWS AFFECTING DECEASED DONORS						
ALL GIFTS	No Limits	No Limits	No Limits	No Limits	No Limits	No Limits
LAWS AFFECTING ORGANIZATION						
INVESTMENT TAX	2% or 1%	2% or 1%	2% or 1%	2% or 1%	2% or 1%	No
SELF-DEALING TAX	YES	YES	YES	YES	YES	YES
PAYOUT REQUIREMENT	5% of Assets	5% of Assets	All Gifts plus Income	All Income	Varies	Varies
TAX ON EXCESS HOLDINGS	YES	YES	YES	YES	YES	YES
JEOPARDY INVESTMENT TAX	YES	YES	YES	YES	YES	YES
TAX ON CERTAIN GRANTS	YES	YES	YES	YES	YES	YES
PUBLIC SUPPORT TEST	NO	NO	NO	NO	NO	NO

*If the donor or the corporation is subject to the alternative minimum tax, the value of the gift may be limited to cost.

AGI = Adjusted Gross Income
FMV = Fair Market Value
Corp. = Corporation

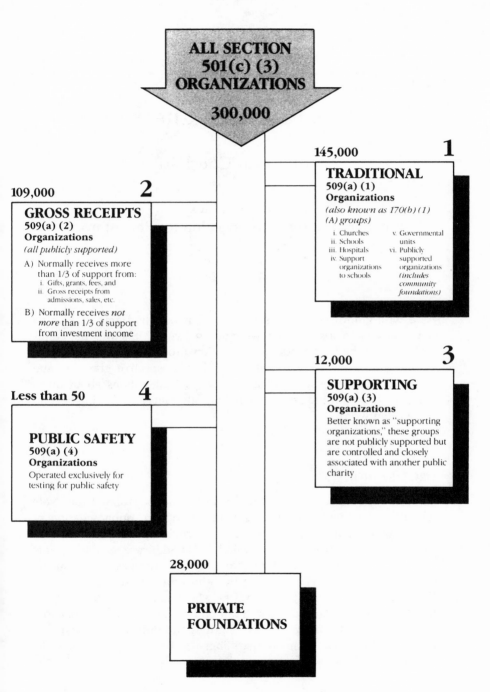

ALL SECTION 501(c) (3) ORGANIZATIONS

300,000

145,000 **1**

TRADITIONAL
509(a) (1)
Organizations
(also known as 170(b) (1) (A) groups)

i. Churches
ii. Schools
iii. Hospitals
iv. Support organizations to schools
v. Governmental units
vi. Publicly supported organizations *(includes community foundations)*

109,000 **2**

GROSS RECEIPTS
509(a) (2)
Organizations
(all publicly supported)

A) Normally receives more than 1/3 of support from:
i. Gifts, grants, fees, and
ii. Gross receipts from admissions, sales, etc.

B) Normally receives *not more* than 1/3 of support from investment income

12,000 **3**

SUPPORTING
509(a) (3)
Organizations
Better known as "supporting organizations," these groups are not publicly supported but are controlled and closely associated with another public charity

Less than 50 **4**

PUBLIC SAFETY
509(a) (4)
Organizations
Operated exclusively for testing for public safety

28,000

PRIVATE FOUNDATIONS

APPENDIX 5

Sample Site Visit Checklists

Site Visit Checklist

Ann Gralnek
Southern California Association for Philanthropy

As a wise grantmaker once said, "You can tell good grantmakers by how many pairs of shoes they wear out in a year." It is true that grantmaking goes beyond reading the written proposal. Grantmaking involves getting out of your office, visiting prospective grantees, and asking difficult questions. What follows are suggestions about questions you may want to ask when making site visits and delving beyond the written word.

ORGANIZATION

Be certain to receive a copy of the IRS determination/ruling letter. Note whether the organization is a private foundation, public charity, or operating foundation. If there has been a provisional ruling by the IRS, check when the advance ruling period ends and be prepared to assume expenditure responsibility until that time. If there has been a name change, find out why, and if the IRS and other appropriate agencies have been notified; and ascertain if tax status remains unaltered. Does the organization being considered fall under an umbrella organization, as is the case with many Catholic charities and university-related programs? If so, receive a copy of its ruling.

PERSONNEL

Do not shy away from subjective responses and have no hesitancy to meet and interview anyone associated with the organization. Be certain to meet with administrative, program support, and the governance personnel.

In meeting with *administrative/management* personnel, you want to get a sense of the leadership: how he or she relates to people and whether he or she is an effective communicator of ideas. Does the person reflect a proprietary interest or is the position viewed as a "job"? How long has the person been in the present position, and what is previous experience? Has there been a change in program emphasis with staff changes? What is the staff relationship and involvement with the governing board, and who is ultimately responsible for meeting the budget and for program expansion/curtailment? What is your sense of the person's ability to respond under pressure, to deal with critical problems as they arise?

Ask similar types of questions of *program staff*. Check for nuances, as goals may differ from the organization's plan. What is the size and makeup of support staff; is the organization overloaded with professionals, or is it understaffed for program efficiency? Look at the growth pattern of the staff, checking for signs of instability, such as a high turnover rate or sudden changes. What use is made of part-time and volunteer support? If there is a dependence on volunteers, is there any difficulty meeting program needs at certain times of the year? Who is responsible for the coordination of volunteer activities?

The *governance* of an organization is critical—the trustees/directors/members of the governing board. Try to get a sense of commitment; are rubber-stamp approvals given, or are needs thoroughly examined? Why are the members serving—to lend professional expertise, as a civic duty, because of personal experience in field, or at a friend's or colleague's request? Is there a strong or reluctant willingness to raise funds? How often does the board meet, and what is the attendance? Who are the pivotal members? If the board is set up by committee, what is the meeting/reporting/action procedure for each? What staff representation is present at board/committee meetings, and does staff have formal vote? Check for imbalance on the board, for example, too much professional expertise and no accounting or legal background. Note the possible discrepancy between a working board and an advisory one; too often the latter lends prestige without input. What is the board's relationship with staff? Is there awareness of problems or an unwillingness to get involved? What controls are placed on the administrator in regard to expenditure responsibility or extraordinary expense approval? Is board being well used?

FACILITY

As you enter and walk through the facility, be conscious of its location and its physical space. Is the *location* easily accessible to the organization's constituency, and is it able to attract and accommodate clients? What factors determined this specific location—availability, outreach, or drop-in services? Does the *physical space* appear to be up to code, and are there any signs of visible needed repairs/improvements/deferred maintenance? Is the space conducive to productivity, for example, adequate lighting, sufficient room? Are there limitations or observable deficiencies to meet program/service requirements? Is too much hardware visible, e.g., copier machine used exclusively, or unnecessary equipment? Do proper office systems/procedures appear to be in place, e.g., if a health care agency, are medical records confidential—is filing system accessible by too many or too few?

PROGRAM

What are the stated *goals and purposes* of the organization and does it appear they are being met? What constitutes "community"—local neighborhood, community-at-large, regional, or national direction? Has the organization bitten off more than it can chew? Has a lesser scale been tried and proven? Are there inconsistencies in goals? What are the *basic program components/services* that will always be provided, and what projects are dependent on funding? What *internal monitoring system* has been established to assess programmatic and administrative problems and successes? How does the organization judge its program performance? What is the frequency of the review process? Note that program accountability is often superficial while hours can be spent on fiscal control/reporting or vice versa. What means does the organization have to avoid duplication of services/programs with other community agencies? Is it unaware of similar work, or is there a willingness to coordinate efforts? What *documents* are available to look at, e.g., staff reports, board documents, administrative memoranda?

FINANCIAL

Look carefully at the *current operating budget* and assume the following built-in biases: underestimated expenses and overestimated income (particularly true of cultural organizations). Scrutinize *the basic* (hard dollar items): rent/mortgage; salary ranges; are they reasonable, too high or too low? Check for disproportionate costs and hidden costs, e.g., deferred maintenance. Look at program needs, *the flexible/soft* dollars: duplication with hard-core items; use of consultants and why; are travel expenses necessities, for whom and why? Where can budget cuts be made, if necessary? Who is ultimately responsible for balancing the budget? Get answers from both staff and board. How is the proper use of funds assured? In checking *income*, weigh percentages of government grants/private funding and other sources, such as fees for service or admission fees. Is there a dependence on a few major donors to sustain the organization, and is it desirable to alter such a skewed position; what are the methods of correcting same? Is public charity status jeopardized by a major long-term commitment? Ask for the audit of the previous year; if not available, look at previous budgets and have someone you rely on give an outside opinion.

All organizations should have a *master plan*, a three-to-five-year forecast. If not available in written form, it should be succinctly verbalized and the organization encouraged to develop a written statement. Does the plan simply include a built-in inflationary spiral, or does it reflect a realistic growth pattern? What increases are legitimate? Does the plan get reviewed periodically? How often and by whom? What changes have been made in plan during past year? Why? It's okay to dream, but working plans should be obtainable. If a claim toward self-support is made, it is achievable? Is growth in revenue-producing services consistent with program goals? If self-support is not attainable, what alternatives have been considered? What willingness is there to curtail services?

There are certain *pitfalls* to be reckoned. Does dependence on government grants cause cash-flow problems? Has government or private funding caused the organization to reorder its priorities to meet donors' criteria, that is, has the opportunity for funding influenced the organization's direction? Are reporting requirements burdensomely time-consuming?

American Honda Foundation
Site Visit Checklist

Background Material Requested: Date of Visit:

Background Material Received: Visitor/Title:

A) **ORGANIZATION NAME:** _____

   ADDRESS: _____

_____ Phone: _____

   IRS Ruling _____ Received _____

B) **NAMES/TITLES OF PERSONS INTERVIEWED:**
   1) Administrative Personnel

   2) Program Support Staff

   3) Governance

   Impressions on above (subjective analysis: e.g., ability to communicate; effectiveness of presentation)

C) **PROGRAM INFORMATION:**
   1) Geographic area served:
   2) Number of people served (unit of measurement; e.g., meals served daily, audience for performances; clients seen by medical staff)
   3) Staff: _____ full-time: _____ part-time: _____ volunteers
   4) Stated Goals and Purposes:
   5) Criteria Established to Meet Goals
      a) Internal review process

Organization: _____ Date of Visit: _____

D) **FACILITY ASSESSMENT:**
   1) Location:
      a) ability to attract and accommodate clients
      b) accessibility to constituency

SITE VISIT CHECKLIST (Continued)

2) Physical Space:
   a) conducive to productivity; observable deficiencies

E) **FINANCIAL:**
   1) Current Operating Budget
      a) Hard dollars (rent/salaries/utilities)
      b) Soft dollars (consultants/program/travel)
   2) Master Plan (3–5 year forecast; review process)
   3) Sources of funding (alternatives)
      a) government
      b) private
      c) earned
   4) Changes in budget from previous year (audited statement for prior fiscal year)

F) **SUMMARY OF FINDINGS:**
   1) Personnel
   2) Management Efficiency and Effectiveness
   3) Sense of Mission
   4) Priority Needs
   5) Ability to Survive/Grow

G. **RECOMMENDATION:**
   1) Suggest organization submit formal proposal
   2) Activities fall outside donor's interest areas
   3) Contact outside consultant for assessment
   4) Check community for alternative services available

APPENDIX 6

Sample Guidelines and Grant Application Forms

William and Flora Hewlett Foundation

ADVICE TO APPLICANTS

Because the foregoing program descriptions are brief and are under continuing review, the most efficient means of initial contact with the Hewlett Foundation is a letter of inquiry, addressed to the president. The letter should contain a brief statement of the applicant's need for funds and enough factual information to enable the staff to determine whether or not the application falls within the foundation's areas of preferred interest or warrants consideration as a special project. There is no fixed minimum or maximum with respect to the size of grants; applicants should provide a straightforward statement of their needs and aspirations for support, taking into account other possible sources of funding.

Letters of application will be briefly acknowledged upon their receipt. But because the foundation prefers to conduct its affairs with a small staff, a more detailed response will in some cases be delayed. Applicants who have not had a substantive reply after a reasonable period of time should feel free to make a follow-up inquiry.

The foundation groups performing arts recommendations by discipline for presentation to its board of directors. This allows the foundation to become familiar with the characteristics and needs in each field. It also assists in planning and in the consistent application of criteria. While the foundation does not expect to be able to adhere rigidly to the following schedule, it will make every effort to do so.

	Application Submitted by	Application Reviewed in
Music	January 1	April
Theatre	April 1	July
Dance	July 1	October
Film/video service organizations	July 1	October

The foundation recognizes that significant programs require time to demonstrate their value. It is, therefore, willing to consider proposals covering years of support. While the foundation will entertain specific projects in its areas of interest and will on occasion provide general support for organizations of special interest, it expects to work primarily through support of organizations active in its main programs. One exception is the regional grants program, under which the foundation will make some small grants for specific projects that meet an immediate community need. Like most foundations, the Hewlett Foundation is unwilling to assume responsibility for the long-term support of any organization or activity.

All inquiries are reviewed first by the relevant program officer. He or she will either (1) in consultation with the president decline those requests that seem unlikely to result in a project the foundation can support, (2) request further information if a decision cannot be made on the basis of the initial inquiry, or (3) present the request to the rest of the staff for discussion.

Applicants who receive a favorable response to their initial inquiry will be invited to submit a formal proposal. Special supporting materials may be requested in some cases, but normally the proposal should include:

1. a concise statement of the purpose of the request, its significance or uniqueness in relation to other work being done in the field, and the results sought.

2. a budget for the program, an indication of other prospective funding sources and the amount requested of each, and a statement of the sponsoring organization's total budget and financial position. Applicants should indicate how they would continue a successful program once support from the Hewlett Foundation ceases.

3. the identity and qualifications of the key personnel to be involved.

4. a list of the members of the governing body.

5. evidence of tax-exempt status.

6. a statement to the effect that the proposal has been reviewed by the applicant's governing body and specifically approved for submission to the William and Flora Hewlett Foundation.

Normally the foundation will not consider for support grants or loans to individuals, grants for basic research, capital construction funds, grants in the medical or health-related fields, or general fundraising drives. It will not make grants intended directly or indirectly to support candidates for political office or to influence legislation.

Grants must be approved by the board of directors, which meets quarterly. Meeting dates are available upon request, but applicants should realize that even proposals that are to be recommended for board approval cannot in every case be reviewed at the first meeting following their receipt. All inquiries and proposals are reported to the board, including those that are declined at the staff level.

Jessie Ball duPont Fund

Mission

Through grants to the eligible institutions, the Jessie Ball duPont Fund seeks to help solve the needs of today's society; especially in the South, and to anticipate emerging issues that may become major concerns in the future.

During her lifetime, Mrs. duPont concentrated a majority of her philanthropy in the South. Carrying on the work of Mrs. duPont, the fund seeks to help the South—with special emphasis in the states of Florida, Virginia, and Delaware where she and Mr. duPont lived—to prepare for its new demographics, its new economic opportunities, and its new national and international leadership roles. Most importantly, the fund wishes to accomplish its mission by accommodating—even encouraging—necessary changes in the region, while seeking to preserve and reinforce features of the South that make it so attractive to those who are native born as well as to its newest immigrants.

The fund can accomplish its mission only through the creativity, skill, and talent of its eligible institutions. The fund hopes that, by working closely with these institutions as partners, it will be able to use its substantial but finite resources to meet society's challenges. While requests always far exceed the funds available, the trustees hope that through attention to a number of articulated priorities and criteria, the grants will make a significant difference.

Objectives

The trustees of the Jessie Ball duPont Fund, in selecting grants that work toward the fund's mission, will pursue the objectives listed below:

- To enable individuals to reach their full potential in today's society and to enable society to fulfill its obligations to its members.
- To support projects that are not adequately funded by other sources.
- To assist and encourage eligible institutions to work with other organizations to address common problems and achieve common goals.

While no single proposal will be able to accomplish all of these objectives, they are general guidelines that reflect Mrs. duPont's interests and the values of the fund.

Further, the trustees reaffirm two objectives of the fund that reflect Mrs. duPont's philanthropic interests and those of the original trustees:

- To enable the eligible institutions to generate additional resources by attracting a broad constituency of donors and volunteer participation.
- To preserve and use our historical heritage.

APPLICATION FORM

Jessie Ball duPont Fund
225 Water Street, Suite 1200
Jacksonville, FL 32202-5176
(904) 353–0890

In order for a grant request to be considered by the Jessie Ball duPont Fund, the applying organization must be eligible by having received a contribution from Mrs. duPont during any of the five calendar years ending December 31, 1964. Proof of eligibility is determined by the fund from examination of Mrs. duPont's personal or tax records or by the applicant presenting written verifiable evidence or a tax record of a contribution during that period.

The trustees of the Jessie Ball duPont Fund meet every other month —January, March, May, July, September, and November—to consider grant applications. In order for one to be considered for a grant, this completed form and the following materials must be submitted:

This application form, completed in all sections, including the required signature.

A proposal of no longer than five pages describing the proposed program as follows:

Need for the program
Objectives and purposes of the program
Activities to achieve the objectives and purposes
Description of the applying eligible organization
Qualifications of the staff of the program
Location and estimated duration of the program
Evaluation plan to determine the results of the program

A budget of one page, identifying the projected expenses and income of the program.

The most recent audit of the eligible institution, including the balance sheet and income statement, if such audits are made.

A list of the members of the governing board of the eligible institution.

Optional materials may be submitted to supplement the application.

About the Applicant

All information on this page pertains to the eligible institution that is applying for the grant and accepting fiscal responsibility for any funds received.

Name _____

Address _____

_____

Telephone _____

Chief administrative officer _____

Organization Summary:

In the space provided, give a short statement of the purpose, size and history of the applying organization.

Signature of Authorized Person:

My signature certifies that the organization named above currently has tax-exemption under the Internal Revenue Service Code section 150(c)(3) and is classified as "not a private foundation" as defined under section 509(a).

My signature is made as one who is authorized to do so on behalf of the applying organization.

_____

Approval of Board Chairman or Executive Officer

_____

Title   Date

About the Program

All information on this page pertains to the program for which funding is requested.

General Information:

Program Title _____

Beginning and ending dates _____

Program Director's Name _____

   Title _____

   Address _____

   Telephone _____

Total Budget for Program $_____

Amount Requested of the Fund $_____

Potential Funding:

What funds from other private or public sources have been received or are under consideration for this program?

   Received   Under Consideration

Future Funding:

If the program is to continue beyond the grant period, what are the plans for funding the program upon expenditure of this grant?

Abelard Foundation:
A Guide to Grantmaking

PURPOSE

The Abelard Foundation's Board of Directors is committed to social change activities that

- expand and protect civil liberties and civil and human rights;
- increase opportunities for the poor, the disenfranchised, and people of color; and
- enhance and expand community involvement in, and control over, economic and environmental decisions affecting members of the community.

The organizations that Abelard supports use a broad range of tools to accomplish social change as they work toward the goal of a more democratic, just, and equitable society. These tools may include community and grassroots organizing, action research, and advocacy. Whatever the choice of tools, the foundation expects that the organization will use them as part of a larger strategy and as aids in developing local leadership and strengthening the skills of its constituency.

The foundation seeks to support groups whose work reflects awareness of broader policy issues, and which demonstrate an understanding of the implications those issues have for the future and for other communities.

GUIDELINES

The Abelard West office makes grants in Hawaii, California, the Pacific Northwest states, the Rocky Mountain states, and the Southwest. Abelard's East Coast office supports urban projects in New York City and rural-based efforts along the eastern seaboard and into the South.

Grant requests should be sent to:

Abelard Foundation/Common Counsel
2530 San Pablo Ave.
Suite B
Berkeley, CA 94702
(415) 644-1904

Types of Grants. Most Abelard grants are small ($5,000–$7,000), reflecting the foundation's limited budget, and may be project or general support grants. The foundation is interested in new projects or organizations addressing issues that traditional philanthropic sources might avoid. By supporting model efforts that can be duplicated elsewhere, and which offer the potential for broader impact, we encourage grantees to use Abelard dollars as leverage in gaining additional support.

Abelard also looks for organizations producing self-help tools that can be distributed to and used by others, or which provide technical assistance to improve the effectiveness of other nonprofits and Abelard grantees.

Technical Assistance. The board of directors believes that its responsibilities to its grantees do not end once a grant has been made. The board has directed foundation staff to be available, when appropriate, to grantees for assistance in their other fundraising and organizational development efforts.

Exclusions. The Abelard Foundation receives many more proposals than it can fund. The board of directors has concluded that it does not choose to support:

- social service programs offering on-going or direct delivery of service;
- medical, educational, or cultural institutions;
- capital expenditure, construction, or renovation programs;
- programs undertaken at government initiative; or
- scholarship funds or other aids to individuals.

Projects whose purpose is primarily to inform in a general way or to study or research an issue for purposes of public education, and with little or no emphasis on policy change or implementation, do not fall within Abelard's funding guidelines. Conferences are supported only when closely related to the initiation of new programs or organizations.

APPLICATION PROCEDURE

Applicants for funding may submit a full proposal or a summary of their request. Letters of inquiry are not necessary. The foundation will acknowledge receipt of all proposals.

Format/Contents. Grant proposals should include the following:

- a cover letter that summarizes the background and purposes of the organization requesting funds, and how the funds will be used;

- a project narrative and description that explains the problem or issue the project addresses, how the project will respond to or resolve that problem, and why the strategy will be effective;
- resumés of people who will do the work;
- a project schedule;
- a detailed budget for the specific project, as well as for the sponsoring organization, if the project is part of a larger, ongoing effort;
- information on fundraising strategy, including the status of current requests and past sources of funding;
- documentation of the project's federal tax-exempt status; and
- a list of board members and other references familiar with the organization's work.

Application Dates. Abelard board meetings are held four times each year, in the months of February, May, August, and November. There are no application deadlines and the foundation will accept proposals on an ongoing basis. The board has authorized the foundation staff to limit review of proposals in any application period to the first one hundred received. Additional proposals will be deferred to the next grant cycle. Applicants are encouraged to submit their materials at least two months before each board meeting to assure that they fall within that "first hundred" limit and that the review process is concluded well before the board meeting.

Proposal Review and Evaluation. Foundation staff will conduct an initial screening of all proposals to determine which fall within Abelard's areas of interest. Organizations whose proposals do not meet these initial criteria will be notified of that decision within eight weeks of the receipt of their proposal.

Proposals that do meet the initial criteria will be evaluated more thoroughly, and staff may request additional information. A site visit or meeting may be scheduled.

The board of directors will review the final candidates for funding. The board will select a limited number of proposals for funding that address most effectively the issues to which the board has given priority.

Renewals. Abelard grantees may apply for renewed funding at the end of their grant year. The foundation does not make multi-year grants, but the board will consider renewal requests for up to three years.

Reporting Requirements. Abelard grantees are required to submit six-month and one-year reports. Renewal requests will be considered only if both reports have been made on a timely basis.

BACKGROUND

Abelard is a small family foundation incorporated in 1958. The foundation's annual grantmaking budget is approximately $280,000. Abelard was located initially in New York City.

In 1978, Abelard opened a West Coast office, seeking to become more active in a region where fewer foundation dollars are available. Abelard now distributes two-thirds of its annual budget through the West Coast office.

The Prospect Hill Foundation

Application Guidelines 1989–90

The Prospect Hill Foundation is a private foundation established in New York in 1960 by William S. Beinecke, the retired chairman of the Sperry and Hutchinson Company. In 1983, the Prospect Hill Foundation merged with the Frederick W. Beinecke Fund, which had been established by the will of William S. Beinecke's father and was later augmented by the will of Carrie Sperry Beinecke, his mother.
Directors and officers are:

William S. Beinecke, Director and President

Elizabeth G. Beinecke, Director and Vice President

John B. Beinecke, Director and Vice President

Frederick W. Beinecke, Director

Frances Beinecke Elston, Director

Sarah Beinecke Richardson, Director

Constance Eiseman, Secretary

Michael A. Yesko, Treasurer

Foundation programs are managed by:

Constance Eiseman, Executive Director

Nettie Foskett, Administrator

The December 31, 1989 asset value of the Prospect Hill Foundation was $39,266,772. Grants paid during the twelve-month period ending December 31, 1989, totaled $1,398,540. Grants paid during the six-month period ending June 30, 1990, totaled $836,000. An employees' matching contributions program made available an additional $97,770 and $61,162, respectively, during those periods.

GRANTS PROGRAM

The Prospect Hill Foundation has a broad range of philanthropic interests. During the eighteen-month period represented by this report, grants were made to organizations active in environmental conservation, nuclear weapons control, and population planning in Latin America, as well as selected social service, arts, cultural, and educational institutions. The directors intend to maintain this breadth of activity in the coming year.

Environmental Conservation

The foundation's environmental grantmaking promotes the conservation of natural resources and environmental quality. Grants are made primarily to organizations that act as catalysts in the protection of environmentally significant public and private lands and advocate improved environmental quality. We encourage proposals that:

- offer strategies for the preservation of public and private lands.
- strengthen public policies for environmental protection.

Nuclear Weapons Control

The foundation seeks through its grants relating to nuclear weapons control to limit reliance on and availability of nuclear weapons, and to enhance the sensitivity of national leaders to their collective responsibility to assure a habitable world. We seek proposals that:

- implement strategies for limiting the proliferation of nuclear weapons, nuclear weapons materials, and the capacity to manufacture nuclear weapons.
- lead to commitments among national leaders to limit or reduce nuclear weapons arsenals.

Population

Concern about unplanned population growth in relation to natural resource availability, food supply, and an opportunity for a satisfying and healthy life for all underlies our giving for population planning. We invite proposals targeting Latin American countries that:

- encourage access to a full range of family planning services.
- promote public understanding of the issues and problems resulting from unplanned pregnancies.
- bring the issues and problems resulting from restrictive family planning policies before those who make and shape policy.
- improve the status of women through increased education and employment strategies.

Youth and Social Services

The directors have allocated a small portion of foundation resources for projects (primarily in the New York area) that provide unique or highly innovative solutions to widely recognized social problems.

Arts, Cultural, and Educational Institutions

Major commitments have been made to institutions already identified by the directors and only a limited number of new grant requests from arts, cultural, and educational institutions receive favorable response. *Applications for such grants should be made only upon invitation.*

APPLICATION REQUIREMENTS AND REVIEW PROCESS

Applicants may submit grant requests to the Executive Director at any time of year. The request should be in the form of a letter (three pages maximum) that summarizes the applicant organization's history and goals; the project for which funding is sought; and the contribution of the project to other work in the field and/or to the organization's own development. In addition, requests should include the organization's total (current and proposed) budget and staff size; project budget; potential sources of project support and a list of the organization's board of directors. The foundation favors project support over general support requests. *Please submit this information in duplicate.*

All material is reviewed by the Executive Director and one or more members of the Board of Directors. Response is generally provided within four weeks. If there is interest in the proposal, more detailed information is normally required including line-item organizational and project income and expense budgets; a list of committed and prospective sources of support for the project; a timetable for completion of the project; qualifications of key personnel involved with the project; a list of other organizations involved in similar projects with a description of how the proposed program is different from or complementary to those efforts; a list of the project's expected result and criteria the applicant wishes the foundation to apply when evaluating the completed projects; the IRS letter determining 501(c)(3) tax status; the most recent audited statement; and the most recent IRS 990 form.

The Prospect Hill Foundation directors meet three to four times annually. Whenever possible, an applicant will be visited by a representative of the foundation before it finally acts on a proposal.

At the termination of the grant year, a frank project assessment in narrative form and a financial report are required. In some instances, interim reports will be requested.

Restrictions

The foundation does not consider grants for individuals, scholarly research, or sectarian religious activities.

Miscellaneous Sample Forms

Sample Request for Proposals

The Meyer Memorial Trust

ANNOUNCING THE SMALL GRANTS PROGRAM

The trust in the summer of 1988 initiated the Small Grants Program. This program recognizes the need in the philanthropic sector to provide assistance to a larger number of worthy organizations with requests for small projects.

Background

In its other programs, the trust tends to provide multiyear grants for relatively sophisticated projects that offer the promise of large-scale, significant results. In this context, small requests for support are seldom successful. In the Small Grants Program, the trust will use different criteria and simpler procedures in selecting grant recipients.

Purpose

The Small Grants Program will provide assistance to a wide variety of worthwhile organizations for small projects that are limited in scope but that are valuable and important, especially to the applicant organization and its immediate community. One of the considerations in reviewing these requests will be how significant the proposed project is for the applicant organization. Because of this, it is not expected that many of these grants will go to large organizations, although such applicants will not be automatically excluded. An organization that is the recipient of a grant under another trust program is eligible to apply, but not for an activity related to the previous grant.

Grant Amounts

Grants will range from a minimum of $500 to a maximum of $8,000. Proposals submitted under this program will compete only with other small grant requests. Every three months, the trust will award a total of approximately $125,000 to organizations selected from the applications received in that quarter.

Geographic Scope

This program is limited to tax-exempt organizations in Oregon and that part of Washington located in the greater Portland metropolitan area.

Application Procedures

The trust's Grant Application Guidelines publication describes how to submit a small grant request, and it also contains a Grant Application Cover Sheet that must accompany all proposals to the trust. A copy of this publication may be obtained by writing or calling the trust office.

There are four application deadlines a year: January 15, April 15, July 15, and October 15. A proposal should not be submitted more than one month prior to a deadline. To be considered for a particular quarter, a proposal must be postmarked no later than the deadline date.

Applicants will be notified of the decision on their proposal within two–three months after each deadline. An organization should not re-submit a declined proposal for at least twelve months, but a different proposal may be submitted prior to that time.

Discussions with trust staff members about potential proposals under this program will not be possible. Only written proposals will be considered.

The Meyer Memorial Trust
1515 S.W. Fifth Avenue, Suite 500
Portland, OR 97201
(503) 228-5512

The Robert Wood Johnson Foundation

CALL FOR APPLICATIONS: PROGRAM FOR FACULTY FELLOWSHIPS IN HEALTH CARE FINANCE 1991

The Robert Wood Johnson Foundation's Program for Faculty Fellowships in Health Care Finance was established in 1984 to help meet the growing need for university faculty prepared to teach and conduct research in this important field. The program is designed to permit selected faculty committed to academic careers in health care finance and administration to gain firsthand and in-depth knowledge of this rapidly changing area. This program provides a unique opportunity for faculty and their institutions to assume leadership roles in the teaching and formulation of policy around an issue central to our health care system.

During the past 20 years, the U.S. health care system has become increasingly complex. This growing complexity has affected the financing of the system, which is critical to such basic issues as who provides care, where it is provided, what incentives exist, and who receives services.

The financing system itself has grown and changed. It has become a complex, fragmented mix of private and public mechanisms, each with its own rules, limitations and exclusions. The system is increasingly confusing, and the extent and rapidity of changes that have taken place have created a number of problems:

(1) Many who are asked to administer this changing system and to help develop public and private financing policy for the future are not equipped to carry out these tasks. This includes both those who manage health care programs and those in government and private industry who set policy. Often they have neither sufficient training in the basics of health care financing nor the analytic tools necessary to develop new policy approaches.

(2) Institutions that provide such training—primarily through health administration, health policy, and public administration programs—may not have sufficient faculty or the appropriate curricula to prepare these individuals adequately. Often health care finance is taught by those whose background is related—such as health policy research, account, business, or public administration—but whose detailed knowledge of health care financing is lacking.

Because the problems with the current financing system are unlikely to be resolved easily, the demand for people—in both policy and managerial positions—with competence in health care finance will continue, as will the need for competent university faculty to train these leaders. The Robert Wood Johnson Foundation's Program for Faculty Fellowships in Health Care Finance is intended to address these requirements and to help create a group of faculty members who not only can teach and do research with greater knowledge of the field, but also can serve as leaders both in their own institutions and throughout the academic world, helping to improve curricula and the level of knowledge about health care financing.

The Program

Under the Program for Faculty Fellowships in Health Care Finance, up to six candidates will be selected for 30-month fellowships in 1991. Successful candidates will generally, but not necessarily, already have a faculty appointment, even if such appointment does not begin until after the fellowship period. Such appointments must be in university programs and departments where there is a desire to develop a strong focus on health care finance.

The Fellowship has three parts:

(1) The Educational Component. Beginning in September of the fellowship year, an intensive four-month educational program will be conducted at The Johns Hopkins Medical Institutions. The educational component provides fellows with the opportunity for informal seminars with national leaders in health care finance and the training necessary to pursue an academic career focused on health care finance, including exploring future research interests in this area.

The educational program provides an overview of current issues and problems in health care finance and instruction in the fundamental disciplines and technical skills bearing on the field (e.g., accounting, economics, statistics, public finance, epidemiology, actuarial science, case-mix measurement, and hospital rate setting). The educational program also offers in-depth study of the finance dimensions of specific topics (e.g., Medicare, Medicaid, regulation and competition in the health sector, antitrust, medical economics, new technology, alternative delivery systems, uncompensated care, and capital) and an exploration of future options. Leading experts in health finance and related fields serve as faculty. A detailed outline of the program is available upon request.

In addition, fellows will participate in research with faculty mentors from The Johns Hopkins Medical Institutions. Time is allotted for both individual and collaborative research on health finance issues. Assistance will be available to the fellows in both carrying out and preparing publishable articles.

(2) The Placement Component. In January of the fellowship year, fellows begin an eight-month placement in a major private or public health care financing organization, medical center, or alternative delivery system. Fellows work closely with that institution's senior officials. The placement experience affords the opportunity for each fellow to explore the impact of major health care financing changes in depth and to develop a related research project.

Fellows select their placement sites in consultation with the program director. Organizations that have been among the placement sites for previous fellows range from private insurers and the Health Care Financing Administration to major health care providers. However, fellows are free to arrange other placements with the approval of the program director. During the eight-month placement, fellows convene to discuss their experiences and research plans.

(3) The Research Component. Grants of up to $15,000 may be made for eighteen months following placement to support completion of the research project—generally at the fellow's home institution. The research project must focus on scientific or policy questions related to changes occurring in health care finance.

Foundation financial support during this phase of the program is contingent upon approval of the fellow's research plan by the program's national advisory committee, the program director, and foundation staff.

All fellows are expected to complete a major research report suitable for publication. The program staff will provide assistance in achieving this goal. In addition, fellows will present their findings at an annual meeting of the National Advisory Committee.

Stipends and Benefits

Stipends and benefits are provided by the foundation through grants to the fellows' home institutions. During the first year of their fellowship, fellows are paid annual stipends equal to their base salaries prior to entering the program, up to $46,300. (Under special circumstances, compensation greater than base salary may be negotiated to avoid unreasonable hardships resulting from higher costs of living in the Baltimore area. In no case, however, will stipends exceed $46,300.) In addition to the stipend, the fellows' existing fringe benefit levels are maintained. Sponsoring institutions may supplement either or both sums. As noted previously, in the third component of the program, up to $15,000 will be provided to fellows for approved research projects carried out at their home institutions during an 18-month period.

Fellows are reimbursed for transportation, temporary living expenses, and moving expenses, within specified limits. Specific information on these matters is available from the program director.

Program Direction

The Robert Wood Johnson Foundation's Program for Faculty Fellowships in Health Care Finance is directed by Susan D. Horn, PhD, professor in the Department of Health Policy and Management at The Johns Hopkins Medical Institutions. June M. Buckle, ScD, RN, is the deputy director. At the foundation, the responsible officer is Jeffrey C. Merrill, vice president and Diane Montagne, program assistant. A National Advisory Committee assists in the review of applicants and the conduct of the program.

Eligibility and Application Procedures

The Program for Faculty Fellowships in Health Care Finance is designed for university faculty members with a firm commitment to teaching and research in health care finance. The program is open to faculty members in graduate programs with a health finance and policy focus—in schools of public health, health administration, public administration, public policy, law, business, political science, economics, medicine, or nursing, where health care financing is an integral part of the department's teaching and research.

Individuals interested in applying should contact the program director's office to obtain an application packet. Members of the program staff are available to discuss all aspects of the program. All completed applications and supporting materials must be submitted to the director of the program no later than September 28, 1990. Finalists will be invited to Baltimore on November 7–8, 1990, at the expense of the program, to be interviewed by the National Advisory Committee. The committee's recommendations regarding candidates will be made soon after completion of these interviews. Final decisions on recommending candidates to the foundation's board of trustees will be made by foundation staff. All awards are made by the trustees.

People who currently do not hold a faculty position may apply if they have obtained an academic appointment to begin immediately following the fellowship experience. However, they must have already had experience in academic settings related to teaching or research in health care policy or administration.

Applicants will be considered on the basis of past academic and other professional achievements, as well as their potential for growth and leadership in the academic world. If selected as semifinalists, candidates will be asked to provide letters of recommendation and have the support of their institutions, as demonstrated by evidence of appointment to a faculty position upon completion of the first year of the fellowship and by a written indication of the school's commitment to teaching and research in this area.

Inquiries

All questions and correspondence concerning the program should be directed to:

Susan D. Horn, Ph.D.
Director, Program for Faculty Fellowships in Health Care
The Johns Hopkins University
624 North Broadway, Hampton House 354
Baltimore, MD 21205
(301)955-6891 or 955-3157

Sample Grant Denial Letters

We acknowledge receipt of your recent inquiry concerning an application for a grant from the —— Foundation.

The Foundation limits its interest to —— County and —— County, New York. Therefore, we are sorry to advise you that we are not in a position to entertain your request for funds.

Sincerely yours,

Jane Doe
President

Dear Applicant:

Thank you for your recent interest in the —— Foundation.

We would like to respond affirmatively to all grant requests coming to the foundation. As you know, we receive far more proposals than can possibly be funded. Therefore, we must identify geographic as well as programmatic areas of concern.

The —— Foundation devotes its resources to the metropolitan area of ——. We are interested in the broad fields of health, education and children. We regret to inform you that your request for assistance is outside the geographical and/or programmatical concerns of the foundation.

While the foundation cannot be of assistance to you at this time, we do wish you every success in securing the necessary funds from other sources.

Sincerely,

Jane Doe
Executive Director

Date

Proposal Name:
Purpose:
Amount requested:

Name
Title
Address
City, State, Zip

Dear _____:

I am very sorry to inform you that the Trustees of the —— Foundation, at their quarterly board meeting on _____, _____, did not approve your grant request for the above-mentioned purpose.

We receive requests for many more dollars than are available, and, therefore, are not able to fund all requests.

We wish you success in your project as you seek other avenues of funding. (If applicable, suggest other sources)

Sincerely,

Jane Doe
Executive Director

cc: Board Chair
    Grants Committee Chair
    Investigating Grants Committee Member

Dear _____:

This will acknowledge your letter of _____ in which you requested funding for _____ (program) _____.

The foundation devotes its resources to the metropolitan area of _____. We regret to inform you that your request for assistance is outside the geographical area of the foundation's concern.

I am sorry we cannot be of assistance to you.

Sincerely,

Dear:

We have reviewed your (*date*) letter (*and enclosures*) through which you request (*statement*).

Although we would like to respond affirmatively to all requests coming to the foundation, we receive far more proposals than can possibly be funded. Therefore, we must identify specific areas within the broad fields in health, education, and agriculture and confine our grantmaking activities accordingly. This means that many important projects, such as yours, cannot be aided by the foundation. Enclosed is an informational statement that describes the types of programs we are currently aiding.

Although the foundation cannot be of assistance, we do wish you every success in securing the necessary funds from other sources.

Sincerely,

Request for Further Information

Dear Prospective Donee:

Thank you for your interest in the ―― Foundation. Your grant application has been received.

_____ Your application is complete and will be presented at our next board meeting, _____

_____ Your application is incomplete and the foundation requests the following:

      _____ A copy of the IRS ruling showing the tax-exempt, nonprofit status of your organization.

      _____ A list of your board of directors.

      _____ A complete budget for the project described.

      _____ The current annual operating budget of your organization.

      _____ An audited financial statement of the previous year's activities.

      _____ The latest copy of your 990 report (if you file one).

      _____ Seven additional copies of the ―― Foundation Charitable Grant Application Form.

_____ Other: _____

_____

_____

No information regarding the foundation's decision on your request can be released until three weeks after the foundation's board meeting. Thank you for your cooperation and effort in this matter.

Sincerely,

Jane Doe
Executive Director

Sample Grant Acceptance Letter

Name   Date
Organization
Address
City, State, Zip   Grant Number

Dear —— :

I am pleased to inform you that the —— Foundation has approved a grant of $_____ to _____ for a survey of social investing activities of private and corporate foundations, and publication of reports based on the survey. This grant is being made in response to your letter to Jane Doe dated _____.

These terms apply to your organization's use of the foundation's grant:

Grant funds will be available over a _____-month period beginning _____.

Payment of the grant funds will be made in full after receipt by the secretary of the foundation of a countersigned copy of this letter. To facilitate your receipt of the payment check, please indicate on the countersigned copy the name of the official of your organization to whom the check is to be sent.

Under United States law, the —— Foundation grant funds may be expended only for charitable, scientific, literary, or educational purposes. This grant is made only for the purposes stated in this letter and the document referenced earlier, and it is understood that these grant funds will be used for such purposes substantially in accordance with the attached approved budget. It is also understood that no substantial variances will be made from the budget without the foundation's prior approval in writing. Any grant funds not expended or committed for the purposes of the grant, or within the period stated earlier, will be returned to the foundation.

A written report signed by an appropriate officer of your organization is to be furnished to the secretary of the foundation at the end of the grant period. The report should contain: (1) a narrative account of what was accomplished by the expenditure of funds, including a description of progress made toward achieving the goals of the grant; (2) a financial accounting, according to the line-item categories of the attached approved budget, which has been certified correct by the responsible financial official of your organization; and (3) copies of any publications resulting from the grant that have appeared or are in preparation. It is expected that these narrative and financial accountings will be submitted as a single report.

In the application of its resources to serve the public interest, the foundation gives high priority to the realization of equality of opportunity for all members of society. Accordingly, it is the foundation's expectation that in carrying out this grant, your organization will take appropriate affirmative action steps with respect to women and disadvantaged minorities.

The foundation may monitor and conduct a review of operations under this grant, which may include a visit from foundation personnel to observe your program, discuss the program and finances with your personnel, and review financial and other records and materials connected with the activities financed by the grant.

The foundation will include information on this grant in its periodic public reports. The foundation may also refer to the grant in a press release, in which a copy would be sent to you in advance. If you wish to make your own press announcement, please consult with the foundation's Office of Reports.

If this letter and the attached budget correctly set forth your understanding of the terms of this grant, will you please indicate your organization's agreement to such terms by having the enclosed copy of this letter countersigned by an appropriate officer of your organization and returned to the secretary of the foundation. It is also understood that by countersigning this letter, your organization confirms that there has been no change in its qualification as an organization exempt from income taxation pursuant to Section 510(c)(3) of the Internal Revenue Service Code or its classification as not a private foundation. If any change occurs, please notify the foundation.

In all correspondence concerning this grant, reference should be made to the grant number designated on the first page of this letter.

On behalf of the foundation, may I extend every good wish for the success of this endeavor.

Sincerely,

Jane Doe
Assistant Secretary

Attachments
ACCEPTED AND AGREED:
Organization

By: _____
Title: _____
Date: _____

Payment check should be directed to: _____

(name and title)

_____

(address)

_____

Grant Contract

Organization: _____

Address: _____ Telephone: _____

_____

Project Director:_____

Address: _____ Telephone: _____

_____

Amount of Grant: _____

Date of Payment: _____

Term of Grant: From _____ to _____

Program Title: _____

Description:

The following terms are agreed upon as conditions for this grant:

1. The tax-exempt status verified in the proposal is still valid; any changes in the organization that could lead to a change in the status will be reported to —— Foundation immediately.
2. The funds will be used by the above-named organization solely for the purposes described.
3. The organization will keep and maintain records of expenditures adequate to check the use of the grant readily. Semiannual reports concerning budget, personnel, and program developments will be completed and returned to —— Foundation. The foundation will send report forms well in advance of their due date.
4. The organization will repay, upon demand, to —— Foundation the amount of the grant if any condition of the contract is not upheld.

5. The organization will send to the foundation copies of any printed publicity regarding the awarding of the grant or the program supported by the grant; the organization may, if it chooses, refer to —— Foundation's support in any such publicity.

6. The following special terms will be observed:

The terms of this contract are accepted by _____

on behalf of _____ and _____
(Organization)

_____ for the
—— Foundation.

_____
(Date)

Program-Related Investments

Excerpt from "Many Happy Returns"

by Melinda Marble

With the help of the Indianapolis Foundation, a center for senior citizens moves into a new building; now it can expand and consolidate services under one roof. In Mississippi, the Phil Hardin Foundation helps to create a vitally needed student loan fund. And in six inner-city neighborhoods around the country, Aetna provides financial and technical assistance to grass roots organizations that implement housing development projects.

Those initiatives have the ring of successful grants—the kind displayed proudly in annual reports. In fact, however, all three were financed not by grants but by program-related investments. The initiatives represent the range of imaginative ways in which the device is currently used by funders.

Just what is a program-related investment? The term is heard frequently in grantmaking circles nowadays—among the initiated, by the acronym "PRI." The PRI has arguably been around since Benjamin Franklin established loan funds for young artisans in Philadelphia and Boston; in the early 1900s, the Russell Sage Foundation and a few others invested in housing development. Basically, however, the practice has become popular only in the past two decades. The Tax Reform Act of 1969 encouraged it but imposed limits on participating foundations.

There is a range and level of activity among funders. While the perception is often that PRIs have been made only by large national foundations—and then usually for ambitious, expensive housing and community development projects—in fact, social investment is not the

Source: *Foundation News*, July/August 1989.

exclusive province of the mighty. PRIs have been made by foundations with endowments of less than $2 million. Corporations with giving programs rather than foundations are also becoming involved.

PRIs range in size from a few thousand dollars to investments of millions. Under the Tax Reform Act, the investment must have a social purpose, that is, it must seek to accomplish religious, charitable, scientific, literary, or educational objectives; it must not have as its goal income production or property appreciation.

While funds disbursed through PRIs are counted against a foundation's payout requirement, PRI payments increase the requirement by increasing the foundation's asset base.

Loans are the most common form of PRIs. Other practitioners prefer loan guarantees or lines of credit, which often encourage traditional financial institutions to get involved in a project. Equity investments are another option.

For any type of PRI, the funder needs to consider standard questions: How much risk is acceptable? Will social investment funds come from endowment or the grantmaking budget? Should investments be made directly or through intermediaries?

Practitioners of program-related investments say that it will never supplant grantmaking as the primary activity of funders. They view it as an addition to tool kit of philanthropy, a broadening and extension of foundation work.

PRI advocates argue, too, that a willingness to look beyond grantmaking provides many benefits:

- enlarging a funder's overall resources for program initiatives by allowing participation in projects of a size that would not be fundable from the annual grants budget;
- recycling charitable funds so they can be reused for new projects;
- leveraging funds from traditional financial institutions and government sources that might not otherwise be forthcoming; and
- with regard to social problems, encouraging the development of approaches that to a significant extent are self-supporting and self-sustaining.

PRIs have been used in virtually every program area of interest to foundations, from generating jobs to supporting the arts. The key word in the term is *program:* The funders are not necessarily interested in PRI as a technique in itself.

For growing numbers of private foundations, PRI has become a standard option, one of several potential forms of support for a project. The

Blandin Foundation, which in the past eight years made 14 PRIs rang-
ing from $45,000 to $2 million, prefers to make a loan whenever there
is the potential for repayment. Says the foundation's president, Paul
Olson, "I don't believe in pure altruistic giving. We're usually helping
people help themselves."

John Kostishack, executive director of the Otto Bremer Foundation,
says Bremer makes PRIs because it "saw a number of instances where
organizations needed financing, but they had the potential to recover
the money and repay the foundation. To make a grant in that situation
when we have so many good requests coming in seemed a waste."

The Phil Hardin Foundation never intended to start a PRI "pro-
gram," but because of a peculiar set of circumstances, President
Thomas R. Ward secured board approval to establish the Mississippi
Private College Loan Program, administered by Millsaps College.

Hardin loaned the college $500,000 at 4 percent annual interest for
10 years to make federally guaranteed loans. In the process, the college
received federal interest subsidy, which it used to pay the administrative expenses of the loan programs. The successful experience led the
foundation to undertake a second PRI involving a faculty development
endowment at Mississippi College.

In order to stimulate economic development, some private foundations use PRIs to make loans or investments in business ventures in
low-income or minority communities. The Mary Reynolds Babcock
Foundation has made several loans to cooperative worker-owned business in rural North Carolina. One $50,000, five-year loan helped a
worker-owned garment factory—located in one of the poorest counties
in the United States—move from subcontracting to direct contracting
with chains such as Sears and K-Mart. The co-op's employment rolls
rose from 25 to 60.

Some private foundations have used PRIs on "once-in-a-lifetime"
occasions, when a project is extremely compelling but requires a commitment that would strain the resources of the grants budget. A good
example follows: the Peter Kiewit Foundation's $10.5-million PRI and
$2-million grant to revitalize the Jobber's Canyon warehouse area of
Omaha, Nebraska. The PRI was made as part of a public–private partnership anchored by a large food processor that had threatened to
leave the area unless it was redeveloped. The foundation's funds will
be used to assemble property. Lyn Wallin Ziegenbein, Kiewit's executive director, says her trustees saw the opportunity as "the perfect hybrid of grantmaking and investment. There is the potential of getting
$10.5 million back with appreciation, although we do forego income.

The trustees decided the opportunity [in downtown revitalization, longtime Kiewit interest], was worth the cost."

Because it often receives requests for loans to acquire open space, the David and Lucile Packard Foundation has set aside $3 million of its principle as a fund for such acquisitions. "We work with organizations we know," says Cole Wilbur, the foundation's executive director, "those that have a track record, and we feel confident of their ability to repay the loan."

Benefits of PRIs
Excerpt from *Program Related Investments: A Primer*

by Staff of the Piton Foundation

PRIs involve a new way for some foundations to think and do business. What motivation is there for grantmakers to begin to make PRIs? The benefits for both foundations and recipients more than justify the time and energy it takes to develop and implement a PRI program. These benefits include:

(1) Revolving of Limited Funds. Any time a foundation can recycle its funds and thereby assist more than one project with a given amount of funds, the community benefits will multiply. The PRI is a means for recycling limited foundation resources for maximum community impact.

(2) Adding Resources Not Previously Available. For foundations that now fund their grant programs from the earnings they receive on their endowment, PRIs represent another way to utilize the foundation's corpus: The endowment itself can be used to make PRIs. Since the principal of the PRI is expected to be repaid eventually, the foundation's endowment should remain intact. Of course, PRIs also can be made from grant funds, or can be made in conjunction with a grant to increase project feasibility.

(3) Building Closer Relationships between Foundations and Recipients. Generally speaking, the relationship between foundation and a grant recipient consists of pre-award interviews and a final report of accomplishments, with little dialogue in between. Many foundations find it difficult to achieve a working partnership in which both the foundation and the recipient share feedback and input. PRIs tend to bring about closer working relationships, similar to those between for-profit companies and their investors and creditors; for example, foundations often help applicants to structure a project to accommodate a PRI and perhaps additional outside financing, loan repayments are usually required periodically, and the foundation must monitor its investment on a continuing basis. In addition, PRIs give foundations a greater stake in helping recipients to identify and address potential managerial and financial problems.

Source: *Program Related Investments: A Primer*, Council on Foundations, 1986.

(4) Strengthening the Capacity of the Recipient. The rigorous financial discipline involved with many PRIs can create a new business environment for the recipient. It is not unusual for an organization to create new or improved financial and management systems when it receives a PRI. Such internal organizational changes will have lasting benefits for a recipient long after the PRI has been repaid. PRIs often help recipients to become more bankable, making it easier to obtain future financing from the private sector.

(5) Leveraging Other Sources of Funds. Commercial investors are unable to invest in many socially beneficial projects because the financial return is too low. However, if a foundation is willing to provide a portion of the needed financing through a PRI with a below-market rate of return (or no return at all), then the recipient may be able to raise the remainder of the financing from commercial investors at a market rate of return. In effect, the market rate investment is blended with the PRI as part of an overall package with a below-market rate of return.

A similar situation arises when a foundation takes a more exposed position in the financing of a risky project. The foundation's acceptance of a disproportionate share of the risk can reduce the financial risks for commercial lenders to an acceptable level. Both direct investments and guarantees can be used to achieve this result.

A PRI can also be used to attract financing from other charitable sources. For example, in cases where no single foundation may be willing to fund a large project alone, several foundations may be willing to join together in making common investments. The Cooperative Assistance Fund is an example of an organization that raises PRIs from several foundations, and invests these funds in minority and community-based development ventures.

About Social Investment
Excerpt from *Social Investment and Private Foundations*

by Melinda Marble

This study showed that most private foundations engaging in social investments pursue two strategies: the program-related investment (PRI) and the recoverable grant.

While PRIs and recoverable grants made up most of the social investment activity found in this survey, a small number of foundations had used their assets in nontraditional ways that did not fit either the PRI or recoverable grant category. A few foundations, faced with a pressing community need, have chosen to use a substantial percentage of their assets to meet that need—making a conscious decision to permanently reduce their assets by 10 percent or more. Their support may be in the form of a grant, but it represents a different use of assets that goes far beyond payout requirements.

Other foundations have used assets to purchase annuities for projects to ensure their long-term survival, or have chosen to forgo investment income by providing grantees with multiyear support up front—allowing their grant to be, in effect, a temporary endowment.

Program-Related Investment (PRI)

A PRI is an investment made by a foundation primarily to further one or more of its program goals. PRIs offer the potential to recycle foundation dollars through loan repayments, interest income, and capital gains. The Tax Reform Act of 1969 specifically exempts PRIs from its regulations on investments that might jeopardize a foundation's tax-exempt status.

PRIs can be made from the foundation's endowment principal or from annual earnings. To qualify as a PRI, an investment must meet the following test:

- The primary purpose must be to accomplish religious, charitable, scientific, literary, or educational purposes.

Source: *Social Investment and Private Foundations.* Council on Foundations, 1989.

- No significant purpose of the investment can be the production of income or the appreciation of property.
- No purpose of the investment can be to carry on propaganda or to influence legislation.

Treasury regulations provide that an investment serves the first purpose if it "significantly furthers" the accomplishment of the foundation's exempt activities and if it would not have been made but for such purposes. It serves the second purpose if commercial investors would not have made the investment on the same terms as the foundation, either because of the risk involved or the low rate of return.

Funds disbursed through PRIs are counted toward a foundation's payout requirement. PRI repayments increase the payout requirement by increasing the amount of the repayment. While many of the largest and most publicized PRIs have been made in the fields of housing and economic development, the PRI vehicle is also appropriate for small scale projects in a variety of fields. PRIs as practiced by private foundations take several forms.

Loans

The most widely used form of PRIs, loans have provided mortgage financing, predevelopment costs of housing and commercial development, cash flow, equipment acquisition, and a host of other purposes. Interest rates charged vary from interest-free to just under market rate. Terms for repayment vary also: payments can be fully amortized, like a mortgage; interest-only, with a balloon payment; or deferred.

A foundation may take a primary position as creditor to a project, ensuring that it will be first to be repaid if the project fails. Many foundations choose a more subordinate position in order to leverage larger conventional debt. If the foundation is willing to absorb more risk by being subordinate to other debt, traditional financing institutions may agree to participate in financing projects.

Loan Guarantees

Some foundations make social investments that may not require initial disbursement of capital by serving as guarantor on a loan or line of credit given by another financial institution. Willingness to do this often serves as an incentive for traditional financial institutions to get involved in a project.

Loan guarantees, like any social investment, have their own set of risks. As a loan guarantor, the foundation is not directly responsible for monitoring the loan, so it may have less direct contact with the recipient. The bank has the first line of exposure and the responsibility for monitoring the loan. In the case of a default, the foundation must pay its funds to make good its guarantee, and may not have adequate security to recover its investment. Also, loan guarantees do not count toward the payout requirement until they are disbursed.

Linked Deposits

A linked deposit is a deposit in an account with a financial institution to induce that institution's support for one or more projects. The foundation might make a deposit in a bank account bearing no interest, in order to persuade the lender to make loans at low interest. Or the account may earn a market-rate return, but still represents available funds to the bank that are less expensive than borrowing from traditional bank sources.

With a linked deposit, the foundation is essentially subsidizing the interest rate, but since its deposit is guaranteed by federal deposit insurance, it does not absorb any project risk. The bank bears full responsibility for collecting on the loan or loans. For the purposes of this study, deposits placed in banks and community credit unions to encourage the institution to make a series of loans in a particular field, rather than a single project, are recorded as linked deposits.

Equity Investments

Equity investments involve the direct purchase of stock in business ventures, and the direct purchase of land, buildings, or equipment by foundations. Equity investments made by foundations in this study ranged from purchase of stock in small business enterprises and bank holding company to ownership of nonprofit office buildings leased at below market rates to nonprofits.

Recoverable Grants

Recoverable grants are grants that function as interest-free loans. They are made by foundations from their grantmaking budget, and are entered on the books as "recoverable grants." If repayment is not received, they are converted to grant status.

There is a great deal of blurring and disagreement within the field about what constitutes a PRI versus a recoverable grant. The decision about how to designate a particular project depends upon the foundation's accounting practices and beliefs.

Many foundations do not consider their social investments "real" PRIs unless they are made from principal; loans from their annual giving budget are thus reported as "recoverable grants." Others report all collateralized loans as PRIs and consider unsecured loans recoverable grants. Still others call interest-free loans recoverable grants and loans that charge interest, PRIs.

More extensive information on the structuring of social investment projects can be found in *Program-Related Investments: A Primer*, published by the Council on Foundations.

Expenditure Responsibility

"It's Easier Than You Think"

by John A. Edie

Expenditure responsibility "can't get no respect." It's the Rodney Dangerfield of grantmaking. Maids don't do windows, and private foundations don't do expenditure responsibility. Yet, a growing number of private foundations are finding the exercise of expenditure responsibility to be a regular and surprisingly routine part of their annual grantmaking.

Last spring in the middle of a speech in New York City, I was asked to explain what steps were required to do expenditure responsibility. When I finished a brief explanation, several members of the audience expressed amazement at how simple it sounded. One questioner said, "We do most of that already with every grant." Despite this common reaction, once the procedure is explained, I am continually confronted with grantmakers who avoid expenditure responsibility like the plague.

The origins of this procedure go back to the landmark Tax Reform Act of 1969, when Congress passed laws to restrict certain practices and to penalize those foundations that violated the new rules. At the time, Congress was reacting to some evidence of foundations making grants to noncharitable organizations for purposes that were far from charitable. Determined to put a stop to this practice, they passed Section 4945 of the Internal Revenue Code—a grocery list of restricted expenditures that, if made, would incur penalties on the foundation (10 percent of the amount involved), and possibly on the foundation managers (2.5 percent of the amount involved). One of the prohibited expenditures is a grant to any organization that is not a "public charity."

The term *public charity* does not appear in the tax code. To be spe-

Source: *Foundation News*, September/October 1990.

cific, Section 4945 penalizes a grant to any organization that is not defined in sections 509(a)(1), 509(a)(2), or 509(a)(3). For convenience, lawyers refer to organizations defined by these three sections as "public charities." To be classified under any of these sections, an organization must formally apply to the IRS and obtain a ruling that it qualifies first as a Section 501(c)(3) organization (which requires that it be organized and operated exclusively for charitable purposes). For public charities, this determination letter from the IRS will also state that the organization is not a private foundation because it has demonstrated enough "publicness" to qualify as a public charity under part 1, 2, or 3 of Section 509(a).

Public charities under these three sections typically include churches, educational institutions, medical institutions, supporting organizations, and a wide assortment of groups that can show that a minimum amount of their total revenue or support comes from a broad cross section of the general public (i.e., they meet a "public support test"). There is one exception to these rules. Units of government (such as public libraries or school boards) also qualify as public charities even though they are not required to obtain Section 501(c)(3) status from the IRS. Governmental units by definition have sufficient "publicness" built into them. In short, Congress was saying that no penalty will apply when a private foundation makes a grant to a public charity. This made the IRS feel comfortable that the funds would be used strictly for charitable purposes for several reasons: (1) the grantee applied for exclusively charitable status with the IRS; (2) the grantee in most cases is required to file a tax return annually; and (3) from time to time, IRS will audit each public charity as part of its ongoing oversight.

MISCONCEPTION

This potential penalty for giving to a nonpublic charity has created the misconception among many in the foundation field that a private foundation can give only to a Section 501(c)(3) organization. This simply is not true. There are many organizations to which a private foundation may make a grant even though the grantee is not a public charity. Examples include chambers of commerce, labor unions, trade associations, fraternal orders (such as Rotary), other private foundations, or even for-profit companies. However, to avoid the penalty when giving to nonpublic charity grantees, the private foundation must, in Congress's words, "exercise expenditure responsibility."

In other words, the private foundation must exercise the oversight job normally done by IRS for public charities. Since such a grant is going to a private foundation or to an organization that is *not* organized and operated exclusively for charitable purposes, the grantor foundation must take the steps necessary to see that the funds are appropriately spent. Before spelling out the basic steps required to exercise expenditure responsibility correctly, it is important to make clear that this process is not as easy nor as safe as simple grants to universities or the United Way. The required procedures and documents must be designed with care and should definitely be approved by your legal counsel. But once established, procedures are very similar to what many foundations already undertake for many, if not all, of their grants. While it is certainly true that staffed foundations are more likely to make expenditure responsibility grants, more and more smaller foundations are finding this procedure to be much easier than they had first thought.

There are four basic requirements for expenditure responsibility: (1) a pregrant inquiry, (2) a written agreement, (3) regular reports from the grantee, and (4) a report to IRS by the grantor. A brief summary of each of these requirements is set out below, and the reader can obtain sample procedures and documents from the Council on Foundations. However, it bears repeating that any system for exercising expenditure responsibility should be approved by legal counsel.

As a first step, a private foundation must conduct an inquiry of the potential grantee that is complete enough to give a reasonable person assurance that the grantee will use the grant for proper, charitable purposes. As Treasury regulations state, such a pregrant inquiry "should concern itself with matters such as (a) the identity, prior history and experience (if any) of the grantee organization and its managers; and (b) any knowledge which the private foundation has (based on prior experience or otherwise) of, or other information which is readily available concerning the management, activities, and practices of the grantee organization." Some foundations design a simple pregrant inquiry check sheet that is completed by a foundation official and kept on file. The regulations also make clear that the "scope" of the inquiry will vary from case to case depending on "the size and purpose of the grant, the period over which it is to be paid, and the prior experience which the grantor has had with the capacity of the grantee to use the grant for the proper purposes."

WRITTEN AGREEMENT

In making an expenditure responsibility grant, the foundation may not simply write a check. Rather, a written agreement (or contract) must be signed by "an appropriate officer, director or trustee of the grantee organization." This requirement for a written agreement is where legal counsel is most vital because the regulations are quite specific about what must be included.

However, once a "form" contract (or "boilerplate" as lawyers call it) has been developed and approved, completing the rest of the blank spaces in the "form" contract is fairly easy. The blanks to fill in can be as simple as name of grantee, name and title of grantee official signing the agreement, the date of the agreement, the length of the grant period, the date (or dates) by which a written report (or reports) on the status of the grant must be submitted, and the grant's specific charitable purpose (or purposes). The regulations are clear in indicating that the purpose of the grant must be spelled out in writing.

The rest of the private foundation's standard expenditure responsibility agreement will never change (unless amended by counsel). However, the regulations require that the grantee sign an agreement that includes each of the following four commitments:

1. To repay any portion of the amount granted that is not used for the purposes of the grant.
2. To submit full and complete annual reports on the manner in which the funds are spent and the progress made in accomplishing the purposes of the grant.
3. To maintain records of receipts and expenditures and to make its books and records available to the grantor at reasonable times.
4. Not to use any of the funds:
   To undertake any activity that is not charitable;
   To carry on propaganda, or otherwise attempt to influence legislation;
   To influence the outcome of any specific public election, or to carry on, directly or indirectly, any voter registration drive;
   To make any grants to individuals for travel study or similar purposes unless such grants comply with the requirements to which private foundations are subject; or
   To make any grants that would require expenditure responsibility unless such grants comply with the requirements to which private foundations are subject.

There may be other provisions of agreement that your legal counsel may wish to include. For example, a foundation may wish to state that the grantee understands that the grantor intends to monitor and evaluate the activities funded by the grant, and that the grantor may discontinue, modify, or withhold part or all of the grant funds when, in its judgment, such action is necessary to comply with the law or regulations.

REPORTS FROM THE GRANTEE

Since Treasury regulations do not spell out the details of what must be included in the grantee's report, it is probably wise for your legal counsel to include them in the "form" contract.

The regulations state, "The grantee shall make such reports as of the end of its annual accounting period within which the grant or any portion thereof is received and all such subsequent periods until the grant funds are expended in full or the grant is otherwise terminated." For example, if grantee X receives a two-year expenditure responsibility grant on May 1, 1990, and grantee X has an accounting period ending on June 30, reports would be due "within a reasonable period of time" after June 30, 1990; after June 30, 1991; and after June 30, 1992. The grantee must make a final report (the June 30, 1992, report in the example above) with respect to "all expenditures made from such funds (including salaries, travel, and supplies) and indicating the progress made toward the goals of the grant." The grantor is not required to conduct "any independent verification" of such reports "unless it has reason to doubt their accuracy or reliability," and may rely on adequate records or other sufficient evidence (such as a statement by an appropriate officer, director, or trustee of the grantee organization).

Finally, if the grantee receiving the expenditure responsibility grant is other than a private foundation, the grantee must agree to maintain continuously the grant funds "in a separate fund dedicated to one or more charitable purposes." In other words, the noncharitable grantee may not simply commingle funds that are dedicated exclusively for charitable purposes with those that are not.

Failure by the grantee to provide the required reports could subject the grantor to a penalty unless the grantor makes a reasonable effort to obtain the reports and withholds any future payments until they are received.

REPORTING TO IRS

Every private foundation is required to file a tax return within four and one-half months after the end of its tax year. For each year in which it has made an expenditure responsibility grant, it must answer "yes" to the appropriate question (Part VII, line 14(a)(4) on 1989 Form 990-PF). In addition, it must add a schedule to the tax return, providing a brief summary paragraph on each expenditure responsibility grant's status. An example, as suggested by the IRS, is Form 990-PF for the hypothetical Oak Foundation:

Grantee: Allen Reid Museum of Fine Arts, 31 Meyers St., Atlanta,
            GA 30301

Date paid: April 7, 1985. Amount $15,000

Purpose: For the partial support of a major renovation and expansion
            of the museum facilities

Amount of grant spent by grantee: $15,000

Diversion: To the knowledge of the foundation, and based on the
            report furnished by the grantee, no part of the grant has
            been used for other than its intended purpose

Date of report for grantee: Final report January 8, 1986

(In addition to its own report covering the use of grant funds, the grantee furnished an independent auditor's report of its operations for its fiscal year ending September 30, 1985. Since this latter report verified the information provided by the grantee, the Oak Foundation, Inc. deemed further verification of the grantee's report unnecessary.)

For some, the requirements of expenditure responsibility will seem more complicated than their normal grantmaking procedures. But many will note that a pregrant inquiry is regularly performed, that their foundation requires use of a standard grant agreement form, and that some kind of written report is required from the grantee. For these foundations, the added steps of satisfying the requirements of expenditure responsibility will be relatively easy to accomplish.

Sample Letter for Expenditure: Responsibility Grant Agreements

The Tax Reform Act of 1969 imposed a series of new restrictions upon the activities and grants of private foundations. These restrictions are enforced by stringent penalties. One provision of the legislation requires grants like the present one to be made subject to a written agreement between the grantor and grantee establishing certain limitations on the use of the grant funds. To comply with the statutory standards, you must make the following agreements with respect to the grant covered by this letter.

1. The grant is to be used exclusively for the purposes specified in this letter. Any part of the grant funds not so used must be returned promptly to us.

2. No part of the grant may be used to attempt to influence legislation [within the meaning of Section 4945(d)(2) of the Internal Revenue Code].

3. No part of the grant may be used to attempt to influence the outcome of any specific public election, or to carry on, directly or indirectly, any voter registration drive [within the meaning of Section 4945(d)(2) of the Internal Revenue Code].

4. No part of the grant may be used for the making of a grant to an individual for travel, study, or similar purposes unless the requirements of Section 4945(g) of the Internal Revenue Code are met. The payment of compensation to your employees does not constitute a "grant" for these purposes, and is not subject to these restrictions.

5. No part of this grant may be used for a grant to another organization unless the provisions of Section 4945(h) of the Internal Revenue Code (dealing with "expenditure responsibility") are complied with if they are applicable.

6. No part of this grant may be used for purposes other than religious, charitable, scientific, literary, or educational purposes or the prevention of cruelty to children or animals.

7. Within a reasonable period of time after the close of each of your annual accounting periods, you will furnish us full and complete annual reports on the manner in which the grant funds are spent and the progress made in accomplishing the purposes of the grant. Upon completion of your use of the grant funds, you will make a final report to us detailing all expenditures made from grant funds (includ-

ing salaries, travel, and supplies) and indicating the progress made toward the goals of the grant.

8. You will indicate the grant separately on your books of account, charge expenditures made in furtherance of the grant purposes against the grant, and keep records adequate to enable the use of the grant funds to be checked readily.

9. You will keep these records, along with copies of the reports submitted to us for at least four years, and make the records available to us at reasonable times.

If you have any questions about the effect of these agreements, or if the requirements outlined above pose special problems for you, we shall be happy to discuss them with you. If, during the course of your use of the grant, you would like information on the application of one or more of the agreements to a particular problem or situation, we shall be happy to consult with you.

Your acceptance of these agreements should be indicated below by the signature of the officer or officers who are, under your bylaws, and the law governing you, authorized to execute contracts on behalf of you. Please return the executive original of this letter to us. A copy of the letter is enclosed for your files.

Very truly yours,

THE FRUGAL FOUNDATION

By: _____

Accepted on behalf of _____ *[grantee organization]* _____

This ____ day of _____, 19___

By: _____
                    Title

APPENDIX 10

Small Can Be Effective

by Paul N. Ylvisaker

When people think, talk, or write about foundations, almost invariably they have in mind the large and very large philanthropies, starting and usually ending with the Fords, Rockefellers, Carnegies, and MacArthurs. Rarely will they be focusing on any or all of the small foundations that actually comprise the overwhelming mass of grantmakers in the United States. Twenty-three thousand of the total of 25,000 foundations in the United States have assets of less than $10 million—arbitrarily chosen here as an approximate indicator of what could reasonably be classified as a "small foundation."*

The Council on Foundations has commissioned this essay in the belief that more attention should be paid to the workings of these smaller philanthropies, as well as to their contributions.

All too little is known about them, but it is doubtful in the climate of rising demand for philanthropic funding and growing sophistication of applicants that they will remain invisible or unnoticed. Concern has already been expressed that increased scrutiny at both state and federal levels might well focus on actual and alleged shortcomings in this sector.

But the Council's interest is more on the positive side. There is vast potential in small-scale philanthropy, and this is a time when that potential needs to be fully released. The dollars held by small foundations, individually and collectively, are a precious resource in a society trying to meet burgeoning needs with increasingly scarce public funds.

Moreover, it is the Council's fundamental belief that the *creative* use of foundation moneys rather than their size and scale constitutes the real potential of philanthropy—"small can be effective." This mono-

---

* Bear in mind that a number of "pass-through" foundations have little or no assets but actually give away sizeable sums and can hardly be classified as small foundations.

Source: *Small Can Be Effective*, Council on Foundations, 1989.

graph, then, is an appeal for creativity, and an attempt to illustrate how small foundations have been and can be both creative and effective.

WHAT IS A SMALL FOUNDATION?—SOME FURTHER BENCHMARKS

In addition to asset size, small foundations might be distinguished by two other criteria: *size of annual grants* and *size of staffs*. Both indicators are arbitrary and approximate.

Foundations that award an annual total of $1 million or less can reasonably be classified as small. Similarly, foundations with five or less paid staff might be thought of as being small. But there are always exceptions that plague an attempt to classify or generalize. For example, the Alden Trust of Worcester, Massachusetts, has over $76 million in assets and awards close to $3 million annually, but operates without staff: Its trustees handle all the normal grantmaking operations.

So it's probably best to deal in approximates, and with a pervading sense of relativity. Small compared to what? To the Ford Foundation with its billions in assets, its hundreds of million in annual grants, its scores of professional staff? In the final analysis, to paraphrase a Supreme Court justice, you know a small foundation when you feel you are one.

WHAT DO WE KNOW ABOUT SMALL FOUNDATIONS?

Most of what we know about small foundations comes from a combination of personal contact—the isolated examples of boards we have served on, individual trustees and staff we have encountered, grants that have achieved high visibility—and from surveys that include some sampling of this sector. One such is the Council's biennial management survey; half of its respondents typically satisfy the criteria cited earlier. But the sampling is surely skewed: It represents only a tiny fraction of all small foundations, and those that respond are members of the Council, displaying all the marks of interest and professionalism that generally characterize Council membership. Still, the results are informative.

To generalize, small foundations:

- differ in board size.
- have more donor and family participation on their boards.
- show more participation by women as trustees.
- differ in their minority participation: Independent foundations have fewer minority trustees than their larger counterparts; small community and public foundations average 15 percent more.
- pay directors' fees less frequently.

- employ a median of two professional or support staff, half of them part-time.
- pay a small percentage of salaries as benefits.
- less frequently have a written vacation policy or a written maternity leave policy, although those who do have nearly doubled in the last two years.
- indicate somewhat higher administrative costs and payout rates.
- display conventional patterns of grantmaking, although with a slightly higher proportion going to religion.

All this is but marginal information. Clearly, what is needed are more systematic surveys, extensive field research, intimate case studies, and critical essays of the kind that have been carried out with respect to the nation's larger and more conspicuous foundations.

THE FUNCTION OF FOUNDATIONS: THREE TRADITIONS

Before answering the question of how small foundations can be effective, one needs to go back to some basics: What are the great traditions within which foundations, large and small, move and have their being? Essentially, there are three.

The oldest and most widely practiced and understood is *charity*. In its simplest form, it is a one-to-one transaction between two parties—one more affluent sharing resources with one more needy, a classic example being the Good Samaritan.

A second and equally ancient tradition is *patronage*, the identification and nurturing of talent. Originally practiced by kings and nobles, the tradition has given us the masters and masterpieces of art, sculpture, and music. In its modern form, it is represented by fellowships such as the Guggenheim and MacArthur awards, and by direct support of cultural and educational enterprises.

The third great tradition is *modern philanthropy*, only a century old and still evolving. It emerged along with the massive fortunes of Andrew Carnegie, John D. Rockefeller, and their kindred barons; it took on the structured character and law of the corporate world, and associated itself with the outlook and professionalism of organized science. It dedicated itself to finding systemic solutions to underlying causes of poverty and other social ills, and over time has become a recognized social process, in effect a set of private legislatures defining public problems, setting goals and priorities, and allocating resources toward general solutions.

Imbedded as we are in the immediacies of that evolution, we perhaps do not fully appreciate the role that foundations are allowed—and increasingly are expected—to play in U.S. society. We have, in effect, been given a "hunting license" as private organizations to participate in what has conventionally been thought of as exclusively a public/governmental domain. And what is even more significant, this is becoming a global development: Societies everywhere, growing in diversity and complexity, have become aware that government alone cannot release the energies and potential of their citizenry without giving room for spontaneous private initiatives. Even the Soviet Union is now encouraging the formation of private foundations.

MODERN PHILANTHROPY—THE CHALLENGE TO FOUNDATION CREATIVITY

Philanthropy in its contemporary form has grown explosively in its potential for social influence and creativity. It now has a multitude of ways in which it can be an effective and generative force for human betterment. These generic functions of modern philanthropy can be listed under five general headings: financial, the catalytic role of philanthropy, the conceptualizing role of philanthropy, the critical function of philanthropy, and the community-building role of philanthropy. The following enumeration illustrates the range and variety of the devices by which foundations, whatever their size, can exercise and maximize their effectiveness. Only a few directly involve the transmission of money—which in itself gives an answer to that provocative, if somewhat mischievous, question, "Who would come to see you if you didn't have any (or much) money?"

FINANCIAL—SUPPORT FUNCTIONS OF PHILANTHROPY

1. **Grantmaking.** Notice how in our times the concept of giving (the older charitable mode), and even the word, have given way to the modernized term of grantmaking. Actually, the process has become one of *negotiated contracts*, in which two parties—the donor and the donee—at least in theory agree on the terms of the exchange. Implicit in this exchange is the equality of the two parties, although there is still the hangover from former days of the superior position of the grantor —and, hence, the oft-cited occupational hazard of arrogance. But if we were explicitly to recognize the "democratization" of an elite institution, we would be practicing the equality of exchange in which money from one party secures the services of another on mutually acceptable terms.

It is in this kind of negotiation that philanthropy at any scale can and should ensure both its effectiveness and its credibility. In being credible, it will be all the more effective—and in making the adjustment to modern thought, it will demonstrate its creativity.

2. **Lending.** Granting money is only one way of extending financial support. A foundation can also lend—and by that device, stretch its resources. Lending may be done at below market or even at no interest; moreover, accepting higher risk—aiding needy nonprofits while not depleting a foundation's financial capacity. Lending has proved an effective way, for example, of covering revenue shortages often experienced by social service agencies whose cash flow position has become temporarily precarious.

3. **Insuring.** Another means of providing financial assistance is by reinsuring commercial loans extended by banks or other sources to nonprofit agencies. Again, it allows foundations to be of assistance without diminishing their financial capacity.

4. **Investing.** The past decades have added still another device to a foundation's repertoire: program-related investments. Once thought to violate the doctrine of prudence, such investments—out of the foundations's corpus and usually at below-market rates of interest—are now generally accepted and increasingly practiced. Again, they enable a foundation to stretch its resources without depleting them.

Another significant use of investments is to make an ethical statement. By screening its own investments through criteria that are socially and environmentally sensitive, a foundation can ensure not only that its own programmatic and financial goals are congruent, but also that its example may have an impact on other sectors of the general public.

THE CATALYTIC ROLE OF PHILANTHROPY

5. **Initiating.** Foundations often diminish their effectiveness by remaining passive, waiting for others to propose while hanging back themselves. Even small foundations can become proactive, taking initiatives that stimulate others to act.

6. **Accelerating.** Social action is usually a slow process. Foundations can speed up the process by stepping in, acting as "society's passing gear." A notable example of this came when then-Governor Terry Sanford created the North Carolina Fund through the help of local foundations. The fund made it possible for minorities to participate in decisions and programs that speeded the adoption and experimentation of a rich variety of solutions to the state's long-festering social problems.

7. **Leveraging.** Small foundations are particularly at a disadvantage not having enough money to fund larger ventures. But they can leverage their funds by bringing other resources into play.

8. **Collaborating and Partnering.** Leveraging usually involves collaborating with others in joint grantmaking—another development in modern philanthropy that is picking up speed. A relevant case in point is the educational partnerships spreading across the country in the last few years. Small foundations are conspicuous in school reform, maximizing their own energies, resources, and creativity.

9. **Convening.** One other mode of foundation activity that has come into vogue is that of bringing together several sectors of the community with a common concern. Convening can be done with or without a financial outlay, but it does require credibility and trust. Foundations are a "natural" in this role: They are usually viewed as nonpartisan, a trusted meeting ground for divergent interests, and their functioning in this role can often have spectacular results. The Fund for the City of New York specializes in this activity. It holds "no-agenda lunches" where both public and private agencies can meet and discuss what's on their minds, regularly resulting in new approaches and joint ventures. It can be one of the most creative—and least expensive—forms of philanthropy, ideally suited to small foundations and their limited means.

THE CONCEPTUALIZING ROLE OF PHILANTHROPY

10. **Analyzing.** Foundations are well known for the research they do and the fact finding and analyses they finance. The role is at once valuable, mostly uncontroversial, and need not be expensive. And it need not in every case be complex or sophisticated, often requiring only some time, asking the right questions, and searching in the right places. Subjects for small foundations cover the whole range of community problems, from assembling data on the incidence of specific diseases to examining the import of demographic changes.

11. **Defining and Redefining.** In a rapidly changing society, one of the most valuable processes is taking a new or another look at issues that have long been, shortly will be, or should be on the public agenda. There is too often a lag in public perception and recognition; foundations can play an effective part in defining and redefining those issues through research, analyses, conferences, seminars, publicity, or simply reporting their own considerations and grant results.

12. **Focusing.** Again, in setting their own priorities for grantmaking, foundations of whatever size can exert a powerful influence on how nonprofits and public agencies concentrate their own energies and objectives. This is a further argument for foundations clarifying their goals and publicly stating/reporting what they hope to accomplish.

13. **Inventing and Testing.** A more familiar part of philanthropy's thinking function is that of devising new programs, new approaches,

and new solutions. Innovation and experimentation early on became synonymous with the modern foundation. Two of our most ingenious solutions to serious social problems came from the pioneering efforts of very small foundations: the practice of painting white lines on the outside edges of roads and highways, radically reducing accident and mortality rates; and the use of lasers to limit the ravages of diabetic retinopathy, and save the residual vision of millions in this and other countries.

THE CRITICAL FUNCTION OF PHILANTHROPY

14. **Commenting.** Foundations, by their reluctance to speak out and their uneven record of public reporting, have all too often passed up what is one of their readiest and least expensive opportunities to be of influence. They have the freedom and the platform not only to inform the public of what they stand for and have done, but also to comment on the state of the community they serve and on the needs they see as not being fulfilled. Small foundations in general are particularly remiss: The infrequency of their public reporting and their seclusion from public awareness have bound them like Lilliput in knots of their own tying.

15. **Approving and Disapproving.** Foundations, small as well as large, carry their own "Good Housekeeping Seal of Approval." Given the public trust and confidence accorded to them, they are looked to as symbols of what has been disinterestedly judged as favorable or not favorable, promising or not promising, a risk worth or not worth taking. The use of that symbol is one to be exercised and guarded with the greatest of care, and with the willingness to be explicit about both purpose and criteria.

16. **Advocating.** Brian O'Connell of the Independent Sector has stated his belief that advocacy is the most powerful and precious of the roles of foundations and nonprofits. But it is hardly the most popular. One has to be willing to live with controversy. Small foundations willing to engage in it, either directly or through grantees, will obviously have to assess the risks; but they should also know of the potential rewards.

17. **Gadflying: Serving as Social Conscience.** This is the "prophetic" role that foundations at any scale can choose to play; they can do it through sponsored studies, commissions, and reports, or through statements and actions of their own. In recent years, small foundations throughout the United States have stirred the conscience of their communities on such topics as hunger, homelessness, and AIDS—not to mention such nagging constants as civil rights and environmental protection.

THE COMMUNITY-BUILDING ROLE OF PHILANTHROPY

18. **Bonding/Unifying.** De Tocqueville more than a century ago noted a virtue in the new nation that might well become its fatal flaw: individualism leading perhaps ultimately to the fragmentation of community. It is a theme recently picked up again by Robert Bellah and his associates, in their volume, *Habits of the Heart*. And for me, it was etched memorably in a friendly argument with Fei Xiao Tong, the noted Chinese anthropologist. "You," he amiably charged, "are the White Devil. You symbolize undisciplined individualism. You define human potential in terms of what an individual can accomplish on his/her own, regardless of whether or not that accomplishment is to the benefit or to the detriment of that person's community."

Strengthening both the sense of community and the tradition of community service may well be the first obligation of foundations, whatever their size—an obligation that goes along with the rare privilege given philanthropy: the freedom to decide privately the means by which the goal of community building is to be accomplished.

19. **Balancing.** Building a community requires conscious efforts simultaneously at *diversifying* and *equalizing*, an essay in social balancing to ensure that disparities and polarization do not get out of hand. Even small foundations can make a difference simply in what they say, how they act, and what they do. Choosing trustees and staff who reflect diverse backgrounds and interests is powerfully symbolic; making certain that grantees are similarly reflective, seeking out, and being accessible to people and agencies struggling at the margin are ways of helping a community achieve a healthy balance.

20. **Leading.** Foundations have no alternative but to accept the leadership position their command of flexible resources places them in. They will lead even when passive and silent; the only question is whether they will recognize and accept the responsibilities of their advantaged position. A foundation is a public trust; it is not simply a private prerogative, to be maintained as a private sanctuary and for private purposes. Why else the tax advantages accorded them by a public that expects public benefit in return?

VAST ROOM FOR CREATIVITY*

By now, it should be evident that foundations do not need a lot of money to be effective: Within the 20 generic functions of modern phi-

---

* It might well be worth the effort if trustees and staff were to review their grants and activities to determine which and how many of the 20 generic functions they have engaged in.

lanthropy, they have all the room they need to be creative. If, indeed, they were to exploit only a fraction of the strategies available to them, their individual and collective impact on U.S. life would be vastly and beneficially expanded. This nation needs what foundations at any scale have to offer; public awareness and expectancy are fast rising.

EXAMPLES OF SMALL FOUNDATION CREATIVITY

Examples of creativity have been scattered throughout the preceding pages; it may be helpful to identify a few more. These are but a sampling of the myriad instances where the generative potential of small foundations has been realized.

The Edward P. Hazen Foundation has distinguished itself over two generations as a powerfully leavening influence both on the U.S. scene and in the philanthropic community. Originally a family foundation, its board has for some time been composed of nonfamily members representing a wide diversity of gender, race, and occupational background. With assets of less than $10 million, its grants have been consistently well considered and often pioneering: For example, its earlier work in values, and its more recent nurturing of a minority scholar (Ron Edmonds) whose work touched off the Effective Schools movement in the United States. The foundation has also risked the calculated decision to invest a considerable part of its income in employing a succession of extraordinarily competent staff, whose personal influence has matched in many ways that of the foundation's program grants.

The Henry C. Frick Educational Commission of Pittsburgh, with assets under $5 million, has for nearly a century been a generative force in that community. With a board of trustees of eleven members representing areas such as finance, law education, and business and community leadership, the fund has served not simply as a grantmaker but also as a program developer, catalyst, broker, and convener. It has carefully focussed its activities, concentrating currently on the alarming turnover of principals and superintendents (in the process initiating the development of a Principal's Academy), on early childhood, and on problems such as teen pregnancy and drug and alcohol abuse.

A dramatic example of what a very small foundation can accomplish came with establishment this past year of the Dan and Inez Wood Fairfax Fund within the Southern Educational Foundation. Created by Jean and Betty Fairfax in honor of their parents, the fund will award college scholarships to black high school students in Phoenix, Arizona, who have persevered through graduation. The original asset contribution was $125,000, an endowment that is expected to grow modestly over the next seven years. It stands as a stimulating example of what minority donors of limited means can accomplish with a well-conceived contribution.

The Albert Kunstadter Family Foundation of New York City, with assets of less than $3 million, has decided that its grants should focus on critical operating needs of a very wide variety of nonprofit organizations; the range of recipients extends from minority educational ventures to agencies working on international development and security. In doing so, the foundation has carved out its own niche: a flexible response at critical times in the life of an organization that has proved its worth. These timely grants rarely exceed $5,000; most are between $2,000 and $3,000.

Finally, the Peninsula Community Foundation of Burlingame, California: It has assets of less than $5 million, and its grants range in size from $50 to $75,000 with the average between $5,000 and $20,000. It has displayed remarkable ingenuity (and parsimony) in its response to local needs; to illustrate, it has:

- created, and with local business support, maintained a Community Resource Library of funding sources, and along with it, a training seminar for those seeking funding;
- in working with local corporations, set up a distribution center for the free disposition of computers, furniture, and other supplies to local nonprofit agencies;
- provided a convening and coordinating point for staff of public and private agencies working on teenage pregnancy, and similarly for the several dance companies;
- initiated (at a total cost of $250) a get-together of the local constabulary and youngsters with cars and motorcycles, dissolving tensions and leading to the holding of a very popular rally and concourse; and
- along with other local funding sources, established a program of internships which adds college volunteers to the staffing potential of local nonprofits.

As Bill Somerville, former executive director, notes: ". . . the challenge lies in how creative one can be with limited resources. Small foundations should be low budget operations but this has nothing to do with how flexible and responsive they can be . . . the San Francisco Foundation is a limousine and the Peninsula Community Foundation is a motor scooter; we both carry people, they can carry more but we can take the corners quicker."

Investing Foundation Assets

"Staying Ahead of the Market"

by Lester M. Salamon

A new study suggests that foundation investment behavior is neither as bad as some critics contend, nor as good as the foundation world might hope.

While much of the foundation community focuses on grantmaking, most of the critical legal restrictions under which foundations now operate—such as the payout requirement, the excise tax, the prohibitions on self-dealing—owe their origins to real or perceived problems on the investment side of the house.

Those issues of greatest concern to government policymakers are those that are generally least understood: How do foundations manage the immense wealth in their control? How does the payout requirement affect foundation investment operations? And what impact has the change in the payout requirement in 1981 had on both the investment and payout performance of foundations?

Thanks to a study commissioned recently by the Council on Foundations, we can begin answering these questions for the first time. With the use of a mail survey distributed to a stratified random sample of private foundations and statistical data compiled from 990-PF forms, an unusual empirical picture emerged of foundation investment operations focusing on four key topics:

1. The process foundations use to manage their investments;

2. The rate of return they have achieved;

3. The process foundations use to make their payout decisions; and

Source: *Foundation News*, January/February, 1989.

4. The payout rates foundations have adopted.

Unlike previous studies, this one consciously sought to cover a broad cross section of foundations, to look at actual performance and not just expectations, to examine a reasonable time span and not just a single year, and to compare foundation performance with that of other investment pools.

THE PAYOUT DILEMMA

The more than $100 billion in assets controlled by private foundations represent at one and the same time a source of support for current charitable ventures and a sizable investment pool to support such activities into the future. Consequently, foundations must continually decide not only which projects are most worthy of support, but also how to balance current claimants against future ones. If foundations pay out more than they earn, over time their assets will decline until they simply cease to exist. On the other hand, if they retain too large a share of their earnings, they'll provoke legitimate questions about the wisdom of granting them tax-exempt status.

Foundations can respond to this dilemma by seeking higher returns on their investments, but this opens them to another dilemma: High-income investments frequently have limited long-term growth potential. Conversely, investments that promise long-term growth yield relatively low current income and relatively high risk.

Under the 1969 payout requirement imposed by Congress, foundations were required to distribute each year in the form of grants or grant-related expenses either all of their annual investment earnings (interest plus dividends), or a given percentage—initially set at 6 percent and then lowered to 5 percent—of their accumulated investment assets, whichever was higher.·

No sooner was the ink dry on these provisions, however, than serious problems surfaced. During the high-inflation/flat-market period of the 1970s, foundations found the payout requirement difficult to meet and still preserve the real value of their assets. This created pressures to increase the levels of risk that foundations had to absorb. In 1981, Congress responded to these concerns by easing the payout requirement. Henceforth, earnings in excess of 5 percent of a foundation's assets could be retained and plowed back into the asset base.

HANDS ON OR OFF

Not surprisingly, one of the study's conclusions is that foundations vary widely not only in size, objectives, and operations, but also in investment objectives, investment strategies, and investment management styles. Nevertheless, it is possible to discern in the welter of data collected two broad patterns of investment management among foundations. The first of these is a relatively aggressive approach. It features active involvement by the board of directors in setting investment objectives and strategies, investment goals defined in terms of "total return" (income plus appreciation or depreciation) rather than just current income, acceptance of at least a moderate level of risk, a multiyear time horizon, and a hands-on management style that often includes multiple outside managers and regular review of performance.

The second approach is far more informal and conservative. it features a much more limited board role in setting investment objectives and strategy, the delegation of investment decisions to inside or outside managers with little clear guidance, concentration on current income rather than total return, considerable risk aversion, and a narrow investment time horizon.

Although accepted practice in the investment field tends to favor the more aggressive of these two broad approaches, most foundations tend to pursue the conservative strategy. Only 46 percent of the foundations report that the full board of directors plays an "extremely important" role in setting investment objectives; less than 40 percent say the board plays an "extremely important" role in determining an investment strategy.

In other areas, 46 percent define investment objectives in terms of "total return," only 50 percent describe their management style as even "moderately active," 4 percent use multiple outside managers, only 28 percent use a time horizon of three years or more in investment decisions, 10 percent subscribe to an outside reporting service, and only 4 percent show evidence of an overall hands-on and aggressive investment approach.

The more active and less risk-averse management style is much more evident among the larger foundations, which control the vast majority of foundation assets, than among the smaller foundations, which account for the bulk of the foundations. This means that a significant share of foundation assets may be managed in the recommended way even though most of the foundations operate more informally and conservatively.

These different patterns of investment management find tangible expression in foundation asset composition. Generally speaking, the larger foundations invest more heavily than the small or medium-sized foundations in common stocks, which have greater growth potential but also greater risk. The smaller foundations, by contrast, are generally more heavily invested in fixed income securities, which generally have higher yields but much lower growth potential.

RATES OF RETURN

The study looked at how these policies and processes affect foundation investment performance, and found:

- The average annual rate of return on foundation assets during the period 1979–1983 exceeded the rate on a control portfolio based on standard market indexes (14.1 percent vs. 13.5 percent). The control portfolio was assumed to contain 60 percent stocks, 30 percent bonds, and 10 percent cash. The stock portion of the index was assumed to vary with the Standard & Poor's 500; the bond portion, by the Salamon Brothers' corporate bond index; and the cash with the short-term Treasury bill index. Even after it was adjusted for inflation, the foundation average yielded a real return rate of 5.7 percent a year, or enough to sustain a 5-percent payout rate without eating into the real value of foundation assets.

- This respectable record was attributable to the performance of the larger foundations. By contrast, the smaller foundations as a group registered considerably lower rates of return.

- Reflecting this, the median rate of return for the foundations sampled was 12.4 percent per year, well below the 13.5-percent rate of the control portfolio. After inflation is adjusted for, this means that the median foundation had a real return rate of 4 percent a year—not enough to sustain a 5-percent payout rate and still maintain the real value of the foundation asset base.

This is all the more striking in view of the generally favorable market conditions that existed during the 1979–1983 period that was the focus of the analysis, when the Standard and Poor's 500 stock index registered an average annual rate of return of 8.9 percent. During the preceding five-year period, 1974–1978, this same index had an average annual rate of return of −3.6 percent; over the entire period, 1950–1978, it registered an average annual return rate of 6.9 percent. Considering all three components of the composite index, the average rate of return during the 1979–1983 period was 5.1 percent, versus −2.8 percent during 1974–1978 and 4 percent during 1950–1978.

RATING PAYOUT

Lower rates of total return are not necessarily a sign of poor investment management. Foundations may consciously choose investment portfolios with low growth potential but high current income in order to support high payout levels. The data shows, in fact, that the smaller foundations, which tended to have lower total return rates, did turn out to have higher rates of income yield (8.3 percent vs. 7.2 percent).

As far as payout rates are concerned, our data show that foundations as a whole had payout rates above the 5 percent minimum during 1979–1983. Among the smaller foundations, however, the annual payout rate was higher than among the larger foundations (8 percent vs. 6 percent).

The facts learned about foundation payout policies help to explain these disparities. For the larger foundations, payout decisions seem to be shaped by investment objectives: The larger foundations seem to be seeking to maximize the value of their assets given the prevailing payout requirement. They structure their investments to pay out only the minimum that the law requires, or slightly above it. By contrast, the smaller foundations seem much more likely to allow payout considerations to dominate their investment decision making and to be content to pay out all of their investment earnings.

These findings imply that the primary beneficiaries of the 1981 change in the payout requirement may not be the foundations with the most active and sophisticated investment styles. The more sophisticated foundations had already arranged their investment portfolios to minimize the impact of the payout requirement on their long-term asset base. Put another way, the foundations most likely to benefit from the change are the least likely to take advantage of it because they utilize a much less active and aggressive investment approach. This expectation finds considerable confirmation in the data. Although the time span available to gauge the impact of the 1981 payout change was too limited to reach firm conclusions at this point, the following was revealed:

- a greater tendency toward a more flexible "total return" approach after the payout change.
- a considerably higher rate of return during 1982–1983 than 1979–1981. However, this was mostly due to dramatically improved market conditions. Interestingly, foundations performed better relative to the market averages during the earlier part of the study (1979–1981) than during the latter part (1982–1983). This probably reflects the generally conservative investment approach foundations pursue, which prevents them from doing as well as market averages during boom periods but protects them against sharp losses during periods of decline.
- Payout rates have not changed much since 1981. Although the median rate dipped in 1984, this was probably due more to a drop in income yields than any change in foundation payout practices.

IMPROVING PERFORMANCE

The findings make clear that foundation investment behavior is neither as bad as some critics contend nor as good as those in the foundation world might hope. Great strides have been made over the last two decades, but as a whole the investment performance could be upgraded with a concerted effort. In this light, the study suggests:

- extension of the 1981 payout change. The 1981 liberalization of the payout requirement appears to have allowed increased flexibility with little if any serious effect on payout rates. The change should therefore be extended.

- multiyear payout computation. Foundation investment and payout practice would likely be improved if the required minimum payout rate were computed on the basis of a three-year floating average of asset values rather than a single year. This would reduce the variability in payout rates that can sometimes cause turmoil in grant decision making.

- more attention to investment management. The ad hoc and somewhat lackadaisical investment approach evident among a large number of foundations suggests the need for greater attention to the investment management function within the foundation.

- a "Common Fund for Foundations." Foundation investment performance could probably be improved through the creation of a Common Fund for Foundations modeled on the similar fund created for college and university endowments. The Fairfield, Connecticut-based Common Fund, founded in 1971, manages approximately $7.5 billion for over 1,000 members.

KEY FEATURES OF FOUNDATION INVESTMENT MANAGEMENT

	% of Foundations		
	All	Large (Assets $50 million or more)	Medium (Assets $10-49.9 million)	Small (Assets under $10 million)
Full board extremely important in setting investment objectives	46%	49%	52%	46%
Full board extremely important in setting investment strategy	37	36	43	37
Use outside managers	42	87	75	40
Multiple outside managers	4	44	40	—
Focus on total return	46	81	65	45
Risk tolerance comparable to stock averages or higher	28	65	42	27
Time horizon, 3 years or more	54	73	65	53
Hands-on management style	12	42	24	12
Overall Active Investment Approach	5	46	19	4

Source: Salamon/Voytek Foundation Investment Study

FOUNDATION INVESTMENT PERFORMANCE, 1979–83

	Average Annual Actual	Total Return Rate Inflation-Adjusted
Control Portfolio	13.5%	5.1%
Large Foundations	14.9	6.5
Medium Foundations	14.7	6.3
Small Foundations	12.1	3.7
All Foundations: Asset-weighted	14.1	5.7
Median	12.4	4.0

Source: Salamon/Voytek Foundation Investment Study

FOUNDATION PAYOUT RATES, BY SIZE OF FOUNDATION, 1979–83

Group	Average Annual Payout Rate 1979-83
Large Foundations (assets $50 million or more)	6.0%
Medium Foundations (assets $10-49.9 million)	6.6
Small Foundations (assets under $10 million)	8.0
All: Median	7.8
Asset-Weighted	6.8%

Source: Salamon/Voytek Foundation Investment Study

Mixing It Up

by Donald W. Trotter

An investment fund's asset mix is a critical factor in determining a foundation's long-term financial health and ability to sustain its grantmaking program.

Navigating a foundation's investment portfolio through the shoals of inflation, current payout policies, and timeline investment constraints has become a lot like tiptoeing through a mine field. Making the wrong decisions can result in a substantial loss of principal or, worse, liquidation of the foundation itself. In an effort to guide the way, this study examines payout policies of foundations—in particular the 5 percent minimum spending policy—and suggests methods of selecting the best possible asset mix for a particular foundation's portfolio.

The importance of the asset mix cannot be overemphasized. It is probably the most critical financial decision foundation trustees make. Various studies have indicated that more than 90 percent of a fund's performance is attributable to its asset mix. For example, the percentage of a foundation's portfolio allocated to stocks has a far greater impact on its long-term financial health than whether or not its stock managers outperform the Standard & Poor's 500 by a few points.

Many foundations, unfortunately, lose sight of long-term asset mixes and become overly concerned with the short-term performance of individual managers. To avoid this, a foundation should have a structured, deliberate, and disciplined process for determining its long-term asset mix. To arrive at such a process, it helps to understand the relationship between spending policy and inflation.

Every foundation aims to maintain funding for its grantmaking programs. But how? A basic formula helps to determine whether a fund is on course or not. To arrive at the foundation's real rate of return, subtract the rate of inflation from the portfolio's total return. In other words, when a foundation's grants exceed the real rate of return earned on its portfolio, it cannot keep pace with inflation. Such a foundation, paying out more than its real return, is in effect liquidating itself.

Source: Foundation News, July/August 1990.

If a foundation's total return averages 11 percent at a time when the inflation rate averages 6 percent, its real return is 5 percent; thus, if it elects to pay out 8 percent in grants, it would eventually be in real trouble. On the surface, its principal appears to grow—earning 11 percent and only paying out 8 percent. In real terms, however, this foundation is liquidating, because its payout of 8 percent exceeds the real return of 5 percent. In just five years, the real value of the foundation and its future grantmaking capabilities would be cut to 86 percent of current value. In 25 years, it would be reduced by more than half—an obvious and very serious problem for any foundation with a perpetual grant-making mandate.

The returns enjoyed during the 1980s gave many foundations unprecedented asset growth. The total return, including appreciation and income, for both stocks and bonds was spectacular. At 17.6 percent, stocks of large companies in the 1980s outperformed those of any of the previous five decades except the 1950s. Bond returns of 12.4 percent in the 1980s were without precedent in any decade. But even more significant for conservative investors, this bond return far exceeded the 5.1-percent inflation rate; a real return of approximately 7.3 percent was the highest yet.

The 1980s' investment return, particularly the real return, is unusual and not sustainable. Foundations could be in considerable trouble if they rely heavily on the results of the last 10 years alone to set their spending and asset mix policies. They must take a longer-term perspective.

ALARMING RESULTS

Our study examines the implications of different payout rates using the actual historical returns produced by the various capital markets. A contemporary portfolio mix, based on a recent survey by Greenwich Associates, was used to examine these historical returns. Because the portfolio is far from conservative—54 percent in domestic stocks, 3 percent in international stocks, 30 percent in bonds, 3 percent in real estate, and 2 percent in venture capital—it is unlikely that the study biased the returns on the low side. Yet, even with this aggressive portfolio, the results of the study are quite alarming.

The accompanying graph illustrates how this hypothetical foundation portfolio would have performed had it been funded with $1 million in 1950 and paid out 5.5 percent annually. This 5.5 percent is intended to represent the minimum 5 percent mandated payout plus .5 percent for expenses—chiefly investment expenses—that foundations

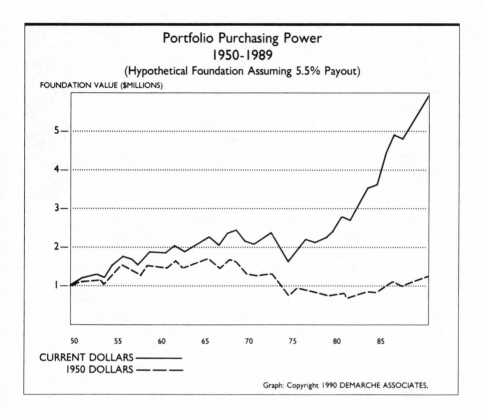

Portfolio Purchasing Power
1950-1989
(Hypothetical Foundation Assuming 5.5% Payout)

FOUNDATION VALUE ($MILLIONS)

CURRENT DOLLARS ————
1950 DOLLARS — — —

Graph: Copyright 1990 DEMARCHE ASSOCIATES,

incur and cannot include in the minimum. The graph's solid line represents the nominal value of the portfolio over 40 years. The line increases nicely, reflecting the impact of a compound annual return of 10.4 percent. However, the value in real terms—the dotted line—does not grow, reflecting the 4.3-percent inflation rate. The real progress made in the 1960s is wiped out by the difficult investment environment of the 1970s. Outstanding returns in the 1980s allow a recovery, but only back to the initial value. The payout of 5.5 percent is about all a foundation could have made and still maintained its real value. A much higher payout would result in a gradual liquidation of the portfolio.

MODELING THE MARKET

The returns used to construct this graph represent only a sample of what the capital markets can produce. Capital markets are not likely to

behave in the future exactly as they have in the past, and it is not sufficient to evaluate them alone. A better process, called "probabilistic
modeling," looks at these capital markets and the entire range of prob-
able results. Computer models are needed to make those projections
and to determine the best asset mix of stocks, bonds, cash, real estate,
and so on. Developing the model inputs is the crucial first step in for-
mulating an asset mix policy, as their quality affects the entire exercise.
The inputs for the model used in our study are based on historical data.
However, the data alone—raw, long-term average returns—can be
misleading. DeMarche undertook a complex process (reviewed in detail
in the full study) to analyze and adjust the historical data to develop its
model inputs.

Three inputs, describing the fundamental financial characteristics of
each asset class, are required to run the model. The first characteristic is
the long-term expected return, that is, what an asset class should provide on average. Second is the asset risk—"risk" being the volatility or
variability of returns, describing the probability of actually getting the
expected return.

The third characteristic, the correlation statistic, is the relation of the
returns of one asset class to the returns of another. Certain asset classes
have returns that are highly correlated; as the returns of one class rise,
the others rise, too. There are also asset classes whose returns are independent of one another or may even have an inverse relationship.
When such assets are combined, they offer excellent diversification
benefits because they can reduce the risk or volatility of the entire portfolio.

The model searches among all the asset classes for the best diversified portfolio, that is, the combination that most efficiently reduces risk.
The accompanying table provides a summarized version of the model
output, showing ten efficient portfolios—numbered one through ten—
that produced the highest return at a given level of risk. Portfolio
number one represents the lowest risk, containing only 20 percent
stocks, but 70 percent cash and bonds. Its expected return is 7.4 percent. Note that return assumptions in this table are based on a 4-per-
cent inflation rate. Subtracting this from the expected return, portfolio
number one produces a real return of approximately 3.4 percent. Such
a low real return will not support a payout rate of 5 percent.

Portfolio number ten is the most aggressive, bearing the highest risk.
It has 60 percent in domestic stocks plus 10 percent in international
stocks and 5 percent in venture capital. It produces a return of 9.9 percent. Again, this return assumption is based on a 4 percent inflation
rate and would support a maximum payout of approximately 5.9 per-

cent. In addition to the ten efficient portfolios, the table shows the representative portfolio based on Greenwich Associates' survey as number 11. This portfolio is not efficient because others offer more return for the same risk, or the same return for lower risk.

RISKY BUSINESS

When choosing its portfolio, a foundation must determine how much risk it can tolerate. The "shortfall risk" concept provides an intuitive bridge between investment statistics and the realm of human experience and understanding. Shortfall risk measures the probability of not meeting a return objective. This model is a tool used to calculate the probability of an actual return either exceeding or falling short of this objective.

Two objectives are used in this study. The first uses a floor return of zero; failure to meet it implies a loss of principal. The second objective is a return of about 9.5 percent, which would support a current payout of 5.5 percent and allow future payouts to keep pace with the 4-percent inflation rate.

The lowest-risk portfolio, number one in the table, has only a 10-percent probability of producing a loss after one year, although it has a 64-percent probability of not meeting the 9.5-percent return objective. On the other hand, the higher-risk portfolio, number eight, has a 21-percent probability of producing a loss. A foundation with a one-year time horizon and a high concern about capital losses will naturally gravitate toward the low risk portfolio. Bear in mind that this foundation will move toward a self-liquidation if its payout rate is 5 percent, because this conservative portfolio is expected to generate a real return of only 3.4 percent.

It is better to adopt a longer-term time horizon. Over a ten-year period, for instance, both portfolios have almost a zero-percent possibility of producing a loss. However, the low-risk portfolio has an 87-percent probability of not meeting the 9.5-percent return objective, while the higher risk portfolio has more than a 50-percent probability of meeting that objective. The foundation that adopts a longer-term time horizon can tolerate more risk and increases its chances of netting a higher return and of supporting a higher payout.

In brief, this study shows that:

- asset allocation and payout decisions are interrelated. If the payout rate exceeds the real return, the foundation will undergo an effective liquidation.

- determining asset allocation is the most critical investment decision trustees make, probably impacting the future of the foundation's assets more than which investment manager is selected.

- only by accepting higher levels of risk can foundations sustain payout rates above 6 percent if they also wish to maintain the purchasing power of their portfolios and future grants. Even to achieve real returns that would support payouts of 5 to 5.5 percent requires more aggressive asset mixes than many foundations currently use.

- the short-term investment horizon of many foundations appears inconsistent with a long-term grantmaking strategy. If foundations adopt a longer-term investment horizon, it would provide them with the risk tolerance needed to adopt more aggressive asset mixes, increase expected returns, and support higher payouts.

APPENDIX 12

Council on Foundations' Principles and Practices for Effective Grantmaking

As the contours of U.S. society have changed dramatically, so has the breadth and nature of organized philanthropy. The philanthropic enterprise is more varied in geography and type. It is more complex. It has entered into many more diverse relations with other U.S. institutions, including the corporate and governmental sectors. It is a more significant factor in forming and implementing public policy than ever. In the course of this evolution, trustees and managers of many foundations and other grantmaking institutions have developed an array of operating principles. Principles have a twofold advantage. They provide a framework for consistent, effective practice, and they afford the public a view of ethical and philosophical values on which grantmaking organizations base their conduct.

Organized philanthropy's voluntary efforts to set standards for accountability and openness follow in the tradition of other independent enterprises dedicated to the public interest. These self-determined measures strengthen and assure public confidence in the distinctive purposes and practices fundamental to the pluralistic world of philanthropy.

The Council on Foundations has served as the primary forum through which grantmakers have debated their views and exchanged experiences. This dialogue led the Council's Board of Directors, in June 1980, to adopt a statement on "Recommended Principles and Practices for Effective Grantmaking." The purpose of the statement is to provide practical counsel to new foundations in establishing their operating guidelines and to existing foundations and other donor organizations that may be re-examining their policies and procedures. In form and substance the statement recognizes the pluralistic nature of organized philanthropy and affirms what has proved useful in the successful handling of grants and in the maintenance of good relations with various publics.

279

In preparing the principles, a special committee drew suggestions from a wide variety of grantmaking organizations. Extended discussions were held at a number of regional associations of grantmakers' meetings. In addition, open hearings were held at the 1979 annual meeting of the Council.

The resulting statement of Principles and Practices for Effective Grantmaking, to which Council members subscribe, therefore represents not only the action of a Board of Directors representative of Council members, but also any number of modifications that emerged from a wide process of consultation throughout the grantmaking community.

In subscribing to this statement, members of the Council affirm their belief in the principles and practices and their willingness to move toward implementing them. While some of the practices refer rather specifically to professionally staffed foundations, smaller foundations and corporate giving programs strive to achieve the spirit of openness and accountability that underlies their principles in a manner consistent with their size, scope, and financial capacities.

Still, the statement is subject to further changes by later boards, and the issues raised in the statement should be topics for an ongoing dialogue. What is enduring, however, is the embodiment in the statement of the philosophy behind a rich tradition of U.S. philanthropy as well as a set of sound practices consistent with the dedication of organized grantmaking to the public interest.

PRINCIPLES AND PRACTICES FOR EFFECTIVE GRANTMAKING

1. Whatever the nature of the entity engaged in private grantmaking, and whatever its interests, it should seek to establish a set of basic policies that define the program interests and the fundamental objective to be served.

2. An identifiable board, committee, or other decision-making body should have clear responsibility for determining those policies and procedures, causing them to be implemented, and reviewing and revising them from time to time.

3. The processes for receiving, examining, and deciding on grant applications should be established on a clear and logical basis and should be followed in a manner consistent with the organization's policies and purposes.

4. Responsive grantmakers recognize that accountability extends beyond the narrow requirements of the law. Grantmakers should establish and carry out policies that recognize these multiple obliga-

tions for accountability: to the charter provisions by which their
founders defined certain basic expectations, to those charitable institutions they serve, to the general public, to the IRS, and to certain
state governmental agencies.

5. Open communications with the public and with grantseekers about
   the policies and procedures that are followed in grantmaking is in
   the interest of all concerned and is important if the grantmaking
   process is to function well, and if trust in the responsibility and accountability of grantmakers is to be maintained. A brief written
   statement about policies, program interests, grantmaking practices,
   geographic and policy restrictions, and preferred ways of receiving
   applications is recommended. Prompt acknowledgement of the receipt of any serious applications is important. Grantseekers whose
   programs and proposals fall outside the interests of the grantmakers
   should be told this immediately, and those whose proposals are still
   under consideration should be informed, insofar as is possible,
   of the steps and timing that will be taken in reaching the final
   decision.

6. Beyond the filing of forms required by government, grantmakers
   should consider possible ways of informing the public concerning
   their stewardship through publication and distribution of periodic
   reports, preferably annual reports, possibly supplemented by newsletters, reports to The Foundation Center, and the use of other communications channels.

7. The preservation and enhancement of an essential community of
   interest between the grantor and the grantee requires that their relationship be based on mutual respect, candor, and understanding
   with each investing the necessary time and attention to define
   clearly the purposes of the grant, the expectations as to reports related to financial and other matters, and the provisions for evaluating and publicizing projects. Many grantmakers, going beyond the
   providing of money, help grantees through such other means as
   assisting in the sharpening of the objectives, monitoring the performance, evaluating the outcome, and encouraging early planning
   for future stages.

8. It is important that grantmakers be alert and responsive to changing
   conditions in society and to the changing needs and merits of particular grantseeking organizations. Responses to needs and social
   conditions may well be determined by independent inquiries, not
   merely by reactions to requests submitted by grantseekers. In response to new challenges, grantmakers are helpful if they use the
   special knowledge, experience, and insight of individuals beyond
   those persons, families, or corporations from which the funds originally came. Some grantmakers find it useful to secure ideas and

comments from a variety of consultants and advisory panels, as well as diversified staff and board members. In view of the historic underrepresentation of minorities and women in supervisory and policy positions, particular attention should be given to finding ways to draw them into the decision-making processes.

9. From time to time, all grantmaking organizations should review their program interests, basic policies, and board and staff composition, and assess the overall results of their grantmaking.

10. Beyond the legal requirements that forbid staff, board members, and their families from profiting financially from any philanthropic grant, it is important that grantmakers weigh carefully all circumstances in which there exists the possibility of accusations of self-interest. In particular, staff and board members should disclose to the governing body the nature of their personal or family affiliation or involvement with any organizations for which a grant is considered, even though such affiliation may not give rise to any pecuniary conflict of interest.

11. Grantmakers should maintain interaction with others in the field of philanthropy, including such bodies as regional associations of grantmakers; the Foundation Center; the Council on Foundations; and various local, regional, and national independent sector organizations. They should bear in mind that they share with others responsibility for strengthening the effectiveness of the many private initiatives to serve the needs and interests of the public and for enhancing general understanding and support of such private initiatives within the community and the nation.

Why the Concern with Principles?

by James A. Joseph, President, Council on Foundations

To speak of principles is to speak of values and virtues that are presumed to be fundamental. At times the word is used literally to refer to rules of conduct, but the Council's statement of principles is much less prescriptive, referring instead to suggested guidelines in pursuit of what are deemed to be responsible and good foundation practices.

Given the ambiguity of moral language, some might argue that it is less than useful to marry the word principles with philanthropy. Yet, it is also possible that the word gives us a symbol with which to grasp and understand what is fundamental when we decide on priorities, choose among grantseekers, commit resources, and otherwise serve a public good.

This use of the word principles makes it a relatively late-born child in the family of virtues in which words like duty, law, goodness, and morality are its much older siblings.

Aristotle began his influential book on *Ethics* with the statement, "Every act and every inquiry and similarly every action and pursuit is thought to aim at some good." The concern with principles and practices in the foundation field is consistent with this claim in that it seeks to keep the eyes of grantmakers on purpose as well as process, on the responsibility *for* public benefit as well as the responsibility *to* private benefactors. And while cognate terms like "good" and "moral" might have been sufficient in the past to describe practices and values considered fundamental, we are likely to look for language that is more precise and definitive.

The most recent effort to engage foundation trustees and staff in a discussion of responsible foundation practices has brought to light the continuing tension between the unique priorities of each foundation and the larger mission shared in common with other grantmakers. Fortunately, this tension has enriched rather than stifled the discourse. But given the difficulty of the task and the lingering uneasiness engendered by any effort to propose standards, it is appropriate to ask, "Why the continuing concern with principles?"

The first answer is that the Council's statement on principles and practices was—and continues to be—an affirmation of pluralism as an essential value. It affirms the freedom of each foundation to choose which public purpose it will serve, while at the same time pointing to commonalities that go beyond our individual program choices. It is our "public-purpose" commitment that is the most persuasive in convincing critics and public policymakers that we should be permitted to hold philanthropic resources in trust for perpetuity.

A second answer is that the Council's statement affirms the goals to which most foundation trustees and staff already aspire. It is, therefore, a public acknowledgement of a private commitment, a demonstration to those who would further regulate an already overregulated sector that additional government involvement is neither needed nor desirable. When self-regulation works, it is not only good private practice, but good public policy.

That reality took on new significance both within and outside of the Council when, in 1983, the Council's board of directors adopted a policy that makes endorsement of the principles and practices statement a condition of membership. The action proved to be a form of enlightened self-interest, given the subsequent interest of Congress in every aspect of foundation activity, but particularly in the public accountability posture of our sector.

The fact that the vast majority of our members had, indeed, affirmed the statement on principles and practices was not lost on our elected officials. No public presentation by the Council or other witnesses was as effective as this demonstration of commitment to responsible foundation practices in making the case for less government regulation.

While there was criticism from a few of our members regarding this policy when it was adopted, the positive response from most confirms that there is a broadly shared set of common values regarding our responsibilities to the public we serve. In the end, the attempt to identify and affirm principles and practices constitutes a marriage of private and public values. This union preserves the social contract between private philanthropy and U.S. society and protects the legal charter that makes each foundation a trustee of the public good. And that is the ultimate answer to the question, "Why the concern with principles?"

Compensation of Directors
and Trustees

Statement Issued by
the Council on Foundations Board of Directors,
December 1989

The Council receives numerous inquiries about foundation practices regarding the compensation of directors and trustees. Among Council members, there is significant diversity of opinion about how we should respond. In light of the concern about this issue, it seems appropriate to provide guidelines to assist members in determining their policy.

It is important to make clear, however, that we are not addressing the practice of reimbursing directors and trustees for reasonable out-of-pocket expense, nor are we addressing the payment of compensation to commercial entities (such as banks, law firms, or trust companies) that may serve as trustees. The board of directors of the Council is firmly against excessive or unreasonable compensation. Even the perception of excessive compensation can be damaging to the whole field of philanthropy.

WHAT ARE THE VIEWS OF THE FOUNDATION COMMUNITY?

Many members of the foundation community oppose compensation of directors and trustees as a matter of principle. They note the long tradition of voluntary service by directors and trustees of nonprofits in general, and believe that compensation (other than to a commercial entity) is not necessary to obtain the services of qualified board members. Moreover, they feel that such payments reduce the funds available for grantmaking.

On the other hand, many foundations believe a fee is appropriate under certain circumstances. They note that responsible board service is time-consuming, that the legal requirements for running a foundation have become increasingly complex, and that compensation facilitates greater board diversity, since not all board members have sufficient means to take time away from other income-earning activities.

After considering these arguments, if a foundation decides to compensate directors or trustees, the following factors should be examined.

The Law

The payment of reasonable fees is lawful; excessive or unreasonable compensation violates federal and state law.

Ability to Attract Qualified Persons

Is the foundation satisfied that it will be able to attract qualified board members either at the current rate of compensation (which may be zero) or at some other level of compensation?

What is Reasonable

Given the extensive diversity of foundations in asset size, spending level and complexity of program, and the different time demands required of board members, no single formula to define reasonable compensation exists. What is reasonable will depend on the facts and circumstances of each case.

DETERMINING REASONABLENESS

In considering the question of reasonableness of compensation, each of the following factors should be closely examined:

    a. What functions are required and actually performed by board members?

    b. What level of skill or experience is necessary to perform these functions?

    c. How much time is *actually* spent by each board member to complete the functions required?

Foundations that do pay or are considering fees to directors or trustees are encouraged to undertake this three-part analysis on a regular basis.

COMPENSATION BASED ON A PERCENTAGE OF ASSETS

The practice of compensating *individual* directors or trustees by providing a fee based on a percentage of assets or income (which is utilized by a few foundations) is inconsistent with these guidelines for determining reasonableness. Percentage fees for individual board members provide a greater potential for excessive compensation and should be avoided.

FEES FOR SPECIFIC SERVICES

In addition to the normal "core duties" of a foundation board such as setting overall policy and overseeing investment management, some directors and trustees provide specific services for which they receive a professional fee (e.g., brokerage fees, legal fees or accounting/auditing fees). Such arrangements can lead to fees that are excessive. The use of outside professionals for paid services is preferable. If, however, board members are paid fees for professional services, the foundation should take care to determine that the fees provided are reasonable based on the three factors noted earlier, and taking into account the prevailing market costs for such services in the community.

Guidelines for Publishing a Minimum Annual Report

This resource paper aims to show that a foundation can publish an attractive annual report at low cost. For example, one format that can be used is a brochure made up of six panels. It will slip easily into a no. 10 envelope, and will contain sufficient facts about the foundation and its grant activities to make publication worthwhile.

The brochure will include the year, as well as the name and location of the foundation on the cover and on panel six. The cover will also state that it is an annual report. It may include a picture, graphic design, logo, or other feature. Panel two, reviewing the year, could include a brief history of the foundation, a president's report, and assessment of the past year's activities, including board changes. There is space on this panel for about 350 words.

Panels three and four describe grant summaries. Each of these panels can handle about 300–350 words, depending upon the layout. Panel five is the financial page, providing for both a balance sheet and a statement of revenues, expenditures and fund balance.

Finally, panel six defines the foundation's interest so the grantseeking reader may know whether or not this foundation is worth pursuing. Guidelines for grant applicants may be included on this panel, as well as a list of the board members and officers. The foundation's complete address and telephone number should also be included. If space permits, it is good to identify board members by their position outside the foundation as well.

DISTRIBUTION

Often an organization prints a certain quantity of material, then considers the question of distribution. Save money, make the distribution plan first. A basic distribution list follows, including:

- trustees and other individuals associated with the foundation or interested in it.

- present and past grant recipients, and other organizations in the community in the fields in which the foundation is involved.

- agencies and individuals with similar program interest, including local and state agencies, and federal agencies in the area.

- other foundations in the community or foundations with similar interests, The Foundation Center, your regional association of grantmakers (if applicable) and the Council on Foundations.

- member of Congress, state legislators, city council members and the mayor, and state governor. The copies sent to elected officials would be more appreciated if accompanied by a brief letter, saying that you wish to call their attention to the report dealing with your foundations's activities, etc.

- local newspapers, both daily and weekly, and radio and TV stations, and specialized journals if appropriate. Targeting these press copies is not difficult. Address a copy to the city desk, another to the editorial page editor, to the education news writer, or whatever. Do the same for the radio and TV people. Include a letter indicating that more information about the projects mentioned in the report is available, and offer an interview.

Now for the report itself.

Paper

Use cover-weight (65-lb) paper for the brochure. Check samples from your printer for texture as well as color. Chances are your press run will be small (500 or 1,000 at most), so you can afford a better grade of paper. Recycled paper is also an option to consider.

Size

The six panel brochure is created from $11 \times 8\frac{1}{2}$ sheet, folded to $3\frac{3}{4} \times 8\frac{1}{2}$. Actually, the printer may suggest that he could make the brochure $4 \times 8\frac{3}{4}$, which is fine as this also fits in the no. 10 envelope.

Typography

Ask to see your printer's catalog of available typefaces or, better yet, samples of printed materials. You will have a choice between serif or sans serif typefaces. Discuss your annual report with the printer, and ask for recommendations regarding the best typeface to use. You should have a good idea of what your finished product will look like and its cost before going into the project.

Cover

The cover can be as plain or fancy as budget permits. Large, bold type superimposed on a photograph is effective, but a cover stating the name of the foundation, and the fact that it is the annual report for a specific year, is sufficient.

Ink

Black is the most economical color; it is also preferable if you decide to use photographs. At an additional cost, you may specify a certain color or the use of two colors.

Sample Contents of the Report

FINANCIAL STATEMENT

Balance Sheet

	Year Ended August 31	
	1985	1984
Assets:		
Cash (overdraft)	$ 568	$ (565)
Interest receivable	1,344	1,248
Loans receivable	2,100	0
Investments	213,266	211,766
Total	$217,278	$212,449
Liabilities and Fund Balance		
Liabilities:		
Provision for federal excise tax	$ 350	$ 440
Grants payable	3,010	0
Total liabilities	3,360	440
Fund Balance:	213,918	212,009
	$217,278	$212,449

Statement of Revenues, Expenses, and Fund Balance

	Year Ended August 31	
	1985	1984
Revenue:		
Contributions received	$ 14,000	$ 10,000
Investment income	17,231	17,754
Grant refunds	11,218	939
Gain on sale of investments	0	4,669
Total revenue	$ 42,449	$ 33,362

Statement of Revenues, Expenses,
and Fund Balance
(continued)

	Year Ended August 31	
	1985	1984
Expense:		
Grants and loans	26,315	24,115
Rent	3,585	3,181
Travel and meetings	2,644	1,681
Professional services	1,555	1,468
Trustee's fee	1,303	1,077
Office expense	1,055	1,607
Communications	837	812
Utilities	756	293
Dues	731	969
Insurance	649	258
Taxes	336	112
Printing	277	473
Postage	150	315
Write-off of note receivable	0	2,000
Miscellaneous	347	65
Total expense	40,540	38,426
Excess (deficiency) of revenue over expense	1,909	(5,064)
Fund balance at beginning of year	212,009	217,073
Fund balance, at end of year	$213,918	$212,009

STAFF

John Smith, executive director

Kay Kauffman, administrative assistant

GRANT APPLICATIONS

The foundation encourages applications on behalf of projects that will benefit organizations in the areas of education, environmental research, health care, social services, and arts and culture. Requests should be in writing and submitted to Mr. John Smith, executive director, the John and Jane Doe Foundation.

GRANT LIMITATIONS

As required by the articles of incorporation (or) . . . In accordance with board policy, established in 1980, grants are made only to organizations in the states of . . . (or) only in the field of . . .

Please send inquiries to:

The John and Jane Doe Foundation, Inc.
123 East Broad Street
Akron, Ohio
123/456–7890

REVIEW OF THE YEAR

President's Report

The John and Jane Doe foundation has traditionally supported five important areas: education, environmental research, health care, social services, arts and culture. In 1985, the foundation was able to provide grants totalling $26,315 to . . .

Board Changes

Two able and enthusiastic members joined the board of the foundation this year. Mary H. Smith, currently executive director of the American University of Women and . . .

Purpose

The purpose for which the John and Jane Doe Foundation was formed is set forth in the second section of its articles of incorporation: "To receive and administer money and other property exclusively for educational, environmental, health, social, and cultural purposes; to make grants, gifts or contributions to associations or trusts, or community chests, funds, or foundations organized and operated exclusively for . . . .

HISTORY

The John and Jane Doe Foundation was founded in 1947. Its principal office was established in the city of Akron, Ohio. Gifts and donations to the John and Jane Doe Foundation are tax deductible as it was declared tax exempt from Federal Income Tax under Section 101 (6) of the Internal Revenue Code on December 23, 1948, and later classified under Section 501(c)(3) of the Internal Revenue Code as of October 20, 1970.

Important: Always list names of grants, city, and state, and the purpose of the grant!

1985 GRANTS

Education

Kent School Advisory Committee $3,665
Kent, Ohio

To aid in planning the curriculum for children ages 6–10 who currently fall below grade level on achievement tests. New methods of teaching will be studied and a report recommending action filed with the school board.

Environmental Research

Wasted Systems Council $5,600
Price, Utah

To cover the costs of doing the necessary research for a bimonthly newsletter to be sent to local industries, governmental units, and concerned citizens.

Health Care

Bergen County Hospital $7,500
Centerville, New Jersey

For general operating purposes.

Social Services

County Respite Care $2,000
Ely, Minnesota

To cover staff time for a new service which allows families with se-
verely disabled children to leave their children under professional supervision on weekends.

Arts and Culture

Music in the School $3,050
Atoochee, Ohio

To cover costs of a series of 24 concerts in the Rook County school system coordinated by the Atoochee Arts Council. The grant was matched
by the Music Lovers Trust Fund of Atoochee.

Craft Days $2,500
Cleveland, Ohio

To cover advertising costs for Cleveland Arts Society's annual Craft
Days event. Held May 3–6, the show drew 300 participants and more
than 10,000 spectators.

10th Annual Poetry Contest $2,000
Elmwood, Ohio

To cover judges fees, miscellaneous costs and prizes for winners. Directed by Smith Junior College, the event drew 312 entries.

Standards for Charitable Organizations

**NATIONAL
CHARITIES
INFORMATION
BUREAU**

Standards in Philanthropy

> The National Charities Information Bureau was founded in 1918 by a group of national leaders who were concerned that Americans were giving millions of dollars to charitable organizations, particularly war relief organizations, that they knew little or nothing about.
>
> Through the years, NCIB has evolved into an organization that promotes informed giving. NCIB believes that donors are entitled to accurate information about the charitable organizations that seek their support. NCIB also believes that well-informed givers should ask questions and make judgments that will lead to an improved level of performance by charitable organizations.
>
> To help givers and charitable organizations, NCIB collects and analyzes information about charities and evaluates them according to the following standards.

Preamble

The support of philanthropic organizations soliciting funds from the general public is based on public trust. The most reliable evaluation of an organization is a detailed review. Yet the organization's compliance with a basic set of standards can indicate whether it is fulfilling its obligations to contributors, to those who benefit from its programs, and to the general public.

Responsibility for ensuring sound policy guidance and governance and for meeting these basic standards rests with the governing board, which is answerable to the public.

The National Charities Information Bureau recommends and applies the following nine standards as common measures of governance and management.

NCIB Standards

Governance, Policy and Program Fundamentals

1. **Board Governance:** The board is responsible for policy setting, fiscal guidance, and ongoing governance, and should regularly review the organization's policies, programs, and operations. The board should have

   a. an independent, volunteer membership;

   b. a minimum of 5 voting members;

   c. an individual attendance policy;

   d. specific terms of office for its officers and members;

   e. in-person, face-to-face meetings, at least twice a year, evenly spaced, with a majority of voting members in attendance at each meeting;

   f. no fees to members for board service, but payments may be made for costs incurred as a result of board participation;

   g. no more than one paid staff person member, usually the chief staff officer, who shall not chair the board or serve as treasurer;

   h. policy guidelines to avoid material conflicts of interest involving board or staff;

   i. no material conflicts of interest involving board or staff;

   j. a policy promoting pluralism and diversity within the organization's board, staff, and constituencies.

NCIB Interpretations and Applications

Fiscal guidance includes responsibility for investment management decisions, for internal accounting controls, and for short and long-term budgeting decisions.

The ability of individual board members to make independent decisions on behalf of the organization is critical. Existence of relationships that could interfere with this independence compromises the board.

Many organizations need more than five members on the board. Five, however, is seen as the minimum required for adequate governance.

Board membership should be more than honorary, and should involve active participation in board meetings.

Many board responsibilities may be carried out through committee actions, and such additional active board involvement should be encouraged. No level of committee involvement, however, can substitute for the face-to-face interaction of the full board in reviewing the organization's policy-making and program operations. As a rule, the full board should meet to discuss and ratify the organization's decisions and actions at least twice a year. If, however, the organization has an executive committee of at least five voting members, then three meetings of the executive committee, evenly spaced, with a majority in attendance, can substitute for one of the two full board meetings.

Organizations should recruit board members most qualified, regardless of their financial status, to join in making policy decisions. Costs related to a board member's participation could include such items as travel and daycare arrangements. Situations where board members derive financial benefits from board service should be avoided.

In all instances where an organization's business or policy decisions can result in direct or indirect financial or personal benefit to a member of the board or staff, the decisions in question must be explicitly reviewed by the board with the members concerned absent.

Organizations vary widely in their ability to demonstrate pluralism and diversity. Every organization should establish a policy, consistent with its mission statement, that fosters such inclusiveness. An affirmative action program is an example of fulfilling this requirement.

2. **Purpose:** The organization's purpose, approved by the board, should be formally and specifically stated.

The formal or abridged statement of purpose should appear with some frequency in organization publications and presentations.

3. **Programs:** The organization's activities should be consistent with its statement of purpose.

4. **Information:** Promotion, fund raising, and public information should describe accurately the organization's identity, purpose, programs, and financial needs.

Not every communication from an organization need contain all this descriptive information, but each one should include all accurate information relevant to its primary message.

There should be no material omissions, exaggerations of fact, misleading photographs, or any other practice which would tend to create a false impression or misunderstanding.

5. **Financial Support and Related Activities:** The board is accountable for all authorized activities generating financial support on the organization's behalf:

   a. fund-raising practices should encourage voluntary giving and should not apply unwarranted pressure;

   b. descriptive and financial information for all substantial income and for all revenue-generating activities conducted by the organization should be disclosed on request;

   Such activities include, but are not limited to, fees for service, related and unrelated business ventures, and for-profit subsidiaries.

   c. basic descriptive and financial information for income derived from authorized commercial activities, involving the organization's name, which are conducted by for-profit organizations, should be available. All public promotion of such commercial activity should either include this information or indicate that it is available from the organization.

   Basic descriptive and financial information may vary depending on the promotional activity involved. Common elements would include, for example, the campaign time frame, the total amount or the percentage to be received by the organization, whether the organization's contributor list is made available to the for-profit company, and the campaign expenses directly incurred by the organization.

6. **Use of Funds:** The organization's use of funds should reflect consideration of current and future needs and resources in planning for program continuity. The organization should:

   a. spend at least 60% of annual expenses for program activities;

   b. insure that fund-raising expenses, in relation to fund-raising results, are reasonable over time;

   Fund-raising methods available to organizations vary widely and often have very different costs. Overall, an organization's fund-raising expense should be reasonable in relation to the contributions received, which could include indirect contributions (such as federated campaign support), bequests (generally averaged over five years), and government grants.

   c. have net assets available for the following fiscal year not usually more than twice the current year's expenses or the next year's budget, whichever is higher;

   Reserve Funds
   Unless specifically told otherwise, most contributors believe that their contributions are being applied to the current program needs identified by the organization.

   Organizations may accumulate reserve funds in the interest of prudent management. Reserve funds in excess of the standard may be justified in special circumstances.

   In all cases the needs of the constituency served should be the most important factor in determining and evaluating the appropriate level of available net assets.

   d. not have a persistent and/or increasing deficit in the unrestricted fund balance.

   Deficits
   An organization which incurs a deficit in its unrestricted fund balance should make every attempt to restore the fund balance as soon as possible. Any organization sustaining a substantial and persistent, or an increasing, deficit is at least in demonstrable financial danger, and may even be fiscally irresponsible. In its evaluations, NCIB will take into account evidence of remedial efforts.

Reporting and Fiscal Fundamentals

7. **Annual Reporting:** An annual report should be available on request, and should include

Where an equivalent package of documentation, identified as such, is available and routinely supplied upon request, it may substitute for an annual report.

   a. an explicit narrative description of the organization's major activities, presented in the same major categories and covering the same fiscal period as the audited financial statements;

   b. a list of board members;

The listing of board members should include some identifying information on each member.

   c. audited financial statements or, at a minimum, a comprehensive financial summary that 1) identifies all revenues in significant categories, 2) reports expenses in the same program, management/ general, and fund-raising categories as in the audited financial statements, and 3) reports all ending balances. (When the annual report does not include the full audited financial statements, it should indicate that they are available on request.)

In particular, financial summaries or extracts presented separately from the audited financial statements should be clearly related to the information in these statements and consistent with them.

8. **Accountability:** An organization should supply on request complete financial statements which

   a. are prepared in conformity with generally accepted accounting principles (GAAP), accompanied by a report of an independent certified public accountant, and reviewed by the board;

To be able to make its financial analysis, NCIB may require more detailed information regarding the interpretation, applications and validation of GAAP guidelines used in the audit. Accountants can vary widely in their interpretations of GAAP guidelines, especially regarding such relatively new practices as multi-purpose allocations. NCIB may question some interpretations and applications.

and

   b. fully disclose economic resources and obligations, including transactions with related parties and affiliated organizations, significant events affecting finances, and significant categories of income and expense;

and should also supply

   c. a statement of functional allocation of expenses, in addition to such statements required by generally accepted accounting principles to be included among the financial statements;

   d. combined financial statements for a national organization operating with affiliates prepared in the foregoing manner.

9. **Budget:** The organization should prepare a detailed annual budget consistent with the major classifications in the audited financial statements, and approved by the board.

Program categories can change from year to year; the budget should still allow meaningful comparison with the previous year's financial statements, recast if necessary.

NCIB believes the spirit of these standards to be universally useful for all nonprofit organizations. However, for organizations less than three years old or with annual budgets of less than $100,000, greater flexibility in applying some of the standards may be appropriate.

National Charities Information Bureau, Inc.
19 Union Square West • New York, NY 10003-3395 • (212) 929-6300

The Council of Better Business Bureaus' Standards for Charitable Solicitations[1]

INTRODUCTION

The Council of Better Business Bureaus promulgates these standards to promote ethical practices by philanthropic organizations. The Council of Better Business Bureaus believes that adherence to these standards by soliciting organizations will inspire public confidence, further the growth of public participation in philanthropy, and advance the objectives of responsible private initiative and self-regulation.

Both the public and soliciting organizations will benefit from voluntary disclosure of an organization's activities, finances, fundraising practices, and governance—information that donors and prospective donors will reasonably wish to consider.

These standards apply to publicly soliciting organizations that are tax exempt under Section 501(c)(3) of the Internal Revenue Code, and to other organizations conducting charitable solicitations.

While the Council of Better Business Bureaus and its member Better Business Bureaus generally do not report on schools, colleges, or churches soliciting within their congregations, they encourage all soliciting organizations to adhere to these standards.

These standards were developed with professional and technical assistance from representatives of soliciting organizations, professional fundraising firms and associations, the accounting profession, corporate contributions officers, regulatory agencies, and the Better Business Bureau system. The Council of Better Business Bureaus is solely responsible for the contents of these standards.

FOR THE PURPOSES OF THESE STANDARDS:

1. "Charitable solicitations" (or "solicitation") is any direct or indirect request for money, property, credit, volunteer service, or other thing of value, to be given now or on a deferred basis, on the representation that it will be used for charitable, educational, religious, benevolent, patriotic, civic, or other philanthropic purposes. Solicitations include invitations to voting membership and appeals to voting

---

[1] Reprinted with permission. Copyright 1982 by the Council of Better Business Bureaus, Inc., 4200 Wilson Blvd., Arlington, VA 22203.

members when a contribution is a principal requirement for membership.

2. "Soliciting organization" (or "organization") is any corporation, trust, group, partnership, or individual engaged in a charitable solicitation; a "solicitor" is anyone engaged in a charitable solicitation.

3. The "public" includes individuals, groups, associations, corporations, foundations, institutions, and/or government agencies.

4. "Fundraising" includes a charitable solicitation, the activities, representations, and materials that are an integral part of the planning, creation, production, and communication of the solicitation; and the collection of the money, property, or other thing of value requested. Fundraising includes but is not limited to donor acquisition and renewal, development, fund or resource development, member or membership development, and contract or grant procurement.

PUBLIC ACCOUNTABILITY

1. *Soliciting organizations shall provide on request an annual report.* The annual report, an annually updated written account, shall present the organization's purposes, descriptions, overall programs, activities and accomplishments; eligibility to receive deductible contributions; information about the governing body and structure; and information about financial activities and financial position.

2. *Soliciting organizations shall provide on request complete annual financial statements.* The financial statements shall present the overall financial activities and financial position of the organization, shall be prepared in accordance with generally accepted accounting principles and reporting practices, and shall include the auditor's or treasurer's report, notes, and any supplementary schedules. When total annual income exceeds $100,000, the financial statements shall be audited in accordance with generally accepted auditing standards.

3. *Soliciting organizations' financial statements shall present adequate information to serve as a basis for informed decisions.* Information needed as a basis for informed decisions generally includes but is not limited to: (a) significant categories of contributions and other income; (b) expenses reported in categories corresponding to the descriptions of major programs and activities contained in the annual report, solicitations, and other informational materials; (c) a detailed schedule of expenses by natural classification (e.g., salaries, employee benefits, occupancy, postage, etc.), presenting the natural expenses incurred for each major program and supporting activity; (d) accurate presentation

of all fundraising and administrative costs; and (e) when a significant activity combines fundraising and one or more other purposes (e.g., door-to-door canvassing combining fundraising and social advocacy, or television broadcasts combining fundraising and religious ministry, or a direct mail campaign combining fundraising and public education), the financial statements shall specify the total cost of the multipurpose activity and the basis for allocating its costs.

4. *Organizations receiving a substantial portion of their income through the fundraising activities of controlled or affiliated entities shall provide on request an accounting of all income received by and fundraising costs incurred by such entities.* Such entities include committees, branches, or chapters that are controlled by or affiliated with the benefiting organization, and for which a primary activity is raising funds to support the programs of the benefiting organization.

USE OF FUNDS

1. *A reasonable percentage of total income from all sources shall be applied to programs and activities directly related to the purposes for which the organization exists.*

2. *A reasonable percentage of public contributions shall be applied to the programs and activities described in solicitations, in accordance with donor expectations.*

3. *Fundraising costs shall be reasonable.*

4. *Total fundraising and administrative costs shall be reasonable.* Reasonable use of funds requires that (a) at least 50% of total income from all sources be spent on programs and activities directly related to the organizations' purposes; (b) at least 50% of public contributions be spent on the programs and activities described in solicitations, in accordance with donor expectations; (c) fundraising costs not exceed 35% of related contributions; and (d) total fundraising and administrative costs not exceed 50% of total income.

An organization that does not meet one or more of these percentage limitations may provide evidence to demonstrate that its use of funds is reasonable. The higher fundraising and administrative costs of a newly created organization, donor restrictions on the use of funds, exceptional bequests, a stigma associated with a cause, and environmental or political events beyond an organization's control are among the factors that may result in costs that are reasonable although they do not meet the percentage limitations.

5. *Soliciting organizations shall substantiate on request their application*

of funds, in accordance with donor expectations, to the programs and activities described in solicitations.

6. Soliciting organizations shall establish and exercise adequate controls over disbursements.

SOLICITATIONS AND INFORMATIONAL MATERIALS

1. Solicitations and informational materials, distributed by any means, shall be accurate, truthful, and not misleading, both in whole and in part.

2. Soliciting organizations shall substantiate on request that solicitations and informational materials, distributed by any means, are accurate, truthful, and not misleading, in whole and in part.

3. Solicitations shall include a clear description of the programs and activities for which funds are requested. Solicitations that describe an issue, problem, need, or event, but that do not clearly describe the programs or activities for which funds are requested will not meet this standard. Solicitations in which time or space restrictions apply shall identify a source from which written information is available.

4. Direct contact solicitations, including personal and telephone appeals, shall identify (a) the solicitor and his/her relationship to the benefiting organization, (b) the benefiting organization or cause, and (c) the programs and activities for which funds are requested.

5. Solicitations in conjunction with the sale of goods, services or admissions shall identify at the point of solicitation (a) the benefiting organization, (b) a source from which written information is available, and (c) the actual or anticipated portion of the sales or admission price to benefit the charitable organization or cause.

FUNDRAISING PRACTICES

1. Soliciting organizations shall establish and exercise controls over fundraising activities conducted for their benefit by staff, volunteers, consultants, contractors, and controlled or affiliated entities, including commitment to writing of all fundraising contracts and agreements.

2. Soliciting organizations shall establish and exercise adequate controls over contributions.

3. Soliciting organizations shall honor donor requests for confidentiality and shall not publicize the identity of donors without prior written permission. Donor requests for confidentiality include but are not limited to requests that one's name not be used, exchanged, rented or sold.

4. Fundraising shall be conducted without excessive pressure. Excessive pressure in fundraising includes but is not limited to solicitations in the guise of invoices; harassment, intimidation or coercion, such as threats of public disclosure or economic retaliation; failure to inform recipients of unordered items that they are under no obligation to pay for or return them; and strongly emotional appeals that distort the organization's activities or beneficiaries.

GOVERNANCE

1. *Soliciting organizations shall have an adequate governing structure.* Soliciting organizations shall have and operate in accordance with governing instruments (charter, articles of incorporation, bylaws, etc.) that set forth the organization's basic goals and purposes and that define the organizational structure. The governing instruments shall define the body having final responsibility for and authority over the organization's policies and programs (including authority to amend the governing instruments), as well as any subordinate bodies to which specific responsibilities may be delegated

An organization's governing structure shall be inadequate if any policy-making decisions of the governing body (board) or committee of board members having interim policy-making authority (executive committee) are made by fewer than three persons.

2. *Soliciting organizations shall have an active governing body.* An active governing body (board) exercises responsibility in establishing policies, retaining qualified executive leadership, and overseeing that leadership.

An active board meets formally at least three times annually, with meetings evenly spaced over the course of the year, and with a majority of the members in attendance (in person or by proxy) on average.

Because the public reasonably expects board members to participate personally in policy decisions, the governing body is not active and a roster of board members may be misleading, if a majority of the board members attend no formal board meetings in person over the course of a year.

If the full board meets only once annually, there shall be at least two additional, evenly spaced meetings during the year of an executive committee of board members having interim policy-making authority, with a majority of its members present in person, on average.

3. *Soliciting organizations shall have an independent governing body.* Organizations whose directly and/or indirectly compensated board members constitute more than one-fifth (20%) of the total voting mem-

bership of the board or of the executive committee will not meet this standard. (The ordained clergy of a publicly soliciting church, who serve as members of the church's policy-making governing body, are excepted from this 20% limitation, although they may be salaried by or receive support or sustenance from the church.)

Organizations engaged in transactions in which board members have material conflicting interests resulting from the relationship or business affiliation will not meet this standard.

Copyright 1982
Council of Better Business Bureaus, Inc.
Publication No. 311-25129
F25 03 90

Philanthropic Advisory Service
Council of Better Business Bureaus, Inc.
4200 Wilson Boulevard
Arlington, VA 22203
(703) 276-0100

APPENDIX 16

Council on Foundations

The Council on Foundations is a membership organization of grant-makers founded in 1949 to promote and strengthen organized philanthropy. Its 1,200 members include independent, operating, community, public, company-sponsored, and international foundations; and corporate giving programs. The Council represents the concerns and interests of grantmakers to public policymakers, the media, and the general public.

Through conferences, publications, educational activities, information services, and special programs, the Council works closely with its members to promote responsible and effective grantmaking, to secure and maintain public policy supportive of philanthropy, to enhance the understanding of organized philanthropy in the wider society, to support and enhance cooperation among grantmakers, and to promote the growth of organized philanthropy both in the United States and internationally.

Government relations, information services, communications, and research are integral parts of the Council's services to members, their trustees, and the grantmaking field. Recognizing that the U.S. population is about to consist of a majority of minorities, the Council has launched a special project to support pluralism in philanthropy.

A board of directors representing all regions of the United States and all types of grantmaking institutions determines council policies. The Council also collaborates with more than 30 regional associations of grantmakers and some 25 special interest affinity groups. By subscribing to a set of principles and practices for effective grantmaking, Council members provide leadership in the area of public accountability.

GOVERNMENT RELATIONS

- active representation of grantmaking interests and concerns to Congress, federal agencies, the White House, and state legislatures
- advisory services on legal and tax matters

- a nationwide Legislative Network, comprised of foundation staff and trustees who closely monitor legislative issues and contact key officials
- up-to-date news and information through *Washington Update*, a periodic newsletter that reports on important legislative and regulatory issues

RESEARCH

- data and analysis of trends that may influence public policy and the management of grantmaking organizations
- biennial survey of compensation and benefits practices among grantmaking organizations—the only source of comparative information on staff and trustee compensation, benefits, personnel policies, and other internal management issues

INFORMATION SERVICES AND PUBLICATIONS

- information and referral services to members
- consultation and materials on such topics as grantmaking practices, administration, foundation governance, corporate community involvement, or starting a foundation or corporate giving program
- publications, such as the *Resources for Grantmakers* series, which provide members with information on grantmaking practices
- communications advice and assistance to members

COMMUNICATIONS AND PUBLIC AFFAIRS

- *Foundation News*, the bimonthly magazine of philanthropy and the nonprofit sector, provides coverage of current activities and issues affecting grantmakers
- *Council Columns*, the biweekly newsletter that contains news and information on grantmaking, including articles on events and activities undertaken by the Council, its members, and the field
- public policy briefings on social and economic issues, conducted for public officials and grantmakers
- editorial briefings, roundtables, and other services to assist the media and promote positive coverage of the grantmaking field
- communications advice and assistance to members

EDUCATIONAL PROGRAMS

- an annual conference focusing on important programmatic, philosophical, and management issues of concern to grantmakers

- workshops and seminars designed especially for staff and trustees on grantmaking, management, leadership, and program issues
- special programs and workshops for community foundations, family foundations, trustees, and corporate grantmakers

INTERNATIONAL AFFAIRS

- technical assistance to U.S. foundations and corporate giving programs engaged in grantmaking overseas
- educational travel to increase global awareness among grantmakers
- training and resources for those engaged in philanthropic activities outside the United States

Council on Foundations
1828 L Street, N.W., Suite 300
Washington, DC 20036
(202) 466–6512

APPENDIX 17

Regional Associations of Grantmakers

The following list contains names of regional associations of grant-makers across the United States. While most on the list are formally organized, some are informal groups. For more information about the regional association in your area, please contact the Council on Foundations.

Arizona Private and Community Foundation Group

Associated Grantmakers of Massachusetts

Association of Baltimore Area Grantmakers

Charlotte Area Donors Forum

Clearinghouse for Midcontinent Foundations (Kansas City, MO)

Conference of Southwest Foundations (serves primarily Arizona, Arkansas, Colorado, New Mexico, Oklahoma, and Texas)

Co-ordinating Council for Foundations, Inc. (Hartford, CT)

Council of Michigan Foundations

Council of New Jersey Grantmakers

Delaware Valley Grantmakers (serves primarily Delaware; New Jersey; Philadelphia, Pennsylvania)

Des Moines Contributions Group

Donors Forum of Chicago

Donors Forum of Miami

Donors Forum of Ohio

Foundation Forum of Wisconsin

Grantmakers Forum (Cleveland)

Source: The Council on Foundations, June 1990.

Grantmakers of Western Pennsylvania

Hui of Foundations (Hawaii)

Indiana Donors Alliance

Maine Grantmakers Association

Metropolitan Association for Philanthropy (St. Louis)

Minnesota Council on Foundations

Nebraska Association of Grantmakers

New York Regional Association of Grantmakers

Northern California Grantmakers

Pacific Northwest Grantmakers Forum (serves primarily Alaska, Idaho, Montana, Oregon, Washington)

Rochester (NY) Grantmakers' Forum

San Diego Grantmakers Group

Southeastern Council of Foundations (serves primarily Alabama, Arkansas, Florida, Georgia, Kentucky, Louisiana, Mississippi, North Carolina, South Carolina, Tennessee, Virginia)

Southern California Association for Philanthropy

Southern Louisiana Grantmakers Forum

Western New York Grantmakers Association

APPENDIX 18

Affinity Groups Associated with the Council on Foundations

Affinity groups provide opportunities for grantmakers with like funding interests to come together to discuss issues, learn more about different areas, and develop professional networks. Some groups are professionally staffed organizations. Others are managed by volunteers. For more information on these groups, or to find out about new groups being formed, please contact the Council on Foundations.

Association of Black Foundation Executives

Communications Network in Philanthropy

Grantmakers Interested in Film, Video, and Television

The Funders' Committee for Voter Registration and Education

Funders Concerned About AIDS

Grantmakers for Children and Youth

Grantmakers in Health

Grantmakers Concerned With Adolescent Pregnancy

Environmental Grantmakers Association

Grantmakers Interested in Religion

Grantmakers Interested in the Arts

Grantmakers in Aging

Grantmakers in Justice

Hispanics in Philanthropy

National Network of Grantmakers

Neighborhood Funders' Group

Precollegiate Education Group

Women and Foundations/Corporate Philanthropy

Working Group on Funding Lesbian and Gay Issues

Grantmakers Concerned About Alcohol and Other Drug Abuse

Southern Africa Grantmakers

Forum on Religion and Public Life

Asians and Pacific Islanders in Philanthropy

Grantmakers Concerned with Mental Illness

Grantmakers Concerned with Immigrants and Refugees

APPENDIX 19

The Foundation Center

The Foundation Center is a national service organization supported by foundations, corporations, and other donors, along with earned income from publications and services. The Center is a unique source of factual information on foundation and corporate philanthropic giving. The Center does not have members. It takes no position of advocacy. It is regarded as an objective, neutral, and authoritative source of information.

The Center's mission is to improve access to information about private grantmaking institutions and the grantseeking process. It does this through a central office, three regional offices, and network of some 181 cooperating libraries and by means of a publications program issuing reference works on funders and grants, technical assistance books for grantseekers, and research and scholarly works on the field. Electronic online databases also disseminate information nationally and abroad.

The Center helps grantmakers by creating a favorable information environment. The existence of the Center demonstrates that foundations are accountable and forthcoming in what they do. Center files of foundation information are always available for public scrutiny, and are frequently cited as a definitive source. The information amassed in Center records underscores the good work of foundations and their benefit to society.

The Center also helps grantmakers by educating the grantseeking public about the funding research process, thereby reducing the number of out-of-scope applications; by acting as a referral point when requests for grants must be declined; and by helping to identify other funders with similar program interests. Center staff respond promptly to questions from grantmakers that can be answered from the extensive public record. In addition, the Center provides the following special services directly to grantmakers (those marked with an asterisk are fee based):

- instruction in the use of its resources by means of group or individual orientations and audio visual presentations

- ready reference service by telephone
- multiple copies of the cooperating collections list
- brochures outlining services and publications in quantity
- photocopying of the Center's paper and microform materials*
- custom computer searches of the Center's databases*
- mailing labels for selected lists of grantmakers*
- rental of the Center's press list*

Center sponsors receive a complimentary copy of *The Foundation Directory* and discounts on other publications.

In 1989 the Center introduced a new grants classification system based on the National Taxonomy of Exempt Entities developed instructional and support materials that enable grantmakers to work with the system.

PUBLIC SERVICES

Each year at least 250,000 people are served directly by the Center or one of its cooperating libraries or indirectly by referring to one or more of its publications. By far the greatest number of users are grantseekers, but the Center also serves foundation and government officials and staff, scholars, journalists, and professionals who work in the field, including attorneys, accountants, and others.

The Foundation Center maintains four libraries which are professionally staffed and make available Center reference books and IRS information returns on private foundations, along with annual reports, newsletters, press releases, newspaper clippings, application guidelines and historical and other research materials:

79 Fifth Avenue
New York, NY 10003
212-620-4230

312 Sutter Street
San Francisco, CA 94108
415-397-0902

1001 Connecticut Ave., N.W.
Suite 938
Washington, DC 20036
202-331-1400

1442 Hanna Building
1422 Euclid Avenue
Clevelend, OH 44115
216-861-1933

The Center also supplies a core collection of its publications to cooperating collections in 181 public, university, government, and foundation libraries in all 50 states, Puerto Rico, the U.S. Virgin Islands, and in Australia, Canada, England, Japan, and Mexico. Cooperating collections are staffed by the host libraries and nonprofit organizations. They contain Center reference works, and many also carry recent books, and reports on grantmakers, along with IRS 990-PF information returns for foundations within their state. For many of the relatively small foundations, they may be the only available source of this type of information. For a complete list of cooperating collections, write to the Center's main office or call 1-800-424-9836.

The Center also operates an Associates Program, a fee based service including toll-free telephone reference for those nonprofits needing frequent and immediate access to information on grantmakers.

PUBLICATIONS

Copies of the Center's more than 100 publications are available for free use in its own libraries and in the core collections at cooperating libraries. These publications include a wide range of reference directories to all types of private foundations, corporate giving programs, and grants; benchmark studies such as *Alcohol and Drug Abuse Funding* and *Crime and Justice Funding*; bibliographies (*The Literature of the Nonprofit Sector*); an annual statistical report called *Foundation Giving*; and guides such as *Foundation Fundamentals* and *The Foundation Center's User-Friendly Guide*.

In addition, the Center publishes a range of monographs on topics relating to foundation or nonprofit management and trusteeship, and to philanthropy and voluntarism. Books may be purchased directly from the Center; for information call 1-800-424-9836.

The Center issues an annual report, a publications catalog, and informational brochures.

The Center's authoritative data on foundations and grants is also available online through DIALOG Information Services. For information on how to access Foundation Center databases on DIALOG, call 1-800-334-2564.

GOVERNANCE AND SUPPORT

The Center is governed by an independent board of trustees consisting of representatives from the grantmaking world, nonprofit organizations, and financial institutions. It receives support from over 500 foundations and corporate sponsors by means of grants to its annual sustaining fund, major gifts, and/or special project funding.

Index